MILLION DOLLAR SPEAKING

THE PROFESSIONAL'S GUIDE TO BUILDING YOUR PLATFORM

ALAN WEISS, PH. D.

New York   Chicago   San Francisco   Lisbon   London
Madrid   Mexico City   Milan   New Delhi
San Juan   Seoul   Singapore
Sydney   Toronto

1 2 3 4 5 6 7 8 9 10 DOC/DOC 1 9 8 7 6 5 4 3 2 1 0

ISBN 978-0-07-174380-8

MHID 0-07-174380-4

McGraw-Hill books are available at special quantity discounts to use as premiums and sales promotions or for use in corporate training programs. To contact a representative, please e-mail us at bulksales@mcgraw-hill.com.

This book is printed on acid-free paper.

Library of Congress Cataloging-in-Publication Data

Weiss, Alan
  Million dollar speaking : the professional's guide to building your platform / by Alan Weiss.
      p. cm.
    ISBN 978-0-07-174380-8 (alk. paper)
  1.   Public speaking—Handbooks, manuals, etc.   I. Title.
    PN4098.W42 2010
    808.5'1—dc22   2010029957

This book is dedicated to those who listen

CONTENTS

PART TWO
Steak

PART THREE
Sizzle   261

PREFACE

THIS IS the follow-up book to my wildly successful *Money Talks*, first published in 1998. A lot has occurred in the last dozen years that has affected and influenced the world of professional speaking. But a great deal has remained constant. I have the luxury herein of introducing the new and reinforcing the true.

I'm writing for professionals. That is, this book is focused on an occupation, not an avocation, a career and not merely good cheer. "Amateur" speaking—in front of community groups, civic associations, religious organizations, and so forth—is important, and one should always endeavor to improve in that pursuit. Associations such at Toastmasters have been helping amateur speakers for decades, and are quite adept in that arena.

But there is a huge difference—a metamorphosis, if you will—in becoming and succeeding as a professional, someone who is paid as an expert who can present important, relevant content in a fascinating, engaging manner. Unfortunately, there are myriad "urban myths" about the speaking business, particularly about how to market your value and how to establish fees based on that value.

Most professional speakers, as I write this, undercharge and overdeliver!

If that hasn't corralled your attention, I don't know what will. My paramount consideration in the pages that follow is that professional speaking is a career—not work, not a job, not a "gig," not a hobby—and that someone engaged in it should expect to earn sufficient money to maintain one's desired lifestyle. This is a business, and you are in business no less than the people whom you address from the platform or the front of the room are in business.

No businessperson wants to hear from a hobbyist or expects to be billed in a nonbusiness manner.

If you want to make a million as a speaker, helping others while you help yourself and your loved ones, read on. As I noted in my first book on this topic, money talks!

—Alan Weiss
East Greenwich, RI
October 2010

ACKNOWLEDGMENTS

Mᵧ sɪɴᴄᴇʀᴇ appreciation and admiration to Patricia Fripp, my partner in The Odd Couple® and one of the finest speakers in the entire world. I've learned a great deal from her in terms of speaking skills and not nearly enough in terms of humility.

I'm grateful to another wonderful speaker and humorist, Lou Heckler, who unselfishly recommended me to a speakers' bureau early in my career. I was hired without hesitation, and also without much keynote experience, based solely on Lou's endorsement.

My thanks also to the old (*really* old) gang at Kepner-Tregoe in Princeton, where I learned how to be a stand-up trainer as well, I hope, as a stand-up guy.

PART ONE

SAVVY

THERE ARE more people trying to provide advice on professional speaking than there are good professional speakers. The ski instructor you choose to follow had better be six yards in front of you on the slope, demonstrating what you intend to be able to do, not sitting in the chalet sipping brandy after giving you a CD and a pep talk.

WHEN ARE YOU A PROFESSIONAL?

AFTER ALL, WE'RE ALL SPEAKING, OFTEN SIMULTANEOUSLY

I WAS speaking at a small business awards ceremony at the Westin Hotel in Providence, Rhode Island. It was a 45-minute after-dinner, post-awards speech, a tough position. I was originally asked to do it for free, since I live 15 minutes away, but I pointed out that the three huge firms that were sponsoring the evening never gave their products away for free, and I was being paid my full fee.

I had prepared my varsity game for the tough closing segment, and 400 people rose (some rather unsteadily) to their feet, either happy with my performance or glad that it was over. As usual, a couple of dozen people waited to chat with me.

"You're the best speaker we've ever had here, and the best I've ever heard," announced the first woman in line.

"I'm sure I'm not, but thank you," I responded.

"No, you are *the* best!" she proclaimed.

"I bet you say that to all the speakers," I said with a smile, trying desperately to move on.

"No, you are unique!"

"Okay," I said, facing my unmoving groupie, "*why* do you think I'm so good?"

"Because you are the *only* speaker we've ever had here who can walk, talk, and hold the microphone at the same time!"

Stunned, I mumbled, "What about my four transcendental points for small businesses?"

She stared back, uncomprehending. "*What* four points?" she asked.

WHITHER GOEST?

For a long time, if you told someone that you were a professional speaker, that person would immediately translate that into "motivational speaker," a phrase that represents everything that is wrong and empty-headed about this profession. Calling an excellent professional a "motivational speaker" is like calling dinner at a five-star restaurant a "meal," citing Willie Mays as an "outfielder," or calling Judy Garland a "singer."

Some phrases just don't do the subject justice.

Historically, professional speakers were evangelical, professional by dint of how they were trying to move the audience, as in Billy Sunday or Oral Roberts. There is a history of superb, moving, inspirational sermonizing and homilies in every religion. There have also been speakers whose intent was to enlighten the audience members about their own potential, not so much by offering pragmatic techniques as by offering stirring messages: "You can be your own best friend"; "You are the owner of the mortgage on your life!" Accompanied by experiences and exercises (taken over from early T-group and sensitivity training[1]), the speech morphed into workshops and "events."

---

[1] For example, falling backward, trusting that your colleagues will catch you and not steal your wallet.

In the 1960s we had Werner Erhart, and in the 1990s, Tony Robbins. In between and along the way, we've had thousands of pretenders to the motivational thrones. But these approaches were based largely on the personality of the originator, no less than the religious, charismatic speaker. (Very few Tony Robbins franchises have ever been successful, so far as I know. I used to mentor one such franchise owner. People wanted to see the master himself, understandably.)

Finally, we have "rallies," wherein an organizer fills an arena, often with the employees of a few companies that foot the bill, and marches out the likes of Colin Powell, George Bush, Zig Ziglar, and whoever else is on that circuit to "wow" the crowd. For a few hours people can hear some stirring commentary, buy some products (which will later gather dust on endless shelves), and return to work under the temporary belief that their company has just invested in their long-term well-being.[2] (It's a lot cheaper than giving them raises or improved benefits.)

Those times have changed.

Oh, you'll still see a group of Goldman Sachs or Prudential senior managers out on some beach racing to build sand castles under the tutelage of an "energy coach" or a "motivation manager." But the only thing occurring there is sunburn.

Today, *everyone* had better be a motivational speaker, but there has to be steak to accompany that sizzle. That is, paying customers are expecting expertise in specific content areas presented in an engaging, provocative, and entertaining manner. Thus, two extremes will not work:

---

[2] There are fascinating tracts in psychology journals about people who engaged in Tony Robbins's famous strolls on hot coals who later needed counseling because their dramatic feat of the feet did not translate in any way whatsoever to their daily lives.

1. Running around like the Mad Hatter trying to thrill people with vapid affirmations, such as, "They can heat you up, but they can't burn you!"

2. Standing rooted in the earth, talking through another boring PowerPoint presentation of 185 slides while people try to see their PDAs in the dark. (If you have enough iPhones, with screens aglow, in the audience during such a tedious presentation, it begins to resemble a silent rock concert.)

Speaking Up: Everyone who is seeking to make big money in professional speaking had better be a "motivational speaker," while also captivating the audience with solid content and pragmatic techniques.

Here is why the market expectations and demands have changed:

- *Increasingly sophisticated audiences.* The mass media and the Internet have created a more intelligent expectation. People can readily watch experts on TED, for example (TED.com), and in 20 minutes (the time limit) be captivated by geysers on the ocean's bottom, synthetic happiness, urban planning, or modern communications devices.

- *Increasingly sophisticated buyers.* Corporate executives and trade association directors demand a return on their investment. They don't need someone to "babysit" the audience for a few hours during a convention; they require topical expertise that can be utilized immediately in conjunction with organizational strategy and tactics.

- *An overabundance of schlock.* There is no barrier—zero—to entry in the professional speaking market. A lot of people have sidled in, managed to get work, and flopped. Still more have decided to position themselves as commodities, charging very little in the hope of achieving for volume, and have done poor (and repetitive) work.

- *The economy contracted.* Some lingering effects even during rebound and growth will be a more zealous analysis of external expenditures. Professional speakers have never exactly proved themselves to be irreplaceable or urgently needed. So the corporate *zeitgeist* has incorporated a "less is more" philosophy.

- *The association and (legitimate) connection with the training business. Most* people who are making big money in speaking are doing so in training. (More on this later in the book.) Very few of us who are noncelebrity speakers can earn big money exclusively from keynoting, for example, and few of us want to, since the travel is ridiculous. However, training and human resources within corporations are increasingly discredited, so approaching through those routes is a rough road.

The profession is changing, but for the better. That's why it's easier than ever to build and sustain a thriving practice.

WHY SIZZLE *AND* STEAK ARE BOTH REQUIRED FOR FINE DINING

There's a wonderful "old world" restaurant in Providence where I love to take clients. It's called Capriccio, it's dark, the captains wear tuxedos, and they are allowed to flambé food tableside, having been "grandfathered in" for this charming but otherwise extinct practice.[3]

Capriccio has both great steak and great sizzle. The ambiance and charm add to the meal (as I'm sure is true of many of your favorite restaurants). If you are intent on an excellent experience, high value for your investment, and finding someplace to which you can confidently return—as I do with clients—you don't want to eat your steak in a parking lot and you don't want to eat gristle in a penthouse.

Assuming that you're salivating, here's the deal: EVERY speaker needs to be a motivational speaker (to have the sizzle) and engage people in a dynamic manner. The steak is your expertise and your ability to convey solid material that is credible, applicable, and flexible.

Take a look at the only four conditions these two factors permit (Figure 1-1).

In the upper right, we have an engaging speaker who has original, informative, and relevant content, as well as appropriate humor, energy, and what we will call "platform skills." By platform skills, I am referring to engaging stage presence and dynamics. In the bottom left, we have a speaker with neither, who will disappoint and disappear.

But we have two dangerous positions in the other corners for those who are seeking to be truly professional

---

[3] How many injuries and how much property damage have been caused by a flambé at tableside? Surely far fewer than those caused by ultraconservative, fearful, moronic legislation.

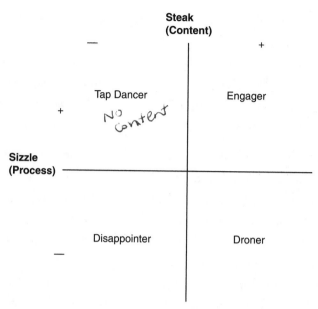

Figure 1-1 Sizzle and Steak

speakers. The tap dancer is the speaker who has virtually no content—no steak—but who tries to dazzle the audience with footwork, telling jokes, playing an instrument, using ventriloquism, doing magic tricks, smashing pumpkins.

The opposite is the true expert whose sizzle was extinguished by a dam bursting years ago and who shows you 120 slides in an hour of unremitting ennui.[4] I took a course in undergrad school at Rutgers during which the professor literally read his dissertation notes, recorded on hundreds of sheets of yellow paper, in every class, mumbling on, turning a page with regularity, nary an inflection nor intonation ever

---

[4] Here are two true stories; you can't make this stuff up. I was on the agenda of a conference where a professor was given a 25-minute segment, showed up with 180 slides, and droned on for 90 minutes, and no one from the organizing team stopped him. And the *New England Journal of Medicine* reported years ago that the speaker at its conference who received the highest participant ratings on the evaluation sheets—perfect 10s without an exception—had canceled prior to the conference and never showed up.

detected. You could, however, hear some snores from the back of the room.

> **Speaking Up: Don't tell people everything you know. Tell them what THEY need to know.**

Too many people who are seeking to speak professionally have a "message" that they feel the universe needs to hear if it is to keep on with its cosmic ticking. (It doesn't.) It's somewhat threatening but nonetheless true that a major event in one's life, no matter how splendid or traumatic, does not always translate into another person's utilitarian need (or even rapt attention). Then there are others who simply love to speak, and feel that the content and subject are irrelevant because they are simply so enthusiastic and emotional. (How long can you really watch the frenetic Energizer Bunny?)

Most, not some, of your teachers, professors, meeting leaders, instructors, and superiors have been less than engrossing speakers. How do I know this?

Because we all make such a fuss when we actually have the good fortune to be in the presence of the exception.

THE TRUE SPEAKER IS NOT A PERFORMING SEAL

This business is about intellectual firepower. Several years ago I was part of a small task force organized by the National Speakers Association to determine what buyers[5] really sought in choosing professional speakers.

---

[5] This refers to "true" buyers, whom I call "economic buyers," not meeting planners and bureaus, which are merely middlemen. See my book *Million Dollar Consulting* (New York: McGraw-Hill, 4th edition, 2009) for discussions of economic buyers and how to recognize them.

Overwhelmingly, we found that they wanted expertise. That's the "steak."

Expertise can be defined as a thorough and encompassing knowledge of a particular subject matter, including its origins, application, strengths and weaknesses, future probabilities, and so forth. It's not about perfection or absolute wisdom, or even a personal repository of global information.

It's about helping others to improve in a given area. That improvement may be in the form of more knowledge, changed behavior, new standards, reduced stress, a more balanced lifestyle, more enduring relationships—whatever.

It's not about jumping through hoops, donning strange clothing, balancing blocks on your nose, juggling fireballs, or reading people's minds. All of the foregoing may be important at times and, if done well, certainly have entertainment value (well, not the juggling), but they are not what professional speakers focus on. Every gimmick you introduce dilutes your educational and developmental message. And there are myriad jugglers and ventriloquists.

But there are relatively few effective and engrossing professional speakers.

So unless you prefer to be paid in herring, here are some parameters for your professional conduct and demeanor.

ALAN'S MILLION DOLLAR SPEAKING PROFILE

- *Focus on the power of your words and reduce gimmicks to a minimum.* You may choose to use visuals or audience interaction, or to play a bit of music. But if these actions are more than 10 percent of what you do (six minutes in an hour's keynote, a half-hour in a morning's workshop), then you're confusing your image, your brand, and, probably, the audience. (Ninety percent of the time, you should not require visuals in an hour's keynote.)

- *Create and maintain a professional image.* If you're wearing strange hats, weird clothing, or outrageous accessories, or if you're selling T-shirts and flip-flops from the stage, you're in the merchandising business, not speaking. (Always dress a step above the group, for example, if it's business casual, dress in business attire; if it's resort casual, dress in business casual.)

- *Don't allow the organizers to dictate your approach or demeanor. You* are the expert in the craft, so *you* decide how you'll approach the stage and leave it, how you'll be introduced, and whether or not you'll take part in related activities. You'll lose your gravitas if you're dunked in a water tank at the company "carnival." (I once had to assertively explain to my client that it was a *very bad* idea to ask for a moment of silence to honor a deceased colleague immediately before I was introduced with the topic of "Innovation for Tomorrow.")

- *No matter how talented you are, don't muddy up your intent.* The fact that you can play the piano, shoot a decent game of pool, sing (most people who think they can actually can't), or create animals out of balloons is nice but hardly relevant. You're not speaking to showcase your ability or to show your vacation slides. You're there to improve the condition of the audience and to meet your buyer's objectives. (I once watched, horrified, as a woman began her presentation by announcing several awards that she had just won, waiting for the delayed applause, and then acting as if she were surprised at the reaction.)

- *Be concerned about, aware of, and willing to change your environment.* In the next section, we'll talk about varying scenarios, but try to understand the milieu so that you can appraise whether it makes sense for what you intend to do. A performing seal will honk and balance balls anywhere the handler takes it. But even the seal is not at home when it's out of the water.

> **Speaking Up: You are not a "hired hand." You're a professional who knows the craft better than the client does, just as the doctor knows medicine better than the patient does.**

THE DIVERSE (AND DAUNTING) SPEAKER SCENARIOS

When I talk about "speaking" in this book, I'm embracing any and all of the following:

- *Keynotes.* The keynote is literally the "key note" to a convention or conference and is properly the opening plenary session. When someone says, "I delivered the closing keynote" or "I was one of the four keynoters," that person is a tad confused.

- *Plenary sessions.* These are general sessions to which the entire conference is invited, and there can be only one or many. The keynote is always a plenary session. Plenary sessions can last from 20 minutes to 90 minutes, but are typically an hour.

- *Concurrent sessions.* These are longer sessions that run simultaneously. Participants generally have their choices of which to attend, although they may be assigned based on need. These generally run from an hour to three hours, but are typically about 90 minutes.

- *Workshops and seminars.* These are full-day and multiday programs. They may be within one organization or be "public sessions" that strangers are invited to attend. They are generally much more oriented toward skills transfer, practice, and application.

Generally, when you work for a large client, you are delivering sessions internally for that client. But when you are delivering public sessions, you are promoting these yourself and charging each individual attendee (although you may be subcontracted to do this by larger seminar training companies, which is like being in indentured servitude—at this writing, some are paying $300 per day).

Here are some variations of these roles:

- *After-dinner speakers.* An after-dinner speaker is addressing a general session with a dozen or a thousand people to conclude an evening. It is one of the most difficult types of speaking in that the audience has usually experienced an open bar, a heavy dinner, wine with the meal, often an awards ceremony, some boisterous banter, and some droning talks by the top executives. It is not for the unconfident, inexperienced, or thin-skinned.

- *Humorists.* These folks may appear anywhere on an agenda to lighten things up (if they're good) or poison things for everyone who follows (if they're not good). They often incorporate information about the organization and the people sponsoring the event into their humor. (Once again, we're not talking about celebrities such as Jay Leno or Jerry Seinfeld, although they'll do this kind of work if you pay them enough.)

- *Character portrayers.* There are people who dress like Ben Franklin, Albert Einstein, Marilyn Monroe, Abraham Lincoln, or, presumably, Zorro who use the persona of their subject both to entertain the audience and to convey some pertinent points about personal and professional development. They frequently provide an exegesis of their subject's famous speeches or roles. These are novelty acts, tightly choreographed, that are often quite successful in schools as well as businesses.

- *Facilitators.* Facilitators facilitate—that is, they are supposed to enable groups to communicate better, to resolve issues more expeditiously, and to deal with difficult issues in a collaborative, constructive manner. The best facilitators allow the groups to do most of the speaking, but they are often required to present summaries, demonstrate what's occurring, describe obstacles, and provoke debate.

- *Moderators.* The moderator is typically the panel emcee who provides brief explanations of subjects and procedures, introduces the panelists, handles questions from the floor, and keeps the proceedings on time.

> *Speaking Up: You can provide a variety of*
> *these roles. Most noncelebrity money in*
> *professional speaking is being made by*
> *trainers.*

Nowhere on my lists do I include the phrase "full-time" or "part-time." That's because those delineations make no sense in professional speaking, despite the fact that so many people seem preoccupied with them. I spoke 50 times last year. Am I a part-time speaker? Would you have to speak every day to be full-time? And speaking is seldom all that you do, especially when you're successful. You're probably doing a little consulting, perhaps serving as a coach, maybe creating and selling products, and generally seeking ancillary sources of income. Full-time and part-time are irrelevant.

Paying the mortgage is relevant.

Finally, there are three types of speakers that I've observed; these are given in Table 1-1.

Table 1-1 Three Types of Speaker Focus

Speaker-Centered	Audience-Centered	Buyer-Centered
Focus		
• What's comfortable	• What pleases the listeners	• What meets the buyer's goals
Risk taking		
• None—always look good	• Mild, but play to the majority	• Always—stir emotions
Humor		
• To get a laugh	• To get them on your side	• To make a point

Stories and anecdotes
- Personal and ego-driven
- To create commonality
- To make a point

Delivery style
- Insincere sincerity
- Choreographed
- Natural and flexible

Reaction to disruption
- Personal affront
- Minimize the effect
- Admit and resolve

Response to questions
- Gives personal examples
- Asks for examples
- Combines examples

Self-disclosure*
- Excessive and irrelevant
- As it relates to listeners
- As it relates to goals

Measures of success
- Standing ovation
- "Smile" sheet ratings
- Buyer rehires

Overall demeanor
- Controlling, in the spotlight
- False "involvement"
- Targets actions

Lingering, most positive effects
- "Interesting person"
- "Great presenter"
- "Let's do it"

---

*Self-disclosure is a much-abused term that which generally means revealing personal aspects of yourself on the stage. It's sometimes used with the equally mysterious *authenticity* or the redundant *self-authenticity*. I'm using it here in the sense of how much of your personal feelings and life you volunteer during a speech.

The trouble is that audiences know what they want, but they seldom know what they *need*. The buyer, presumably, knows what the audience needs, and if he or she doesn't, then it's your job to provide still more value and help the buyer discover what those needs are. Audience-centered speakers are often quite popular, and sometimes that's good enough.

THE VAGARIES OF THE TRADE

The odds are that most of your college professors were deadly dull. That's because they were (and are) compensated for performing a task, which is to hold a class session and deliver information. If teaching is defined as imparting knowledge, few of them actually teach, since precious little knowledge is transferred and only a scintilla is retained, let alone utilized, after the examination.

Most speakers approach our profession in the same manner. They believe that they are being paid to deliver a speech. Nothing could be farther from the truth. Yet that is what most speakers convey in their interactions with the buyer, and that is what most of them cite in their fee schedules. Speaking has become a commodity business, with bureaus (and speakers themselves) providing hourly or daily rates for the presence of a body on stage. That's roughly the equivalent of a doctor who charges by the hour for performing open-heart surgery or an architect who charges by the size of the building. Plumbers, who do charge by the hour, do noble work, but it's much more difficult for me to ensure that my speaking pipes will hold water.

Speaking is a business that provides for the enhancement of the buyer's objectives in return for remuneration to the provider. So let's establish some definitions and parameters prior to delving into the rest of the book and its specific techniques.

The buyer is the person who signs the check or causes it to be signed. The buyer is rarely the meeting planner, although that is the person with whom some bureaus are most comfortable working, which is one of the weaknesses of that system. A buyer is not necessarily the CEO, although he or she may well be in smaller companies or in larger ones that are organizing a top-level meeting. When I spoke at GE, Jack Welch didn't hire me. People five levels down hired me, but they were able to make the decision and cut the check. The buyer is inevitably that person whose objectives are to be enhanced. He or she "owns" the *outcome of the event*.

Whether you are pursuing an organization or responding to a contact that the organization has initiated, try to find the buyer. If you can do so, you can connect your involvement to his or her desired business outcomes, thereby increasing not only your chances of obtaining the assignment, but also your ability to obtain higher fees.

> *Speaking Up: The more you focus on objectives and end results, the more valuable you are. The more you focus on events and tasks, the more vulnerable you are. A client can easily replace a one-hour talk with another one-hour talk. A client can rarely replace "the ability to close sales at a faster rate" or "the improvement of customer service to decrease failure work" quite so easily.*

Objectives are the results that are to be achieved through your participation. Delivering a keynote, speaking after dinner, facilitating a breakout group, and conducting two concurrent sessions are not results. They are tasks, and therefore they are commodities, subject to tough comparative shopping. This is why you'll hear a meeting planner so often say, "We've got $5,000 for this slot. Who can you get for us?" It's the height of absurdity. The real question is, "Here's what we want to achieve. What value do various alternatives provide so that we can make an intelligent ROI (return on investment) decision?"

Listen carefully. The mere act of helping to explore, understand, and clarify the buyer's objectives will add tremendous value to your contribution. That's why you should relentlessly pursue discussions with the buyer and submit your proposal directly to that person. Only the buyer has the volition and capacity to arrange for investments based upon return. (Meeting planners merely have budgets and have incentives to stay within those budgets, and they sacrifice quality for economy every day.) A key aspect of what consultants call "process consultation" is that a collaborative, diagnostic approach is itself intrinsically valuable. Many buyers tell me that they aren't sure that the objectives have been formally articulated. "Well," I respond, "wouldn't it be useful to do that now so that you have a standard by which to measure success?" It's hard not to get the business after that.

The process you engage in is more valuable than your actual time on stage. The reason that the heart surgeon is so valuable is not the hours that it takes to remove diseased arteries. The value is in the 20 years of practice, the continuing study, the experiential base, and the superb judgment that enable the surgeon to perform such a delicate operation in those few hours. Doctors don't get paid by the blood vessel, and you shouldn't get paid by the adverb.

The process behind virtually any speech includes the following:

- Initial talks with the client to determine the desired outcomes and your contribution to those outcomes
- Often, additional conversations with intended audience members to determine their points of view and their challenges, and to develop some client-specific examples
- A study of the industry in general, the competition, and the client's role within that scenario
- Design of the actual speech, which may consist of 50 percent standard points that you make, 25 percent specific client-centered material, and 25 percent audience exercises, interactions, new material, and so on
- Discussion of your speech with the client and coordination with what precedes and follows you, as well as with any other speakers on the agenda[6]
- Preparation of visuals, handouts, and/or performance aids
- Practice
- Actual delivery of the talk

[6] When I offer to call both participants and other speakers to coordinate and customize my message, the client is always highly impressed. This enables me to cite higher fees because additional value is already established in the buyer's mind. There's another pragmatic reason: I once opened my talk, only to find from the audience that a speaker two days before me at the conference had covered the first third of my 90-minute session. I improvised quickly and resolved never to appear "blind" again.

- Postsession follow-up with the client to determine what else may be necessary (e.g., another copy of some of the visuals), what the reactions were, how well the objectives were met, and so on

If you emphasize the process—and you may well have additional components—then the buyer can understand the comprehensive contribution you can make to his or her objectives. If you emphasize the 60 or 90 minutes, or even the full day, that you're on stage, then the buyer perceives that payment is due only for that relatively brief duration. You have the ability to educate the buyer, but you can't do that if you're not talking to the buyer and/or if you don't understand your own value in terms of that process.

SUMMARY

Professional speaking is a craft that revolves around the use of words to meet buyers' objectives. The outcome of a successful speech should be an overjoyed buyer, whose resultant testimonial is a paean to your skills. You manage and guide this process by focusing on the outcomes, understanding the overall value of the process that culminates in your time on stage, and dealing with people who make investment decisions based upon value delivered, not minutes spent.

Professional actors aren't speakers. While it's important for you to be thoroughly prepared, it's sterile to be so tightly orchestrated that the audience perceives an off-the-shelf performance rather than an engaging interaction. People choose the plays and professional performances that they attend, but they usually have their speakers chosen for them. If you do a thorough job at the front end, understanding the audience and basing your value on the difference you can make in the members' personal and professional lives, then you'll be positioned to reap huge rewards. Ego-needs fulfillment, product sales, and adulation will follow as by-products. They should never be pursued as primary goals. When speakers appear primarily to meet their own needs, they are as obvious as a ham sandwich (emphasis on the *ham*).

Now that we have some common understanding of what professional speakers do and why, let's take a look at how to choose a market and why most speakers inexplicably foreclose options rather than expand them.

CHAPTER 2

ESTABLISHING YOUR MARKET

WHOM DO YOU WANT TO LISTEN?

Speaking is about listening. Remember the tree falling in the deserted forest? If only the squirrels hear it, has it made a sound?

If you're speaking to an empty auditorium with only the service staff listening (or to a full house that is sound asleep or busy texting because you're totally irrelevant or insipid), are you speaking?

It's vital to determine two facts:

1. Who are the members of your audience? Whose actions and behaviors do you wish to improve?
2. Who are your buyers? Whose condition can you improve by appearing in front of those audiences?

Note: None of this is about YOU. It's about THEM. If they are not improved, you are not successful, no matter how many stories you tell, how much applause you receive, or the "good vibes" that you experience.

CREATING VALUE PROPOSITIONS

A value proposition is the point on your marketing arrow. It provides aerodynamics. (Too many speakers have a value proposition that's more like a flying barn.) It is NOT an "elevator speech or pitch."[1] It keeps you and the prospect focused.

Here are its characteristics: it is

- Brief
- Output, not methodology, oriented
- Broad enough to embrace many buyers
- Brief (Did I mention that already?)

Some examples of poor and excellent value propositions are

P: I have a six-step sales process that I teach the audience.

E: I dramatically decrease sales closing time at less cost of acquisition.

P: I provide humor and entertainment throughout the conference.

E: I reduce stress and create superior learning environments.

P: I facilitate strategic retreats.

E: I help your senior team select optimal goals and create accountabilities to ensure that those goals are reached.

You get the idea. Your value is in the outcome, not the input. It's about the new actions and behaviors that you can engender, and the improved condition for the buyer that they create. (Behind every professional and/or corporate goal is a personal goal. If I want you to improve teamwork, it means that I'm weary of acting as referee between the teams.)

---

[1] This is one of the most often cited and completely ridiculous techniques in the world. Anyone who "pitches" me on an elevator is going to get off on the next floor.

You might have a single, generic value proposition. Mine is, "I improve individual and organizational performance." Now, that's pretty wide, right? But if someone says (as someone always does), "What does that mean?" or "How do you do that?" I reply, "I guess it is a tad vague, so why don't you give me a couple of examples of areas where you'd most love performance to be improved and I'll give you an idea of how I'd create a speech (or workshop or event) to do that."

The key is not to defend or explain, but to engage the buyer in the diagnostic. Let's both talk about how I can help you.

Speaking Up: If you have a value proposition that appeals to true economic buyers, you are already ahead of the game. This is primarily the marketing business.

Some definitions:

- *Economic buyer.* The person who can write a check or cause one to be produced by the computer. In a small business, it is usually the owner. In a large business, it is typically someone with P&L (profit and loss) accountability, a division or department head, and so forth. In Fortune 1000 companies, there are scores or even hundreds of economic buyers within the organization. In trade associations, the economic buyer is usually the executive director, and sometimes the program or education director.

- *Feasibility buyers.* These are people who contribute to the decision to buy in terms of finance, culture, technology, trust, programming, or whatever. *They can say no, but they can't say yes. They are often gatekeepers, barring the way.* You must circumvent them or blast through them. Human resources people and training people are feasibility buyers 99 percent of the time.

- *Meeting and event buyers.* Although these people are ostensibly in charge of creating and running an event, it is never *their* event. They are minions and organizers for the real economic buyer. Always ask, "Whose meeting is this? Who initiated it?" Although industry organizations such as the National Speakers Association place a premium on meeting planners and bureaus, these are people who are charged with *conserving budget*, not *getting results*. They will continually ask, "Can you do it for less? Can you do several things for one fee? Will you wash the windows?" You are wasting your time with these people.[2]

- *Speakers' bureaus.* These are middlemen dealing with middlemen. (Forgive the gender exclusivity, but "middle people" sounds like something from *The Hobbit* and Middle Earth.) They work with meeting planners. They take 25 to 35 percent of your fee, but they rarely market you effectively. In the past decade, they've had such a rough time that they've begun to charge the speakers and not the clients (for critiquing video demos, inclusion in catalogs, "showcases," special mailings, and so on). Anything you get from a bureau is gravy, but bureaus should not be a primary marketing focus. Later in this book, when I show you

---

[2] Years ago I keynoted for the annual conference of Meeting Planners International. I also did a special session for the board ad executives. Half the board was unemployed at the time. Meeting planners are among the first to go in tough economic times.

how to turn a speech into a process and quintuple your fees, you'll see why bureaus are like stegosauruses.

Thus: value proposition, audience, true buyer. Now, how do we approach them?

GET THE DUMMY OFF THE COVER

A few years ago, I was speaking at a "marketing laboratory" sponsored by the National Speakers Association in Tempe, Arizona. The audience was composed of professional speakers who wanted to broaden their appeal and, commensurately, increase their business. I had addressed the need to allow a wide variety of buyers to contact them, a concept that I call "enabling the buyer to buy." For example, on the practical side, a buyer can't buy from you if he or she doesn't know how to reach you. On the conceptual side, the buyer can't buy if you don't appear to cover the appropriate topic areas, know the industry, have the experience, and so forth.

It's startling how speakers interpret the infinitive "to market." They will plaster their pictures all over their materials, but that doesn't create more appeal or a peer-level relationship. How many corporate buyers have you seen with their photo on their business card and some kind of motivational nonsense written on the back? Not many.[3]

---

[3] Someone should do a sociological study of the tchotchkes and ancillary doodads that speakers either give away or sell. There is an array of laminated cards with fortune-cookie wisdom, bumper stickers, bookmarks, self-published vanity books, can openers, paperweights, wall hangings, and peculiar club memberships (e.g., The International Association of Mighty Thinkers). If all that energy went into increasing fees rather than creating tangential dust collectors, the entire industry might improve its revenues.

At the conclusion of my presentation, one of the participants asked if I would critique his promotional materials. He told me that he wanted to appeal less as an entertainer who appeared after dinner and more as a change agent who appeared as a general session speaker or keynoter at business conferences. His proposition, which was quite logical, was that his entertainment was merely a vehicle to convey his techniques about managing change, and that he was not a humorist per se.

He handed me his brochure, which was an expensive 9×12 piece. On the cover was a picture of him seated in a chair with a large dummy on his lap. It turned out that his entertainment was ventriloquism. (I believe they are called "dolls" in the profession, and Terry Fator has made a fortune with them, but no one refers to him as a professional speaker.)

Here was a talented guy who was energetically engaged in turning off buyers.

"Lose the dummy," I suggested.

"You mean move that aspect of my act to the inside?" he ventured.

"No, lose it altogether. As long as it's here, you're a ventriloquist, and you'll have to work mightily to convince any buyer that you also can deliver a powerful message about change that will be the focus of your value. And stop talking about your 'act' unless your buyer is the manager of the lounge at Caesar's Palace."

> *Speaking Up: Your materials reflect how you see yourself. The buyer has no choice but to accept that image if he or she has no other knowledge of you.*

He made the changes and thanked me profusely for the advice. Whether we're new to the business or veterans of the platform, we all get too close to our "act." We see ourselves from the inside out, yet buyers can see us only from the outside in. Perceptions are reality. The bad news is that our perceptions of ourselves are almost always different from the potential buyer's. Longfellow pointed out, "We judge ourselves by what we feel capable of doing while others judge us by what we have already done." The good news is that we can manage that process if we care to take an objective look.

What follows in the next section are the logical, simple steps for choosing the scope of your markets. Notice that I didn't say "your market." I advise you to be as broad as possible in casting your net. Experience and circumstances will intelligently narrow it as needed, but that winnowing process is often a gentle erosion around the edges, not a sharp knife slicing a pie into eighths. These steps are equally applicable for the neophyte and the veteran. (In fact, those with a few years' success in the business might find that they've been arbitrarily and unconsciously limiting their growth.)

There are, unfortunately, more speaking coaches than there are good speakers. Most of them make their living giving theoretical and usually bad advice, since they've never been successful as professionals themselves. Some examples of what you should run from:

- *Specialize or die.* Why on earth would you want to exclude buyers? Generalize and thrive.
- *Fees are about supply and demand.* No, they're not. Do you want to work 365 days a year? Fees are about your value and the degree to which you improve the client's condition.

- *Audience reaction is the most important metric.* No, the buyer's reaction is the sole metric. Often you're brought in to discomfit and provoke an audience, not make its members jump to their feet applauding.
- *Every speech must be customized.* Most speakers merely change the name of the speech when they offer "customization"! Your key points might be the same every time. Change the examples to suit the environment and the audience.
- *You must have "bureau-friendly" materials.* Fuggeddaboudit! Bureaus are like bank loans. When you need them, you can't get their attention. When you're successful, they come running to you.

ALAN'S 12 STEPS TO CREATING MARKET "REACH"

Here are the steps to defining your market scope—that is, how to determine the extent of your appeal to buyers. The wider the appeal to the more buyers, the better off you are. "Specialize or die" is nonsense.[4]

1. *Determine your value-added for the client.* How are the buyer and the buyer's intended audience better off once you leave? A workshop, keynote, seminar, or "presentation" is merely a delivery vehicle. How are people actually improved?

---

[4] Nearby (to me in Rhode Island) New Hampshire's license plate says, "Live free or die." What a horrible world of absolutes. How about, "Live free or fight to be free"?

Example: Your people will be able to identify a true buyer earlier and establish a peer relationship faster. For you (the buyer), it will mean far less time spent on corrective action and failure work.

2. *Establish who your likely buyers are.* In a larger organization, a buyer may have P&L responsibility or head a department or business unit. In a smaller operation, he or she may be the owner or CEO. In a trade association, the buyer may be the executive director or chair of the board.

Example: For the value proposition in point 1, your buyer would probably be the vice president of sales, the vice president of product management, or the owner of a medium-sized business.

3. *Examine whether you should focus on particular markets.* You may choose to stay within your general geographic area because of child-care needs, an aversion to travel, or a richness of local prospects. You may choose to focus on IT functions or manufacturing firms or financial services organizations because of your background and/or your affinity for them.

Example: You may focus on insurance sales because you began your career in insurance, you still have contacts there, and you are near the headquarters of large insurance companies.

4. *Begin to create a body of work.* Buyers are attracted to expertise. Start to write, speak, network, create blogs, record podcasts, conduct teleconferences, and so forth to build public examples of your expertise.

Example: Begin a newsletter on selling insurance services and products that you distribute electronically for free: *The Insurance Assurance.*[5]

5. *Call everyone you know.* Once you have begun to create a body of work that displays your expertise, contact everyone you can: family, friends, professional colleagues, suppliers, vendors, past clients, community acquaintances, and so on. Explain the value you are now providing, and ask if they—*or anyone they know*—can avail themselves of such value.

Example: Send an e-mail to all those people to whom you recommend others—doctors, dentists, designers, accountants—so that they can reciprocate when appropriate.

6. *Ensure that you are accessible.* Make it easy for people to find you and do business with you. Have a quick and easy answering machine message and recording option. Allow people to send you e-mail via your Web site. Use a *full* signature file, including your physical address, in your e-mail. (If someone wants to hunt you down and kill you, that person really doesn't need to rely on finding your address in your e-mail.)

Example: Return all your calls within three hours, and all your e-mails within a day. Responsiveness is a key catalyst for new business.

7. *Watch your language.* Speak in the buyer's language of results and outcomes.

See Table 2-1 for examples.

---

[5] That's an actual title that I helped Scott Simmonds develop for his practice in Maine. People complain that there are "too many newsletters." Yes, because people enjoy reading them.

> *Speaking Up: Shop your own business. Is your Web site user-friendly, or is it full of "philosophy," "history," and "background"? Does your voice mail allow for a quick message, or does it insist that the caller hold on for two minutes listening to some motivational pap?*

Table 2-1 Translating Speaker Terms to Buyer Terms

Speaker Terms	Buyer Terms
• Conduct sales training	• Improve sales closing rates
• Deliver the keynote	• Create a need to listen and learn
• Entertain after dinner	• Alleviate the day's stress, emphasize camaraderie
• Talk about stress reduction	• Improve productivity
• Deliver my message of hope	• Enable people to resolve their own problems
• Provide a motivational talk	• Challenge participants to exceed higher goals
• Convey time-management skills	• Improve productivity
• Introduce quality techniques	• Reduce failure work that erodes profitability
• Instill a customer service attitude	• Improve customer retention rates, cut attrition
• Describe my battle with illness	• Broaden solution options for personal tragedy
• Provide investment advice	• Maximize financial security
• Teach interpersonal skills	• Reduce conflict on the job

8. *Learn the present and future "hot buttons."* What are the current and short-term greatest needs of the markets and buyers that you've identified? How can you meet and exceed those needs? How can you go beyond just "fixing" (which is of moderate value) and find ways to raise the bar (which is of tremendous value)?

   Example: How can senior management best organize, encourage, monitor, and reward a global sales force that it seldom sees, or telemarketing people who work from their homes?

9. *Reach out through others.* "Cold calling" doesn't work in this business, even though you'll hear people boast about calling someone out of the blue and obtaining business. (Do *you* buy investment securities from the people who call you at home at 8:30 at night?) But finding someone who knows someone who knows the buyer does work. Establish and treasure precious networks of lead sources.

   Example: Someone in your club or church or soccer league works somewhere that is attractive for your plans. Ask if this person can introduce you to someone who knows someone who . . .

10. *Plan for success, not failure.* Too many professionals try to protect themselves against failure, but never plan to exploit success! Look for long-term potential in the markets that you examine and seek to penetrate.
    Examples:
    - Ability to sustain high fees within your value proposition
    - Multiple booking potential (corporations with numerous sites)

- High-level audiences composed of potential buyers (trade associations)
- International potential for expansion (global organizations)[6]
- Exposure in parts of the country where you haven't worked (travel is welcome)
- Ability to purchase added products or services (books, consulting)
- Potential for additional value propositions beyond the original
- Trend setters and early adopters in their industries or professions

11. *Focus on process, not content.* Processes (e.g., decision making, conflict resolution, sales techniques, influence, and so on) are applicable across industries and markets. You are always better off with that orientation than with a narrow one, such as "doctor/patient relationships in public hospitals."

    Example: It's far too difficult to master content, but processes are easier. I've spoken on leadership and strategy for the National Fisheries Association, National Cattle and Feed Lot Association, American Radiological Association, Hewlett-Packard, and Bank of America. Only the examples were changed.

12. *Go get bloodied.* Some people make plans forever. Others go out, try, fail, learn pragmatically, and succeed the second or third time. Find some lower-threat buyers at first (a small trade association, a medium-size business) and try some of this out.

[6] This is increasingly popular and likely; see my book (with Omar Khan) on the subject, *The Global Consultant* (Hoboken, N.J.: Wiley, 2009).

That's how you'll advance.

Example: Put all of this in your calendar and try it locally, at the very least. Find out what you're already good at and where you need more development.

In the old *Cheers* television comedy, the bartender named Coach once told one of the leads, Diane, that he had been working on a book for six months. Diane was amazed and said, "I didn't know you were a writer."

"A writer?" asked Coach. "I've been trying to read it."

It doesn't take six months to read a book (or to write one). Even veterans procrastinate about that book they want to write, that tape series they want to record, and that radio show they want to host. This afternoon or this evening, start it. There's no one stopping you.

THE LITMUS TEST OF REAL, IMAGINARY, AND "WOO-WOO" MARKETS

You need three elements to speak successfully:

1. A market need that you identify, create, or anticipate
2. The competency to meet that need
3. Passion

If you have need and passion but no competency, someone else will always get the work. If you have competency and passion but no need, you have a message that no one wants to

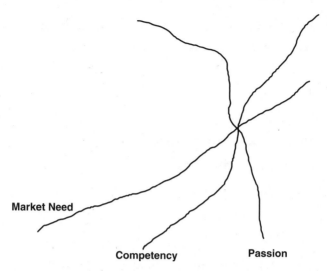

Market Need

Competency   **Passion**

Figure 2-1 Where Do These Paths Intersect?

hear; and if you have need and competency but no passion, that's what I call a nine-to-five job.

There is preexisting need, such as areas of teamwork, strategy, sales, customer service, and so forth. There is need that you create, which might be using the Web to create electronic commerce. And then there is need that you anticipate, which might be having to manage people globally who are never together physically. (No one told Akio Morita at Sony that anyone wanted a device carried on the belt that played music through earphones. But the Walkman was a huge hit and the grandfather of the iPhone.)

Competency is the continuing self-development and creation of intellectual property that allows you to at least competently address client issues and, even better, raise the bar to new levels of performance.

Passion is the desire and resilience to keep going because you believe deeply in your ability to help the audience and the buyer, and because the job is so often about rejection.

With these elements in place and correctly oriented, you can address markets such as

- Corporations
- Small businesses
- Educational institutions
- Nonprofit institutions
- Government agencies
- Self-help organizations
- Charities
- Public service firms
- Boards

If your expertise is a process, such as strategy or team building, then you can usually address many markets, since only the content changes. If your expertise is content, such as growing corn or conducting a census, then your markets are severely limited to those who are involved with such content.

Of course, in many instances, you may have expertise in both process and content. The greater your content knowledge (e.g., of the health industry) and your process expertise (compensation practices), the better the results you can generate (higher morale at cost-effective levels).

Content Knowledge ×	**Process Skills** =	**Results**
Autos	Decision making	Profit
Chemicals	Problem solving	Productivity
Insurance	Negotiating	Morale
Banking	Interviewing	Safety
Electronics	Coaching	Image

> *Speaking Up: If you insist on stacking the deck, at least do it in your favor. Learn to speak the client's language; don't try to be better versed in the client's business. Learn to focus on process needs, not content details. Show me an organization that doesn't need better communication skills, better teamwork, and improved profits, and I'll show you that it's merely a CIA cover.*

The litmus test for a legitimate market versus a "woo-woo" market[7] would include the following:

- Are there people already in this market (which indicates that there is value and the ability to pay—competition broadens markets)?
- Are there common needs spread over a critical mass of people?
- Can the buyer be clearly identified and accessed?
- Is the issue remediable and/or improvable?
- Do you possess the intellectual property, methodology, and approaches to address the topic?
- Is there sustainable business over time (is the population large enough)?

---

[7] My scientific term for a market that has been artificially created in the speaker's mind to justify speaking on a topic that is of great importance to the speaker but to virtually no one else. For example, you're going to speak to the homeless about finding a job. Who will organize this? Where will it happen? Who will pay?

- Are people willing to pay, and will they be able to see improvement?
- Are the interests sincere and nonconflicting (we want you to improve morale while we lay off half the workforce)?
- Is the solution to the need such that speaking or training can be an effective intervention?

I've had speakers try to convince me (because they had convinced themselves) that they could make money speaking to college seniors, high school seniors, union workers, attorneys, dentists, theme park operators, and so on. To name just these few, those are very tough markets.

In fact, there are two equally dysfunctional extremes: to talk about something that is merely important for you to talk about and that other people don't need, and to talk to people about something that is very helpful to them, but that they perceive they don't need.

ORGANIZING YOUR APPROACH: THE EASIEST ROUTE IS USUALLY THE BEST

William of Occam formulated in the fourteenth century that the easiest route is usually the best, no matter what your goals. This has come down to us through the ensuing half-millennium as "Occam's razor." In my terms, too many people travel completely around the block just to arrive next door.

You want to reach true, economic buyers, and/or enable them to reach you. We've established that already. So what are your easiest routes?

First, start speaking. Wherever you can, within reason, take on speaking assignments. Speak at the local Rotary Club or facilitate a meeting of your Little League board of directors; moderate a panel at a town meeting; teach as a guest instructor at a community college. Don't go around the block. Knock on the doors next to you.

This kind of speaking has quite a few salutary effects:

- You can hone your skills through practice.
- You can try out new material.
- You can ask others for solicited feedback.
- You can record the sessions.[8]
- You can develop relationships with potential buyers and recommenders in the room.
- You can garner testimonial letters.[9]
- You can obtain referrals from the participants.
- You can send out a press release about the appearance.
- You may be interviewed or write an article for the organization's newsletter.
- You can invite potential buyers to see you.
- You can provide handouts giving your Web site, blog, products for sale, and so forth.
- You can assess the relevance and attraction of your topic and approach.
- You can network before and after the event.

---

[8] This allows you to calibrate your progress, create "demonstration" audio and video, create future products, and so forth.

[9] Someone watching you who sends you (perhaps at your request) a testimonial letter from Acme Bank results in a testimonial letter with Acme Bank on the letterhead!

I think you can see that, even if you're not paid a cent, there are diverse and attractive marketing advantages to simply getting out and speaking wherever you can where wise people gather.

Speaking Up: There are speaking opportunities all around you. Just open your eyes and your ears.

My dog, Koufax (named after the greatest baseball pitcher in history—American Kennel Club registration: Sanford Van Koufax of Ebbets), is a German shepherd, and is basically a sight dog. That is, he runs out in the yard and looks around immediately to see what's up. His partner, Buddy Beagle, is a scent dog, and he hits the backyard with his nose to the ground. Between them, they cover a wide variety of clues and information as to what's gone on out there since their prior visit.

You need just such extra senses to augment your own. I'm not suggesting that you have dogs hunt down speaking opportunities, but I am suggesting that you can let your friends know that you're seeking them. You can visit major hotels and see who is holding meetings there. You can check the newspapers for listings of meetings. If your town has a convention bureau, let the people there know that you're a speaker and provide your topics, so that if there is a need for a last-minute replacement at a conference (illness, canceled flight), you might be available (at the same rate as the speaker you're replacing, by the way).

Use your networks, your friends, community events, and similar sources to help you "sniff out" opportunities to speak. *One of the primary errors of new speakers is that they are always waiting for the "right opportunity" rather than seizing every opportunity.* The previous list offers very formidable marketing clout with nary a cent of investment. *One of the primary errors of veteran speakers is that they become stuck in the rut of their past clients and successes.* While veterans shouldn't be speaking for free (with the exception of true pro bono work), they should be constantly seeking new markets and new opportunities.

At the outset of your career, don't limit the markets you pursue, because you want to maximize the opportunity to find buyers. Don't arbitrarily exclude any true buyer. The more adjectives you use in describing your value, the worse off and narrower you will be.

For example, "I help you accelerate sales closing time while reducing the cost of acquisition" is powerful and attractive to a wide array of buyers. But if you add to it, "in the telemarketing, real estate investment field in New England," you've just switched from a trawler's net to a single fishing pole with a worm on the hook!

If you're engaging in the kind of marketing I'm recommending—speak wherever you can and allow buyers and recommenders to see you while you improve your craft—you'll be seriously expanding your opportunity to appeal to the broadest number of needs.

Once you've established a successful career, you should have the savvy and the experience to significantly broaden your appeal. Too many veterans fail to do this, but instead simply try to get better at what they're already quite good at. Moreover, the narrower your focus, the more the rug can be yanked from under you by more powerful brands (a well-known author and speaker writes a new book on your subject), newer technologies (people are downloading, not buying, CDs today and may be doing something else entirely by the time you read this), loss of interest in the topic (diversity), changes in perception (wisdom of financial analysts), traumatic events (recessionary times), and obsolescence (Y2K).

Organize your approach to the market so that it is broadly appealing, simple, and easy. Make William of Occam proud.

SUMMARY

The genesis of a successful speaking career is: "First, there was value."

Focus on how the client's condition will be improved as a result of your contributions (not merely "the speech"). Once you know that, you can both attract people to you and reach out to form relationships with them. But you must focus on real markets, not ones that you imagine or that someone claims to be pursuing at some professional chapter meeting. (I've often felt that most professional association annual conventions serve the purpose of members getting together to lie to each other about how well they're doing!)

Keep it simple. William of Occam was right. Your market approach, your dealings with the client, and your delivery should be simple (though not simplistic). Great athletes have the capacity to make the most difficult positions, plays, and performance seem commonplace. We learn how difficult these things are only when *we* try them (which is why I was such a lousy shortstop).

Keep your focus on your value (how you can improve your clients' conditions), the true economic buyer (who can pay for that value), how you will pursue such buyers (outreach), and how they will be attracted to you (market gravity).

That's how the best athletes play this particular game.

POSITIONING AND BECOMING AN OBJECT OF INTEREST

TELL THEM WHAT THEY NEED TO KNOW, NOT EVERYTHING THAT YOU KNOW

BUYERS ARE drawn to expertise. That means that the smarts between your ears (your intellectual capital) must be manifest as a pragmatic means of improvement for others (intellectual property). The more you produce that unequivocally helps others over the long term, therefore, the more you are going to be sought by buyers. And when you're sought by buyers because they find your intellectual property to be of value, you do not have to spend long hours on building relationships, and fees are not important (value is important).

Do I have your attention?

BEING AROUND A LONG TIME MAKES YOU OLDER, BUT NOT NECESSARILY BETTER

There is a tremendous debate among professional speakers as to how one should progress from part-time to full-time status. In fact, there are two deeply revered beliefs among veterans of the business, and like many deeply revered beliefs, they are egregiously false. As Oscar Wilde observed, a thing is not necessarily true just because someone dies for it.

- *Deeply Revered Belief 1*. You are not a professional—indeed, you haven't "made it" in the business—unless you are engaged in it full-time.
- *Deeply Revered Belief 2*. The longer you have been at it, the better you are.

I recall attending my first speakers' conference. All of the "big names" were there, and as I tended to my drink during the cocktail reception, a legend in his own mind walked over to introduce himself. Seeing my "newcomer" nametag, he gratuitously informed me that if I watched the veterans carefully, accessed them as mentors, and generally paid them the proper homage, I just might be as successful as they were someday, fates willing. At the time, I was making about a half-million dollars a year, wasn't spilling my food on myself, and could utter comprehensible sentences. But his criteria for success were longevity and membership in the "in crowd."

My criterion for success is pleasing people who can write checks that clear the bank. Peer recognition—if it is based on merit and not on slobbering adulation—is wonderful, but it doesn't pay the mortgage, and it seldom impresses the buyer. Don't tell me about the industry awards you've garnered and the strange initials after your name. Tell me about how you'll improve my business.[1]

---

[1] The speaking business is the only one I've ever observed where people are so desperate for image, credibility, and recognition that many of them place their master's degree after their name in print, as in Jane Jones, MA. I used to think a disproportionate number of them were from Massachusetts until I caught on.

It doesn't matter how often you speak *because we're all part-timers*. No one is speaking 5 days a week, 50 weeks a year—at least, not for money. If your fee were $10,000 per speech and you spoke once a week, that would earn you a cool half million for getting out of bed just 20 percent of the time. Sound ridiculous? Well, $5,000 twice a week does the same thing, and even $1,000 twice a week will earn you $100,000 and leave you with 3 days plus the weekend. (Yeah, I know about marketing, preparation, networking, practice, and all that time investment. We'll get to that. It's not as bad as most people would like to make it.)

For most of my career, I've spoken about 30 times a year, which has been my average over the past 5 years. I did not pursue any of the engagements, and bureaus booked me for very few; the preponderance came from people calling me. If one's average fee for these engagements is $7,000, that's $350,000. (My lowest keynote fee is $15,000 at this writing.) Over the past decade, speaking revenues have moved from a quarter to a third of my total income (with consulting and coaching work representing about 60 percent and publishing about 10 percent).

I'm a part-time speaker. A lot of people could live nicely on those 30 days of income alone.

> *Speaking Up: It's not how much you speak or how long you've been speaking that's important. It's how well you speak and how effectively you meet the buyer's objectives. Oh, and it's also a matter of charging for it.*

We'll discuss fees in the next chapter, but while we're on the subject of the "full-time fallacy," let's debunk one more piece of horrid advice. There's an industry rubric that states that you should raise your fees when demand exceeds supply. That's roughly akin to saying that you should swim away from the beach until you can see land again. There's an awful lot of water out there.

And there's an awful lot of time in a year. In this case, is supply 5 days a week? Actually, you might be able to speak twice a day, and even on weekends. Maybe supply is 700 speeches a year? Supply and demand are commodity measures. They are not measures of value. Raise your fees— no matter how many times a year you speak—when your value to the buyer increases. *And never forget that wealth is discretionary time; money is merely fuel.* A lot of speakers work so hard earning money that they erode their wealth (never see their families or engage in leisure activities).

If full-time/part-time isn't the indicator of speaking success, does that mean that one can (*shudder*) work at another job and also be a speaker? Of course it does. Let's take the most extreme case. Suppose you're holding down a conventional 40-hour, nine-to-five career. However, you've managed to secure local speaking opportunities in the evenings and on weekends (or during vacations). *If you're paid for them, you're a professional speaker*, and you might be quite happy with the arrangement.

The definition of professionalism isn't your lifestyle or how you choose to spend your time. The point is whether you earn money for working on the platform. I know a dental hygienist named Denise who is married with children. She works full-time in her field. She also addresses dental groups, medical offices, conventions, and trade associations as her schedule permits. She's funny, effective, and highly regarded. She chooses her assignments based upon the demands of her professional schedule and her family's needs. Denise is an excellent professional speaker, a fine dental hygienist, a wonderful mother and wife . . . well, do you get my drift?

Too many speakers waste too much time trying to determine how to leave their present occupations and/or reduce their other time commitments so that they can spend more time on professional speaking, *as if that were an end in itself.* If speaking is to be your total calling, you'll naturally gravitate there because the gratification, job offers, and involvement will result in that evolution. But you can't force it.

People who pursue other interests or have additional careers (which I do, as a consultant, and Denise does, as a hygienist) are also speakers. They are not poor stepcousins of professional speakers; they *are* professional speakers, no less than someone who tries to speak every day and travels 95 percent of the time.

Fish swim. Speakers speak. No one challenges a fish at rest with, "I see you're not swimming, so for the moment we're not going to accept you as a fish."

Don't be awed by the size and scope of this industry. There are people who have been embraced by the bureaus, who have the connections, and who are most visible at industry conventions. But many of the newcomers I've seen are a lot better than the veterans who seem to rely on name recognition and a hackneyed "act" rather than trying to meet the business challenges of their contemporary customers.

There are approximately 10,000 or so trade associations, labor unions, professional societies, and technical groups that hold conferences each year, and many of them hold dozens of conferences annually.[2] If we add over

---

[2] Most of these groups are covered in an extremely useful publication and online guide called *National Trade and Professional Associations of the United States* (New York: Columbia Books). See the resources guide in the appendix for more information.

120,000 businesses in the nation and their conferences and meetings, even eliminating those that have no need for external resources, we can realistically assume there are in excess of 100,000 meetings a year utilizing professional speakers. (After all, 2,000 per week is only 40 per state, or eight per state each day; there are probably hundreds every day in New York City alone.)

The meeting "industry" is in need of new talent. No executive investing in a meeting wants to present the "same old, same old." Don't make the mistake of assuming that you have to earn your merit badges through long apprenticeships and careful climbs to the top. If you want to climb the mountain, fine, but there are choppers available.

One of the worst fates for an actor is to be typecast, which means that people can credibly accept that actor only in a type of role that he or she has been identified with before. That's a career-limiting dynamic. Some can escape this fate— Tom Hanks went on to diverse, award-winning roles after starring in a vacuous television sitcom. But Shelly Long has had a much tougher time post-*Cheers*. The jury is still out on James Gandolfini post-*Sopranos*. Similarly, veterans in the profession have often stumbled into a success trap, in which they were able to establish a niche but then fell victim to it. Speakers shouldn't be typecast either. If you're relatively new to the business, you have the advantage of being lighter on your feet and more versatile.

So disregard both of the deeply revered beliefs that we began with. It doesn't matter how many speeches you make a year, and it doesn't matter how long you've been in the business. All that matters is that buyers hire you, you meet their objectives, and you're paid for doing so. The degree and amount are up to you. But I know of no full-time speakers.

TRANSFORMING INTELLECTUAL CAPITAL INTO INTELLECTUAL PROPERTY

If speakers are sought because of their expertise, then it's fairly important that you make your expertise manifest. That is, no one really knows what's between your ears—and often, that includes you!

Just as we (incorrectly) expect that our prospects will appreciate our abilities, wit, and singing quality as much as our clients who know us well, we often assume that our prospects somehow, magically, can immediately sense all of our distinguishing assets and strengths.

That doesn't happen. Consequently, *you have to transform what's in your head to what's on the table.* (If there's not much going on inside your head, then thus far in this book you've probably been looking only at the pictures.)

Intellectual property is a marketing tool as much as a delivery mechanism. Here are just a few examples, from the ridiculous to the sublime:

Books	Booklets	Position papers
Teleconferences	Podcasts	Video clips
Chat rooms	Manuals	Tip sheets
Conversation	Visual aids	Handouts
Workshops	Web site	Blog
Articles	Newsletters	Reference materials
Downloads	CDs	DVDs

You get the idea. The things you say, depict, explain, represent, and so forth are tangible expressions of your intellectual property. It's never too soon or too late to improve and expand on these. You can protect them through trademarks, service marks, registration, and copyrights, which we'll talk about later. You can find my intellectual property expressed in every single medium I've listed.

> ***Speaking Up: Never fear disseminating your intellectual property. It's better to run the risk of someone stealing it than to appear to have nothing to say.***

I'm asked all the time why I produce so much of my intellectual capital in so many forms, so easily accessed. The reasons are threefold:

1. I want to appear as an object of interest to others through provocation, new ideas, and even controversy.
2. Intellectual property in any form is always a calling card for the engaging, informed, interactive speaker in front of a group.
3. I want to create zero barriers to entry, which means that there must be inexpensive, accessible routes for people to become involved with me.[3]

To create intellectual property, such as that described in the preceding lists, proceed through this sequence:

1. How can I help people improve (their performance, self-worth, productivity, leadership, strategy, teamwork, and so forth)?

---

[3] I'll describe the Accelerant Curve later in the book.

2. What specific ideas (models, approaches, techniques, methodology) do I or can I provide to create that improvement?

3. What forms best convey those ideas (print, audio, video, experiential, periodic, interactive)?

4. Are these forms best used for marketing, delivery, or both?

Here's an example. Let's say that you improve teamwork by changing what is normally a committee structure, with competing interests, to a true self-directed group that "wins or loses" together.

Let's decide that you can write an article for the trade press on the differences between a true team and a committee, you can create a checklist to audit the structures in your organization for marketing purposes, you can produce a keynote highlighting the differences and why they are crucial to performance, and you can design a workshop to transfer the skills.

Voilà! You now have two free marketing devices and two highly lucrative delivery mechanisms. It's that easy.

Some caveats: make sure that you use solely your own intellectual property, and that anything you "borrow" you have permission to use and you duly attribute it. This is important not only for ethical reasons, but also for pragmatic ones: too many speakers use secondary sources (other speakers) and focus on patently false information. (The Chevrolet Nova didn't sell in Mexico because *"no va"* means "no go" in Spanish. See Snoops.com for the bursting of such urban myths.) Also, there are too many of the same stories going around ("When I was watching the electric parade in Disneyland . . . " or "A boy found a sand dollar on the beach . . . "). Please.

For the record, anything you write that is originally yours is automatically copyrighted in your name. You may add, as most of us do, © Alan Weiss 2010 or Copyright Alan Weiss 2010 (you don't need both the word and the symbol). The only reason to file with the commissioner of patents and copyrights—which is tedious, given all that we produce—is that if you ever sue someone for infringement, you can't collect punitive damages if you haven't thus filed. I've never bothered, but talk to your own trademark and copyright attorney to see what's in your best interests.

A trademark (TM) and a service mark (SM) refer to protection for phrases, models, materials, techniques, and so forth. The registration mark (®) indicates that the protection is finalized after a period of 6 to 12 months without challenge. Do *not* use Web-based software to save money when you try to trademark your work. Use a good attorney who specializes in the field, not your uncle's cousin Louie. The cost is almost always less than $1,000. (And you'd be surprised at the law. You can't, for example, protect a book title.)

Produce and protect your intellectual property. No one else is going to do it for you.

ESTABLISHING VIRAL INTEREST

These days it's easier than ever to create viral interest in your work. By this I mean that it's highly productive to get people talking, but not always in the manner you think.

First, let me debunk social media platforms as effective viral marketing tools for speakers. (I told you, intellectual property is about causing controversy!)

This is an unscientific, undocumented, and probably unpopular analysis of what I'm learning as King of Social Media. (I'm reminded of a great review of a leading actor in *King Lear* by Eugene Field: "He played the king as though under momentary apprehension that someone else was about to play the ace.")

Here are my anecdotal observations.

If people visit LinkedIn twice a day for 15 minutes each time, that's 2.5 hours in a five-day week. (I'm discounting weekends, although I shouldn't, because social media wandering is clearly a full-time avocation, but I want to be conservative here.)

If they visit Facebook four times a day for 10 minutes each, that's roughly 3.3 hours.

If they Twitter six times a day for five minutes each time, that's 2.5 hours. (Or 12 times at 2.5 minutes each—you get the idea.)

If they post on their blogs three times a week (it's rather important to keep a blog active and interesting), and if the creation and posting of the item takes 30 minutes (and I think I'm really lowballing this one), that's 2.5 hours. (Blogging can be very useful in moderation.)

And now I'm going to add just two hours to the week to accommodate reading others' blogs, replying to commentary, following up social media stuff offline, updating profiles, uploading photos, and so on.

Drum roll, please: during a five-day week on a conventional 40-hour basis, we now have about 13 hours used to engage in what are somewhat inappropriately termed "social media." I understand that those hours may well extend into evening or early morning time. On the basis of a 40-hour week, that's 33 percent devoted to this stuff, but even on the basis of a 12-hour day, the percentage is 22 percent.

> *Speaking Up: If you want to find a conventional job, use the social media sites. If you want to find speaking assignments, find real buyers. Would YOU hire a speaker who was promoting on a social media platform?*

If you were to devote less than half of those 13 hours, say 6 hours, to other professional marketing pursuits, I estimate that you could do any one of the following during that week:

- Write two or three chapters in a book.
- Create 10 to 12 position papers and post them on your Web site.
- Call, at a moderate pace with follow-up, 30 past clients and/or warm leads.
- Send out a dozen press releases.
- Engage in a full day of self-development or a workshop.
- Create three speeches or a complete multiday workshop.
- Create a new product to be sold on your Web site.
- Create, and develop a marketing plan for, a teleconference.
- Create and record three podcasts.
- Create and tape a video.
- Contact 30 prior clients for testimonials, referrals, or references.
- Attend two networking events.
- Create and distribute two newsletters.

- Complete at least half of a professional book proposal for an agent.
- Respond to 50 or more reporters' inquiries on, say, PRLeads.com.
- Seek out two high-potential pro bono opportunities.
- Contact and follow up with five trade associations for speaking opportunities.

You get the idea. Don't forget that, in my unscientific analysis, I've halved the number of hours that I think are really being invested in full-fledged social media activity based on an already conservative estimate of what they truly are. And I'm not even counting other networks or platforms, just the four I've mentioned.

And over the course of a couple of months, you can easily do ALL of the bullet points if you have a mind to do so. I'm allocating six hours a week, just over an hour a day.

My current evaluation is this: don't confuse occupation with avocation. I've never said that social media are evil or that they will not help someone find a buyer somewhere at some time. Heck, I've become an avid blogger, and I visit Facebook and Twitter daily. Yet I can still do all of the bullet points listed earlier and work only 20 hours a week.

If you're serious about corporate consulting and coaching, and my blog IS located at contrarianconsulting.com, then I'll continue to advise you that you're not going to find those buyers on social platforms. Is it impossible? No. Have some people done it? They claim so. But if you're engaged in social browsing at the EXPENSE of those bullet points, then that's not a good disposition or apportionment of your time. If you can do both, and still live a balanced and fulfilling life by your terms, then go for it.

I post intellectual property—for free, of course—on Twitter, just as I do here. I do find that these platforms are a great way to pay back, to contribute, and to share. You have to be judicious in your selections, however, since some people just want "airtime," and you only have so much air.

If you want to engage in viral marketing, use my bullet points and not the social media platforms, which are too often reminiscent of a bad bar just before closing, when everyone is surly and hard to comprehend.

NINE BEST PRACTICES TO INCREASE YOUR BUSINESS

Here, then, is a brief discussion of nine best practices for the novice or the established speaker who wants to increase business dramatically and take an easier way to the top of the mountain.

1. Never Respond to the Question, "What Do You Speak About?"

Your orientation should always be on what you *accomplish* for the client. Don't focus on what you do; focus on how the customer benefits. Don't talk about why you're good; talk about what the buyer needs. Above all, don't prematurely and arbitrarily narrow your appeal, which a "topic list" will invariably do.

2. Prepare Well, but Not Fanatically

It's as important *not to be perfect* as it is to be well prepared. No speech that you or I will ever make will mark the turning point of modern civilization. With luck, your speeches might mean a bit of improvement in a person's professional and/or personal life. The difference—to the customer—between your being 90 percent prepared and 100 percent prepared (whatever that is) is infinitesimal. It is not perceived. But the energy expended in moving from 90 percent to 100 percent is immense, much more than that required to move from 75 percent to 95 percent.

Heresy? I know. But it's time we took apart the fantasy of perfection in this business, along with its attendant fanatical preparation. We are not building the space shuttle. We're not even trying to build a Toyota. There's just no need for frenzied anticipation. At 90 percent, your slides are rehearsed and placed correctly, you have a backup plan if the projector fails, your examples have been adjusted for the audience, and you can alter your timing given the progress of those before you. Enough.

I once heard a very well-known speaker tell a crowd that he gave the same speech about 100 times a year and that he never failed to practice it *every time* prior to delivering it. The speech was three hours long, and he spent three hours practicing *the same speech* every time. He claimed that this was the path to success.

I call that a learning disability. My immediate reaction was that either he was deliberately lying to create false standards of preparation for others or he was the slowest learner I had ever encountered. The Gettysburg Address was written on the back of an envelope.

One of the best ways to prepare is to record your speech a week or so earlier and then listen to it a few times. Practice some current humor to throw in each time, think about how you'll manage the visual aids during each segment, and work on making smooth transitions. When you're tired of listening to it, you're done practicing.

3. Adhere to Basic Adult Learning Needs

There are those who will tell you that there is a formula to a speech: you open with a humorous story, make a point, tell an anecdote, repeat your point, and close with a deeply personal revelation. That might help you deliver a speech in a choreographed manner, but I think you can see it coming a mile away.

Adult learning generally occurs in the sequence depicted in Figure 3-1. This sequence shouldn't be a lockstep formula, but it does reflect what we know about human learning. We are presented with potentially useful information, practice with it to explore its utility, receive feedback on our use or performance, and then apply it in real life. Without the final step, all else is academic.

The discussion aspect can include humor, audience participation, and a host of other devices. It needn't be simply a "talking head" (although that's what it usually was in school). The practice element can include exercises, role-plays, games, and simulations, or it can be as simple as focusing someone on how a concept might be applied. The feedback constitutes the need to provide insights for the practice, and it can be self-feedback, feedback from colleagues, or feedback from the

Discussion	→ Practice	→ Feedback	→ Application
lecture	alone	oneself	immediate
interaction	in teams	partner	delayed
demonstration	mentally	speaker	independent
example	in writing	delayed	with others

Figure 3-1 An Adult Learning Sequence

speaker. Application means that the audience has done something more than merely sit through your presentation.

These steps apply more to a workshop than to a keynote, but they have applicability for all adult learning. Even in a brief keynote, you want to present ideas and instill action in the participants. (This is why keynotes require different skills and can sometimes be more difficult to craft than much longer presentations.)

4. Understand Your Role as a "Motivational Speaker"

There is a difference between motivation and inspiration. To be inspired is to be spiritually moved, emotionally involved, and uplifted, and to take solace in words themselves. Its derivation is from theology. There's nothing wrong with being inspired, but it's usually a temporary, euphoric feeling, not a long-term focus on action.

Motivation is intrinsic. It comes from within. It is a willingness to act based upon a belief that the actions are important and will be gratifying. I cannot motivate you; you can only motivate yourself. However, I might be able to help establish an environment and atmosphere that are conducive to your becoming motivated. (Which is why motivation in the workplace is most directly a function of the immediate leadership and environment. It's plain silly to have a speaker try to motivate an audience that will then be returning to a gulag.)

Every good speaker is a motivational speaker because he or she helps people to take action. Motivation and self-esteem are intertwined, and self-esteem is heightened when someone receives tangible skills that, when used, will add to the person's success, encouraging him or her to apply those skills repeatedly (see the adult learning sequence in the previous section). In essence, the more successful I am, the better I feel about myself, and the better I feel about myself, the more successful I am. But that's a tautology. The key to influencing that circle is to provide discrete skills that I can rely on for success.

To the extent that we impart those skills to others, we are all motivational speakers. I've never known how to reply when someone asks, "Well, are you one of those 'motivational' speakers?" I guess I'd better be.

Motivational speaking has developed a bad name because it's sometimes delivered as an empty, quasi-inspirational talk filled with platitudes, bromides, and the bathos of personal struggles, delivered by an empty suit. "You can't take away my best friend, myself," and "You can knock me, but you can't reach me" are cute phrases, but they are hard to apply in

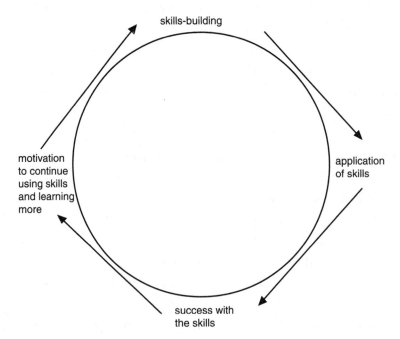

Figure 3-2 The Motivation Circle

the workplace the next day. On the other hand, learning a technique to resolve conflict with a coworker or learning how to influence the boss's delegation style can help me tangibly and immediately.

What's more motivational: being told that I'm my own best friend or being able to eliminate some of the stress in my life?

5. Self-Disclose Only if You Have a Point

Among professional speakers, the personal revelations known as self-disclosure have moved from a minor technique to the main attraction. When we involve ourselves and our experiences on the platform, we've too often moved from modest litotes to egocentric hyperbole. Here's a satire I use with my mentees to make the point:

> The astronaut had traveled to the moon with only a tenth of an inch of metal between him and the void. He had landed a quarter of a million miles away and walked tentatively but triumphantly on the cratered surface. Now, he was to return home in the final, tiny stage of his rocket that awaited him.
>
> But something went terribly wrong. Instead of heading for Earth, he tumbled out of control in the direction of deep space. All attempts to correct his errant capsule failed, and he sailed, helplessly, into the abyss.
>
> Ladies and gentlemen, I am that astronaut . . .

Believe me, it's not so far-fetched. I've seen speakers break down in tears on stage (always in the same spot, night after night, as sincerely as you can imagine, trying to regain control for exactly 46 seconds), speakers invite parents that they hadn't spoken to in 10 years to join them on stage, and speakers reveal more about their personal lives, struggles with disease and loss, and intimate problems than I'd ever want to know. I've heard more from speakers 60 feet away on a stage than I've heard in the privacy of my own living room. It's not a pretty sight.

Self-disclosure works if there's a point that the audience members can use to improve their condition. Telling me that you were born poor and now you're not (presumably because you're making money telling me this story) does not help me unless I can relate to the *techniques* you used to make that transition. Sharing your heartbreak, disease, loss, or vicissitudes with me may help you unburden yourself weekly, but it doesn't help me unless I can translate it to my condition and my life.

I always face an audience with the belief that its members *are not damaged*. All of us, of course, have experienced the vagaries of fate. We all have had tragic times as well as wonderful times. But that's simply a condition of human existence. There's no need to turn yourself inside out or violate my privacy by violating your privacy unless there's a pragmatic set of skills that results.

There usually isn't. While I'm happy with your reunion or conquest of adversity or recovery, I'm a lot better off longer term with something that I can use tomorrow to close more sales, better manage my time, communicate better with others, or lead teams more adroitly.

Some "experts" actually claim that the speaker's relationship with the audience is a function of the audience's need for help and the speaker's need for approval. That sounds like a bad case of codependency to me. I believe that the speaker-audience relationship is based upon shared values (we'd like to improve), trust (the speaker is factual), pragmatism (these are useful techniques), and relevance (this applies to us). If, as a speaker, you need approval, see a therapist.

> *Speaking Up: If you're lonely, get a dog. If you want to practice, get a volunteer audience. Only if you think you can improve an individual's and/or an organization's well-being, however, should you try to get a client.*

6. Have Something to Say before You Write, Then Write Often

I once heard a speaker advise others, "If you have a speech, you have a book." Well, you might have a very, very brief book.

Don't use secondary sources because they're often actually farther removed than that and can be highly misleading. Find your own sources. More important, form your own opinions. Look around in awareness and digest what you see. Are people more stressed when they work at home? Are decisions actually of poorer quality when they are made participatively? Does most training accomplish next to nothing six months later?

Don't be afraid to be contrarian, but be scared out of your mind to be trite. It's better to stand out in a crowd through controversy than to blend into the wallpaper through blandness. Your favorite color shouldn't be plaid.

Writing will enable you to express your thoughts, examine your cognitive processes, and anneal your concepts. It doesn't matter whether you get published, although your odds are strikingly higher if you have written something as compared to having written nothing. Writing and speaking are synergistic and symbiotic. John Updike once explained that to understand how people speak—to be able to write dialogue—you have to understand how they think. I believe that to speak to people, you have to understand how *you* think.

7. Develop and Use Only Personal Anecdotes and Stories

Everyone is sick to death of the boy who throws the sand dollar back into the ocean.[4] The naval ship that keeps requesting the lighthouse keeper to move to avoid a collision is about as old. These stories were poignant and funny once. So were silent films.

All around our personal lives revolve stories, incidents, circumstances, and travails of family, friends, and strangers. Jot them down, record them on tape, or create reminders for yourself (I keep an "anecdote file"). Go through them periodically to select those that have the potential to prove a point or highlight a concept. Feel free to embellish—after all, it's your story, and the key is the audience's improved condition, not personal historical veracity.

Never discard an anecdote. Even those that seem to hold no promise may emerge as brilliant departure points as you mature, your speeches evolve, your clients change, and society diversifies. In the worst case, the anecdote takes up some space, but if you discard it, you lose it forever.

Personal stories immunize you from being copied and keep you unique no matter who else is on an agenda. No one

---

[4] A passerby says that the effort can't make a difference because there are thousands of sand dollars washed up on the beach. "But it made a difference to that one," says the now-stereotyped, philosophical child.

can tell your stories as well as you can, and no one has your personal history and experiences. Collect and nurture the stories of your life. They are your continually renewing resource.

8. Subordinate Your Ego

Stop trying to be the center of attention every time. I was invited to speak in Atlanta once, and the group's officers hosted a dinner for me the night before, presumably to meet me on more intimate terms and to learn what they might. However, the association's president waltzed in, and she promptly dominated the discussion. When one of the group raised a basketball question, she even had some irrelevancies to insert about a game that she had never played and didn't care to watch.

That woman was incapable of sitting quietly and listening because she judged her success by how often she opened her mouth. Our success is actually a function of communication, which, the last time I checked, is a dialogue. If you're not on the platform, don't feel that you have to be the center of attention (and even if you are on the platform, you're only a conduit and shouldn't be a hero).

You might have a better story than the one that was just told. Save it for another time, rather than practicing one-upmanship. You might have visited more places, earned higher fees, worked with tougher audiences, and had a more harrowing travel experience. So what? Allow others their moments in the light of their friends' attention.

The best speakers I've ever seen are terrific listeners. They don't need to be on center stage when they're not on the stage. They don't have to continually tell you what they've done because their accomplishments speak for themselves.

I love the airline pilot who, with superb talent and comprehensive experience, has just landed a $400 million 747 filled with 500 people after a transoceanic flight and comes on the public address system to say, "Thank you for flying with us. We really appreciate your business and hope you'll choose us again." That's humility. It's a rare trait.

9. Understand that Sometimes It's the Audience, and Get On with Your Life

I've had a few speeches that I wish I'd never accepted. Both the client and I had acted in good faith, but conditions (or client judgment) deteriorated. For example, I've faced audiences who have just arrived from a two-hour open bar; who have been awarded prizes and trophies after grueling competition and pressure; who have had terrible news presented to them (deaths, layoffs, divestitures—I kid you not); who have been exposed to too many speakers or activities, some of which were dreadful and dull; and who were just plain ornery for no good reason at all.

I don't hold it against the client, and I *certainly* don't hold it against myself; I do the best I can, and I leave. That's all that I can do, and I'd propose that there's little more that you can do.

If you haven't prepared, blow your lines, are hung over, or become insulting, you're at fault, and you should return the client's money. But if you've done everything you can to the best of your ability, go home to work another day. The money has been earned much more than when you're hot and having a great time for yourself. Some audiences can't be pleased, no matter what you do. All you can do is your best.

No speaker I know of who has been successful in turning around a very difficult crowd ever went to the buyer and said, "That was much tougher than I expected, but I turned them around, so I want you to pay twice my fee."

Conversely, no buyer should say to you, "You did your best, but they were tough and you didn't make any headway, so I want my money back."

Occasionally, what you have carefully prepared doesn't work. The only real downside to this is if you allow it to affect you in the future. The longer you're in this profession, the more of these immovable obstacles you'll hit. I hit one every year or two, bounce off, spend the money, and move on. This business is not about somebody else's idea of perfection or arbitrary credential. It's about preparing well and doing your best. Just think about what a world this would be if everyone, with every client, prepared well and did his or her best every time.

IF YOU DON'T BLOW YOUR OWN HORN, THERE IS NO MUSIC

This section of the chapter is for those of you who are relatively new to the profession *or who seem to be stalled at a low level of activity*. Once you're moving with some headway, it's relatively easy to change direction. But as long as you're becalmed, you're helpless to follow a course.

There are many options available to create your own power. They include

- Working for a seminar training firm
- Obtaining sponsorship
- Securing another speaker's cast-off business
- Volunteering your services in return for exposure
- Broadening your scope
- Serving as a backup

Working for a Seminar Training Firm

These firms include organizations such as Vistage and Fred Pryor Seminars. Quite a few very successful speakers began with these companies. They offer very inexpensive seminars (typically $39 to $99) and/or meetings for owners of small firms, for a limited duration, around the country, drawing from a cadre of speakers and trainers who make up the "faculty."

The true seminar companies either create or purchase their course content independently; the instructor doesn't need to bring his or her own material (in fact, they prefer that you don't). You learn the content, practice teaching with a veteran, and you're off and running. You'll be asked to commit to a basic number of days—say, 10 per month—in return for that guarantee from the company. The pay is dreadfully low, generally about $300 per program at this writing, although there are some exceptions for high performers and commissions on book and tape sales. (The firms that organize "management meetings" often forbid you to market to the participants! I've met people in the National Speakers Association Hall of Fame who take on this low-paying work; such are the struggles of some careers.)

The advantages include exposure all over the country, accolades for your press kit ("Lou was the highest rated CareerTrack trainer for two years in a row!"), experience dealing with diverse audiences, a guaranteed cash flow, learning new concepts (you can teach several different programs), and at least half of your time free to market yourself as a professional speaker.

The disadvantages include a demand on half your time (reducing your flexibility), considerable travel (which is part of our business anyway, however), very low pay, constraints on what you can and can't do in the seminars, and continual monitoring—these firms are paranoid about instructors developing their own prospects during the courses, and with good reason.

All things considered, these arrangements are quite helpful *if* you see them as temporary bridges to the next step in your career growth. As a permanent job, they're roughly equivalent to the rowers in the Roman galleys. No matter how hard you work or how well you row, they're going to kill you.

Obtaining Sponsorship

Some organizations will pay a speaker to appear on their behalf. For example, Apple Computer might hire someone to address school groups on the best uses of technology in the classroom, a communications company might hire someone to address police and fire departments about crisis management, or a health maintenance organization might employ someone to address community groups on the benefits of early screenings for certain illnesses.

These are not sales pitches. They are informative presentations whose sponsors want to increase their profile, goodwill, and long-term business through their support of such efforts. Utilizing a professional speaker rather than a company spokesperson creates much less of a sales environment and much more of a professional presentation.

The advantages include guaranteed work, exposure, the ability to use your own concepts and techniques in support of your sponsor's needs (the sponsor might ask you to help design the session), and a firm client to cite. Depending on the nature of the organization, the pay could be menial or meaningful. The disadvantages include a probable lack of buyers for your future speaking in your audiences and the potential of being cast in a narrow niche (she's a health-care specialist).

Sponsorships virtually never seek you out. Your best bet is to find a firm that is using such tactics (or that could benefit if it did) and present your case to the buyer. Relatively few people do this aggressively, and you could have their undivided attention if you make a strong case, again, *toward their objectives.*

Merck placed me several times as the keynote speaker at various medical and hospital conventions. The firm was simply listed as the sponsor of my appearance. Enough said.

Securing Another Speaker's Cast-Off Business

All of us who have arrived at certain levels of success receive inquiries about business that we don't want to pursue. This is usually because the client can't afford the fee, it's in an area in which we're not sufficiently relevant, it calls for travel that isn't attractive, and/or it conflicts with other professional or personal activities. It happens to me at least several times a year, so it's happening out there every day as you read this.

Reach out to speakers who are in this situation. I don't mean that you should call them once a week and ask for a handout, because that's what it would be if there's no quid pro quo. Develop a relationship as you would with a client, bureau, or banker. Can you do some research for the speaker in return for the first call on appropriate business that he or she can't handle? Does the speaker need some office help, some temporary staffing, some computer work? Can you walk the dog and wash the car? (All right, I'm kidding, but not by much.)

Establish that kind of relationship with three or four busy speakers, and you might get their castoffs on a regular basis. If you're good, you'll be able to address the topic and earn credibility with the audience (which won't always be the case in these situations). Your fee will be no problem, since you'll be a bargain compared to the original, and you'll probably receive a higher fee than you would if you had been contacted directly.

The advantages are in the association with proven pros, the ability to work with firms that otherwise would never have called, and the opportunity to "test the envelope" in terms of your versatility and appeal. There are few disadvantages if you are able to establish a truly trusting relationship, and you're not simply around for legwork and as a "hanger on." One person who took on castoffs from me was able to work at a fee twice what she otherwise would have demanded, put days into preparation, and blew the client's socks off. He told me that, no offense, he really didn't see how anyone (meaning me) could have been better for him.

He was probably right.

Volunteering Your Services in Return for Exposure

Every service organization, community group, social club, youth group, and local professional society can use speakers, especially if they're for free! The key to volunteering for these roles is that you want to do it for groups that will have potential customers in the audience. The ironclad rule for addressing these groups is simple: always bring a lot of business cards and handout collateral.

The Rotary, for example, typically has both owners of small businesses and managers from larger organizations, as well as community leaders. Civic organizations will have, by design, top people from large businesses on their boards and committees (e.g., the Greater Peoria Business Improvement Coalition). Occasionally, these entities will pay at least an honorarium. But it's more important to achieve the exposure to the people in the group than it is to make small change.

Once, I spoke pro bono for the board of a shelter for battered women, helping it to define the organization's strategy and goals. One of the board members was the chief of police of the second largest force in the state, and he immediately hired me to do the same session for all of his senior officers—he had a federal grant! These things happen all the time. But they can't happen if you're not in front of these groups.

Broadening Your Scope

Try to look at your skills on a much wider basis. As a speaker, you can be a panel moderator, an emcee, a visiting college lecturer, a spokesperson, a mediator, a facilitator—just about anyone of whom communication skills and stage presence might be required.

One day, flying home from San Francisco, I returned a message from my wife from the airplane.

"What are you wearing?" she asked.

"Maria, not here," I whispered.

"Knock it off. Are you wearing a suit?"

"Well, no. You know I travel casually."

"Okay, listen. As soon as you land, rush home, put on a suit, and meet me at the public television station outside of Providence."

"Why? Is there a benefit or a fund-raiser?"

"No. You're hosting tonight's debate for the League of Women Voters."

It seems that the local television anchor who usually emceed the event was sick, and the backup was on vacation. My wife, a committee member, confidently volunteered me. When I arrived 30 minutes prior to airtime, the director was nearing meltdown. But when he realized that I could walk, talk, and follow stage signals, he recuperated. (The host from the League refused to introduce me as a consultant, because she said that if she did, everyone would assume that I was out of work! She introduced me as a "business executive.")

The show went flawlessly, and I was subsequently hired to do a local awards banquet as the after-dinner speaker at full fee. I never considered that I couldn't host that show. You can do a variety of things if you let people know. They might not all be perfectly consistent with your speaker's image, but they will provide opportunities for you to shine in front of people who will require that image later.

Serving as a Backup

Here's a technique that most new speakers miss. Provide your name, credentials, and abilities (it's always about relationships) to organizations that can be seriously hurt if they have a no-show. (In areas hit with hard winters, this is particularly relevant.) Provide your name to local speakers' bureaus, hotel banquet managers, company meeting planners, service organizations, newspaper columnists, talk-show hosts, visitors' bureaus, and anyone else who might hire, or influence the hiring of, outside speakers.

You will be competing with no one else, in my experience. Tell people that you're not expecting them to hire you for the gig, but that having a backup is always prudent, and that you'll work for the original speaker's fee if you're called upon at the last moment.

I appear on radio all the time. Locally, I'm interviewed in the studio. One day, the host of a talk show I had appeared on twice told me that she was going on vacation. "You're really good on the air," she said, "so how about pinch-hitting for one day?"

Thus, I became a talk-show host for three hours. The producer kept whispering through the earpiece, "Don't forget to promote your latest book."

Yeah, I think I can do that.

FISH SWIM, BUT DIFFERENT STROKES FOR DIFFERENT FOLKS

There is no single way to make it in this business. Bertrand Russell once said, "Don't ever be absolutely sure of anything—not even if I tell you."

Professional speakers help people and organizations improve their condition. They do it in a wide variety of ways, employing a vast array of talents. You have to decide what your "playing field" is and what kinds of plays make sense once you're on it. Ignore the stentorian, dire pronouncements of those who, with fingers pointed skyward, proclaim that you must specialize, you must speak only for a fee, you must speak full-time, you must work with bureaus, you must have a demo video, you must eat bran every day.

The only "must" is to be flexible and not rule out options that may be useful to you as you advance your career. And we are all trying to advance our careers every day, newcomer and veteran, high profile or low. Some of us are simply less part-time than others.

Speaking Up: Nothing succeeds like success. Don't listen to vacuous directives. Instead, watch what a variety of successful people have done. Then do that.

Observe what people whom you respect have done. (Don't just listen to advice because it's too easy to give it.) And watch a wide variety of people. Adapt those techniques that seem most relevant to you, and perhaps a few that will help you to stretch. Through this exploration, you can determine your true value to the client, and that will help you establish your fees, commensurate with that value.

Someone once asked me why I didn't farm out all of my administrative work, such as sending out invoices.

"Are you mad?" I raved. "That's one of the truly great pleasures of the profession, setting up that invoice and sending it to the client. That's the apotheosis of the work, the tangible evidence that you're providing so much value that the client deems it a worthwhile return on the investment."

You can't help others until you effectively help yourself. So let's turn now to the chapter that most of you may have already begun with: how do you establish fees?

SUMMARY

"Thought leadership" is the latest trendy phrase to describe an immutable condition: people are drawn to objects of interest, to expertise, and to power. No matter where you are in your career, you have the ability to create this kind of repute.

One primary requisite is to be concise. Tell people what they need to know, not everything that you know. You are a professional speaker in business environments, not a raconteur in a salon. A speaker who tells the same tired stories and uses shopworn examples year after year may land some jobs, but he or she won't build a career.

Your greatest asset is between your ears: intellectual capital. You must instantiate this so that it is manifest as intellectual property. IP takes many forms, speaking merely being one (and most speeches aren't immediately copyrighted unless you provide some written transcription, which is rare).

You can increase your business in diverse ways, and you should follow the best practices for doing this, not attempt to reinvent cold beer. That increase will add to your reputation as a thought leader, which enhances viral marketing and mention. In this technological age, that is easier than ever, though not on some of the most touted platforms (social media).

At the end of the day, however, if you haven't blown your own horn, there probably hasn't been much music.

ESTABLISHING FEES

HOW MUCH DO YOU CHARGE? HOW MUCH HAVE YOU GOT?

FOR THOSE of you who turned immediately to this chapter upon opening the book, my warmest welcome. When you get the chance, you may want to visit the preceding chapters.

Professional speaking is a business. What you make is far less important than what you keep.

THE THREE BASIC FEE RANGES YOU MUST CREATE

Nobody is worth all that much by the hour. My auto mechanic makes about $125 per hour for his shop, some speakers command $7,500 for a keynote, and Colin Powell, the former chairman of the Joint Chiefs of Staff, commands about $75,000 for an hour appearance at a convention. That's 10 times the average keynoter fee and 600 times the mechanic's rate. How can this be? Does Colin Powell have 10 times or 600 times their life experiences, skills, preparation, intelligence, and abilities?

The fact, of course, is that the hour (or half day or day) that we spend on the platform is not the value of what any of us brings to the client, *yet we insist on charging fees for that time commodity, rather than for our true value.* In reality, the mechanic is able to charge $125 an hour because of the experience, training, expertise, and talents that enable him or her to fix your car, provide the proper preventive maintenance, and ensure that the proper performance endures long after you're out of the shop. That same process applies to you, me, and Colin Powell as well.

People in the audience come to hear an hour keynote,[1] but the buyer is paying you to deliver it because of some combination of the following factors. I call it the "value list" because it represents those aspects of what you do that the buyer finds of worth.

Alan's Value List for Speakers

- Your repute in the field
- The talents you bring to bear in delivering each speech
- Your singular knowledge or approaches
- Your particular platform skills
- The visual aids or demonstrations that you provide
- Your ability to speak to that particular industry
- The skills that you'll impart to the audience
- Your experiences, stories, anecdotes, and/or humor
- The behavior change that will ensue
- The improvement in the business that will result
- The reference point that you create, which will be an ongoing focus
- The provocation to reconsider positions
- Your perspective from other companies

---

[1] This logic applies equally well to speeches of any duration, including multiday training sessions. I'm simply using the hour keynote as the most dramatic example.

- The motivation that people will generate from your message
- The sense of unity, direction, and purpose that you can provide
- Your credibility
- Your personal accomplishments and results
- Your ability to serve as an exemplar
- The client's intrinsic trust in you
- Your special intellectual property
- Your fame, e.g., a commercially published, successful book

The more of these factors that apply, the more valuable you are. If you think about it, Colin Powell delivers virtually all of them. That $7,500 keynoter delivers a lot of them. How many do you deliver?

Note that my list of valuable attributes focuses mainly on the past and the future. While there are some items that are strictly in the present, such as platform skills and delivery, even these are the result of your past training, experience, and practice. In other words, there are two major aspects under-lying your value to the buyer:

1. The combination of past experience and development that has produced the qualities that you convey today
2. The long-term results that the client will realize as a result of your time on the platform (or in the front of the room)

Your real worth is in the unique combination of factors that has resulted in your current value to the client and in the skills, behaviors, beliefs, and approaches that the audience will apply after your presentation that will benefit them and the business permanently. *The hour itself is incidental, being nothing more than the delivery vehicle that enables your own past to benefit the audience's future.*

> **Speaking Up: The platform is simply a vehicle that enables the speaker to transfer his or her own value—gleaned from past experiences—to the audience's future.**

A taxi ride from the airport is not worth $35. However, being conveyed from the airport, where you don't need to be, to the office, where you do need to be, is worth $35. A bus can take you for only $5, but it's slower, is less reliable, makes more stops, and is far less comfortable. A private limo can take you for $65, with more comfort, a private phone, better climate control, and door-to-door service. We all invest in the kind of ride that makes the most sense, and the kind that we perceive we deserve.

On a per-hour basis, a keynote is far more expensive than a full-day seminar. Someone who charges $5,000 for a keynote isn't going to charge $40,000 for a full day ($5,000 times 8 hours) if he or she offers both types of sessions. That person will probably charge around $7,500 for the full day. A keynote is much more expensive on a commodity basis because it's the limo ride—in far less time, in far more comfort, people are arriving at the destination that the buyer has chosen.

The basic process involved in speaking, from the buyer's perspective, has to be the one in Table 4-1. It is your responsibility to educate the buyer that his or her value list is being achieved not through an hour or half day of your time, but

Table 4-1 The Value Process

Speaker's Past	Current Intervention	Client's Future
experiences	keynote	higher productivity
education	workshop	lower attrition
accomplishments	seminar	higher morale
development	facilitation	improved image
travels	training	better performance
work history		greater market share
beliefs		greater profit
victories/defeats		more growth
risks/adversity		more innovation
experimentation		problems solved
happier customers		
superior service		
process flow		

through the substantial body of work that has taken place in the past and through the results that will accrue on an ongoing basis well into the future. Few name-brand drugs that we buy cost very much to manufacture—certainly nowhere near their purchase price. However, Merck and Pfizer and Johnson & Johnson have spent billions on the research and development that finally brought the drug to the consumer in a safe, reliable, convenient form. And the drug's effect will have a long-term impact on your condition, either curing it or ameliorating it. (Eventually, both generic drugs and generic speakers pop up.)

The speaking process is no different from that of pharmaceutical research and manufacturing. We're not paying for the aspirin capsule, we're paying for the work that brought it to us and the salutary effect that it will have on our health. Buyers shouldn't be paying for the hour's speech, but for the long-term processes that created its value and the longer-term salutary effects on the organization.

Here is the secret to a value mindset: We use the power of our past with a transfer mechanism in the present to greatly improve the client's future. Got that? If you can understand that process flow, you'll never have trouble charging high fees.

The key to establishing high fees is to establish high future value in the eyes of the buyer. (The future could be tomorrow or next year.) Let me make this absolutely clear because most speakers focus on the wrong results. Value has very little to do with standing ovations and "smile sheets" that rate the speaker a 9.9 on a 10-point scale. The only thing that matters to the buyer is how well his or her objectives are met, and that seldom involves audience ratings *unless the speaker is the one who emphasizes them.* There is far more value in improved sales, lower attrition, and greater innovation in the business than there is in a speaker's rating by the audience. The rating applies to a relatively brief moment in time. The results apply to the company forever.[2]

Most speakers, including those who "coach" and give all the advice, are charging for the first or second column in my process flow—the wrong columns! They are inputs, not value.

No company or corporate buyer has ever said, "Remember Mary Speaker? She received a 9.9 rating. What a great contribution to our business." But buyers do tend to say,

---

[2] Let me make it clear that I'm talking about legitimate corporate buyers, who are usually line managers or executives. I'm not talking about meeting planners, who often are solely concerned with saving money and audience ratings because that's how they themselves are evaluated by their company. Line managers are paid to get results, and money is seldom an object if the results are significant enough. For an in-depth discussion of buyers and approaches, see my book *Million Dollar Consulting: The Professional's Guide to Growing a Practice* (New York: McGraw-Hill, 1992, 1998, 2002, 2009).

"Remember the sales improvement that resulted from Mary Speaker's work? Maybe it's time to get her back in here again." Focus on your own ego, and you might get stroked. Focus on the buyer's results, and you will get repeat business.

So, it's vital to do the following to this point:

1. Understand your own value proposition.
2. Work only with true buyers.
3. Translate your value into long-term results for any given client.
4. Educate the buyer so that he or she reaches the same conclusions.
5. Only then suggest your value options.

Let's start with a simple fee system for now: a keynote, a half-day workshop, and a full-day or multiday seminar. Thus, if your keynote fee were $7,500, then your half-day fee would be $10,000, your full-day fee $15,000, and every ensuing full day $12,000. But that's just for now. We're going to quintuple that before the end of this chapter.

Ready to read on?

TAKING OUT THE MIDDLEMEN: DEALING ONLY WITH TRUE BUYERS

Note that I seldom use the word *customer* or *client* when I allude to obtaining business. That's because the buyer is the key, and speakers often don't have a clue about who the true buyer is. A buyer is someone who can authorize a check (or, in noncomputer cultures, actually sign one). The buyer is usually near the top of the hierarchy in smaller organizations, but can be anywhere in larger ones. Titles are highly deceiving. (Everyone in a bank today is at least a "vice president," but nary a one of them has the authority to even waive a fee on your checking account. I call this "title inflation.")

In the speaking industry, there has been a great deal of focus on the role of the meeting planner. In most cases, a meeting planner is actually a feasibility or implementation buyer, not an economic buyer. By that I mean that the meeting planner is given a strict budget (by the real buyer) and is paid and rewarded for conserving it. Meeting planners tend to be low-level people; they are rarely involved in corporate strategy or departmental missions, and they invariably evaluate speakers as commodities to fit time frames and budgets.[3] Meeting planners love to evaluate potential speakers by viewing demo tapes for a few minutes, making visceral decisions based on such ephemera as a funny story, stage movement, and appearance. I have had meeting planners tell me, without blinking an eye, that they didn't want a woman to address their group (this from a woman planner), they thought one candidate was too old, they felt that another was "too New York," and they felt that still another had too much content.

Speakers' bureaus tend to deal through meeting planners, middlemen (consistency with "middlemen"?) dealing with middlemen, sort of like "Middle Earth," and kind of like hobbits. If you work with bureaus, you won't miss these potential buyers because the bureau will find them for you.

---

[3] Please send your cards and letters elsewhere. I know that there are fine meeting planners and that some of them are actually closely tied to key business goals. But that is the overwhelming rarity. Speakers who focus on meeting planners as their primary buyers will never be able to escalate their fees dramatically because the value/results dynamic is simply not important to those buyers.

But for your own approaches, eschew the meeting planners and focus on the economic buyers, who themselves are focused on results. They are the ones to whom you can make your value/results appeal. Since they are paid to achieve results themselves, they will find the money to pay for anyone who can help them engender those results. The equation for them is simple: ROI (return on investment).

Whenever possible, market and sell to economic buyers. If you find that you've been introduced to a feasibility or implementation buyer, use that entry point to gain access to the economic buyer. Bureaus will otherwise attend to the meeting planner market, although the good ones will pursue economic buyers as well. Your strategy should look something like that depicted in Figure 4-1.

The primary thrust of the speaker (and of any marketing or staff personnel who are employed in these pursuits) should be to establish a relationship with the economic buyer. A secondary thrust should be toward those bureaus that can place

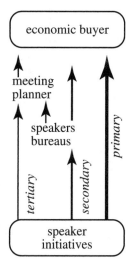

Figure 4-1 Speaker Marketing Priorities

you with economic buyers, although they will invariably also work with meeting planners. Only a tertiary thrust—meaning if there is time or as a result of serendipity—should be geared toward the meeting planner on the chance that this path may lead to the economic buyer. In my experience, most speakers reverse this sequence, thereby securing a poor return on their scarce resources.

So, our steps might really look like this:

1. Understand your own value package.
2. Translate your value into long-term results for any given client.
3. Find the economic buyer in your target customer.
4. Educate the buyer so that he or she reaches the same conclusions.
5. Only then suggest your value options.

How do you know a true buyer when you see one? Is it like the yeti, something that is rarely seen, but leaves just enough tracks in the snow to suggest a sentient being? Or is it Waldo, hidden in some crowd awaiting your scrutiny?

My economic buyers have had titles such as director, manager, business process consultant, vice president, owner, and, of course, CEO. At higher levels, it's fairly easy to tell. You might be talking to the vice president of sales who is interested in a speaker for his or her sales conference. There's not much detective work required. But what if you're talking to a sales director who tells you that she has been given the task of securing the speakers for the meeting? How do you tell if this is the economic buyer or merely a feasibility buyer, without offending her?

Speaking Up: The reason it's imperative that you find the economic buyer is that he or she is the only person who can appreciate your value in terms of the results generated and will make an investment decision on that basis. Otherwise, you'll be purchased like pens, packing material, or produce.

Here are the questions I've found useful in ferreting out the real economic buyer. You don't need to ask all of them, and you should choose those that best fit your style, since I'm prone to simply ask, "Are you the one who's investing the money?"

Alan's Questions to Find the Economic Buyer

- Whose budget is supporting this investment?
- Who will evaluate the final results?
- To whom do the participants all commonly report?
- Whose objectives are at stake?
- Which executive will open and/or close (be featured at) the meeting?
- Who approves the final agenda?
- Will you make a decision or a recommendation to someone else?
- If there are conflicts over the agenda, who makes the final call?
- Who is most affected by the success or failure of the participants?

Committees are seldom economic buyers. By definition, they are evaluators and recommenders. You can ask these questions in as blatant (New York) or subtle (California) a fashion as you wish, as long as you do ask them. Too often, we're so delighted merely to have been considered for a speaking engagement that we fall all over ourselves trying to impress whoever will see us. That's fine if we want to secure jobs, but it doesn't contribute anything if we want to create a million dollar business.

(Incidentally, sometimes we find ourselves magically with the economic buyer at the outset. Here's some complex advice: don't leave. It's not uncommon for the speaker to react to the initial contact by accepting delegation to a feasibility buyer. If you actively participate in the intent to delegate yourself downward, you'll experience a vertiginous drop through the organization, landing dazed and bruised in the office of someone who will ask you, as soon as you've revived, "So, how much can you reduce your fee if we cut the slot from 2 hours to 45 minutes?")

And what happens when we meticulously apply the questions and discover that we are, indeed, dealing only with a gatekeeper who resists allowing us to talk to the economic buyer? We've all encountered the palace guards who bloviate about how busy the management is, but whose sworn duty is to protect the decision makers from actually receiving information that might lead to a high-quality decision. Do we resign ourselves to the ignominy, or do we scale the ramparts?

Get out your ladders and climbing gear. Here's how you convince the gatekeeper to either open the gates or get out of the way while you open them.

Leverage Points to Get to the Economic Buyer

- I have to ensure that his or her objectives are met.
- I have to be sure that there are no unreasonable expectations.
- I have to ensure that the full value of what I can deliver is understood.
- I must tailor my approach to his or her style/theme/philosophy/agenda.
- Ethically, I must see the person who is investing the money.
- It's unfair for you to do my marketing for me.
- There are technical details that only I can explain.
- It's imperative that I hear his or her strategy and tactics.
- You and I can collaborate once we've both received his or her advice.
- I do this with every client. It's why I've been recommended to him or her.
- This is what outstanding professionals do in this business.
- It's for his or her protection. Objectives sometimes change.
- It's a strict quality policy, and I can't work with him or her unless we meet.

In the event that all of these fail, you may want to simply contact the economic buyer and advise that person of the same types of issues. You do risk irritating the gatekeeper and perhaps losing the potential business. However, no risk, no reward. It's simply that important to find the economic buyer and secure your agreement with him or her because only that person can appreciate your value package and the long-term results for the organization in terms of an appropriate investment.

PROVIDING THE CHOICE OF "YESES"

I've spent the entire first half of this chapter leading up to fee structure, and we're not quite there yet. That's because your fee strategy is irrelevant if you're dealing with the wrong people or if you're not in a position to establish value and results. On the assumption that you've accomplished that, however, we're at the final step:

1. Understand your own value package.
2. Translate your value into long-term results for any given client.
3. Find the economic buyer in your target customer.
4. Educate the buyer so that he or she reaches the same conclusions.
5. Only then suggest your value options.

You never want the buyer to be making the decision as to whether or not to use your services. You want the buyer to be making the decision as to how to use your services. To accomplish that, you must provide the buyer with options. You control this dynamic. If you provide options, the buyer will consider them. If you don't, it's unlikely that the buyer will say, "Why don't we develop some options that provide me with a range of ways in which to use you?"

This is not abstruse reasoning. The buyer will do what's in his or her best interest. You must manage the relationship so that what's in your self-interest is in the buyer's self-interest: hiring you.

An Example

Let's suppose that the buyer is considering you for a two-hour concurrent session at an annual conference. The buyer has budgeted for six speakers at $3,500 each in the three concurrent sessions and $6,500 each for keynoters to open and close. Here are some options you might propose:

- Conduct one concurrent session as planned for $3,500.
- Conduct two of the concurrent sessions on different topics for $6,000, saving the client $1,000.
- Present one of the keynotes and a concurrent session for $8,000, saving the client $2,000.
- Present the concurrent session and facilitate breakout groups when the participants are later divided into working teams for $5,000.
- Present the concurrent session and moderate a customer panel that the client had planned for later in the program for $5,000.
- Use any permutations of the foregoing options.

Speaking Up: Remember, the discussion should never be about fee, solely about value.

However, there is a far more powerful way to build speaking fees into project riches.

TURNING AN EVENT INTO A PROCESS AND TRIPLING YOUR SUCCESS

A standard exercise that I insist on in my coaching of speakers is to create a list of everything that they can do prior to, during, and after a session. Many speakers include these elements anyway, since their low self-esteem drives them to throw in everything but washing the dog to justify their fee. None of this will be terribly new, until you see what I'm about to do with it.

Here is a synopsis of what most people tell me. Your lists may differ based upon your topic, background, and focus.

Prior to Event	During Event	After Event
Interview attendees	Deliver presentation	Debrief with buyer
Interview customers	Provide visuals aids	Follow-up sessions
Interview suppliers	Provide handouts	Web page access
Shop the business	Book signing	Coaching by e-mail
Shop the competition	Partners' program	Coaching by phone
Survey	Breakout groups	Survey
Customize materials		Electronic summaries
Interview board[4]		Newsletter
Submit plans/review		Send best practices
Talk to other speakers		Follow-up materials
Critique the agenda		

You can see where this is going. Instead of an "event," you now have a process for improvement. Instead of throwing

---

[4] Especially important and a huge marketing aid if you're dealing with a trade association, where board members are likely to also be your potential buyers.

the kitchen sink into the pot, you're offering the buyer a menu of options.

"What will the fee be?" you're asked.

"I can't tell yet, but why don't you select the value that appeals to you during our overall time together, and I'll create a fee based on your needs and preferences."

I guarantee you—guarantee you—that if you take this structure and organize every speaking opportunity, whether keynote or training, around it, you will quintuple your fees over the course of a year. That means that you must overcome the mentality that "I'm not worth it" and adopt the mentality that "I have tremendous value to offer, and I'd be remiss if I didn't provide everything I can for the buyer's consideration."

Note that this doesn't work unless you're talking to a buyer. A human resource person will simply ask you to do it all for the lowest fee possible.[5]

Buyers may love to reduce fees, but *they hate to reduce value.* Once you introduce significant value, buyers want it. This is an emotional decision. Logic makes people think; emotion makes them act. On the trust "pyramid," you'll find this progression:

Emotional

Intellectual

Affiliative

Expert

Referral

[5] I'll send you a free, autographed copy of any of my books if you can find three full-time, career HR executives who were promoted to CEO of a Fortune 500 company between 2000 and 2010, a full decade. There's a reason that general counsels, actuaries, vice presidents of sales, and COOs become CEOs, and HR people don't!

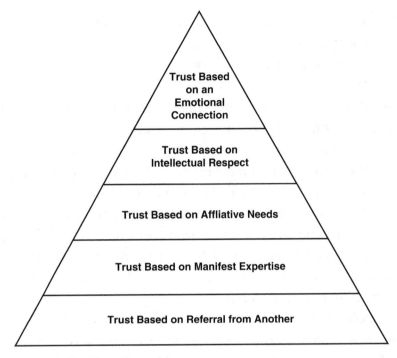

Figure 4-2 The Trust Pyramid

Being referred by a trusted source is important; being seen as an expert is comforting; filling a desire to have an affiliation is significant; holding high intellectual status is imposing; but creating an emotional bond is invaluable.

I once thought that as value increased, fees could increase. I was incalculably wrong. The lines actually cross as trust and a brand are developed, *because people expect to get what they pay for!*

No buyer says, "Listen up, I was able to get the cheapest speaker in the country. I might have obtained his services for less, but I felt sorry for him. I want you to hang on his every word."

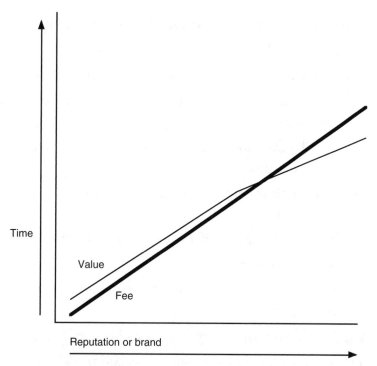

Figure 4-3 When Value Follows Fee

Instead, they say what Curt Nelson, CEO of Silicon Space, said when he asked his people how much they thought I was costing to address them for a few hours at a meeting. Their guesses ranged from $1,500 to $3,500, with one executive wondering if that included lunch.

"He has charged me $18,500," said Curt, "so listen up!!"

Buyers have egos, too.

40 WAYS TO INCREASE YOUR FEES

Here are 40 ways to increase your fees, in addition to the model I've already provided:

1. Establish value collaboratively with the client.

2. Base your fees on value, not on the task.

3. Never use time as the basis of your value.

4. Don't stop with what the client wants—find out what the client needs.

5. Think of the fourth sale first—fees are cumulative, not situational.

6. Engage the client in the diagnosis—don't be prescriptive.

7. Never voluntarily offer options to reduce fees.

8. Add a premium if you personally "do it all."

9. If you're forced to consider fee reduction, reduce value first.

10. Provide options every time: the choice of "yeses."

11. Always provide an option that is comprehensive and over budget.

12. As early as possible, ask the QGTRIHF (Question Guaranteed to Result in Higher Fees): "What are your objectives?"

13. Broaden objectives as appropriate to increase value.

14. Ensure that the client is aware of the full range of your services.

15. If something is not on your playing field, subcontract it.

16. Always ask yourself, "Why me, why now, why in this manner?"

17. Determine how many options the buyer perceives other than you.

18. Use proposals as confirmations, not explorations.

19. When asked prematurely about fees, reply, "I don't know."

20. If you must lower fees, seek a quid pro quo from the buyer.

21. Do not accept troublesome, unpleasant, or suspicious business.

22. When collaborating or subcontracting, use objective apportionment.

23. Any highly paid employee must bring in new business, not merely deliver.

24. Seek out new economic buyers laterally during your projects.

25. It is better to do something pro bono than to do it for a low fee.

26. Fees have nothing to do with supply and demand, only with value.

27. If you are unaware of the current market fee ranges, you're undercharging.

28. Psychologically, higher fees create higher value in the buyer's mind.

29. Value can include subjective as well as objective measures.

30. Introduce new value to existing clients to raise fees in these accounts.

31. Do not accept referral business on the same basis as the referent.

32. When forced into phases, offer partial rebates to guarantee future business.

33. At least every two years, consider jettisoning the bottom 15 percent of your business.

34. Start with payment terms that are maximally beneficial to you every time.

35. Offer incentives for one-time, full payments.

36. Never accept payment subject to conditions to be met upon completion.

37. Focus on improvement, not problem solving.

38. Provide proactive ideas, benchmarking, and best practices from experience.

39. Practice stating and explaining your fees.

40. Always be prepared to walk away from business.

You'd have a hard time convincing me that at least half of these points don't apply to your situation and business.

INCREASING FEE VELOCITY

There's one more aspect to improving fees that most speakers neglect: the *velocity* of the fee. This means that you want to get your fee into your bank as rapidly as possible, but the default position of speakers is often "pay me whenever you feel like it." The terms and conditions of your engagement should be stipulated after conceptual agreement on outcomes and value so that they are merely an afterthought for the buyer. But if you don't establish payment terms, some purchasing agent in the bowels of the client organization is ready—and paid—to do so.

Always try to get paid in full in advance. You won't always be able to, *but you will never be paid this way if you don't ask*. Simply state that your policy is full fee in advance to secure the date and begin any preparatory activities, such as presentation design, materials customization, participant interviews, and so forth.[6]

If you can't get your full fee in advance, you may want to try a soft incentive, such as a 5 or 10 percent discount if the fee is paid in advance. (Don't offer this if the presentation date is imminent.) Such a discount is important for two reasons:

1. You will be holding the money *and using it* for a long period, sometimes as much as a year in advance.

2. The client cannot cancel your engagement if you are holding the money.

Note: Many bureaus have a "policy" of holding your fees "in escrow" until after you deliver the presentation and the client is happy. Simply don't do business with someone with this kind of benighted mentality. The client is YOURS, not the bureau's, which is merely the middleman. Your payment terms are up to you. (Some dopey bureau principals will ask, "How do I know you'll still be here on that date?" I reply, "There's a lot better chance of my being here than of your being here!")

I have a myriad of letters from speakers and consultants testifying to the wisdom of this advice, providing examples of contracts that would have been canceled or delayed because of internal client changes if the fee had not already been paid.

Demand, as a minimum, a 50 percent deposit, with the balance to be paid *prior to the time of the presentation.* That's right, you get an envelope before you show up. Some bureaus will demand a 50 percent deposit *and keep all of it until your*

---

[6] Expenses should be billed at the conclusion of an engagement, or monthly if the engagement is ongoing, and should be payable upon receipt of your invoice.

presentation as a "guarantee." Tell them to take a walk. If a bureau collects a 50 percent deposit, it should keep its 25 percent full commission and forward the balance to you immediately.

> **Speaking Up: Payment terms are often subject to your policy. If you don't have one, the client's policy will prevail, and it certainly won't be one of paying you as quickly as possible.**

If a bureau places you and collects the deposit, the balance should be payable to you at the presentation, not to the bureau (which will further delay payment, sometimes for months—some bureaus even demand that expense reimbursement go through them).

I don't advise ever accepting less than a 50 percent deposit, or a bureau collecting its 25 percent commission, with the remainder being received on the presentation date. Anything less is not a collaboration and leaves you vulnerable to cancellation, delay, late payments, disputed costs, client internal turmoil, and so forth.

Guarantee your work in writing, but make your contract noncancelable in writing as the quid pro quo. This is a business. Businesses turn a profit. (I had four such full deposits prior to 9/11. I offered every client its money back in the wake of the tragedy. Every one told me that it would reschedule; some took over a year to do so, but each one did, and I kept the money and the clients.)

To summarize: base your fees on the value you bring to the client's objectives; provide for options (value packages) in the context of a process flow, so that the client can decide how best to use you and not whether to use you; and increase the velocity of the ensuing payment in every way possible through aggressive terms. If you do that, you'll have the processes in place to make a million dollars. Let's turn now to how you attract that kind of business.

SUMMARY

Fees should be based on value. Even a "bare bones" keynote request has the potential for advance work, concurrent work, and follow-up work. Don't view what you do as an "event," but rather as a "process."

At a minimum, set your fees aggressively for a short, medium, and longer presentation. These fees should not be based on your tenure in the profession, but rather on your brand, your intellectual property, and the value you deliver. The easiest, best, and most lucrative way to do this is to deal directly with economic buyers, not with middlemen.

Speakers' bureaus and meeting planners are not organized to maximize your fees or even to maximize your success. The former work on a volume basis, trying to place as many people as they can in the mistaken belief that the client belongs to them and that speakers are merely hired hands instead of talent. The latter are paid and given incentives to minimize costs, irrespective of quality or results.

You can get so good, so much in demand, and so talked about that value will follow fees—buyers will expect to get what they pay for, just as they do with a Bentley car or a Baume & Mercier watch.

If you want to make a million in the speaking profession, focus on these two keys: work only with true buyers, not middlemen; and focus on the process and its outcomes, not the time or event. If you do, you'll be ahead of about 85 percent of the speakers out there.

MODERN MARKETING

I DON'T CARE ABOUT THE COST; GET ME JANE JONES!

IT'S IMPORTANT that you attract business because

- Very few people buy from "cold calls" in this business.
- You don't have to prove yourself or present credentials.
- There is minimal cost of acquisition.
- Fees simply don't matter.

I could go on, but that's more than enough. You want to attract the right clients—those that are amenable and appropriate for the fee structures discussed in Chapter 4. Fortunately, I can help you do that right here.

THE MAGIC AND MYTH OF THE INTERNET

Let me annoy as many of you as I can immediately: your Web site is *not* a sales tool.

Oh, my, what about all those Internet marketing gurus? Well, they're wrong about Web sites (and a lot of other stuff, but we don't have time for that here).

Your Web site is a *credibility statement*. That is, buyers—true buyers—might go there to get some additional information once they hear of you, read something about you, meet with you, and so forth. Only nonbuyers "troll" the Internet looking for speakers, and they will send a generic communication, such as: "We are looking for presenters at the National Hot Air and Persiflage Association annual convention. If you're interested, please go to www.gasbag.edu and fill out the presenter's form."[1]

What this means is that your site needs to do only two things—two things!—well and quickly: tell the buyer what's in it for him or her, and justify it with testimonials from his or her peers.

Speaking Up: You must appeal to the buyer's self-interest and provide a level of comfort through peer-level endorsements.

Alan's Formula for Web Site Success

1. State your value proposition prominently (e.g., "I reduce the cost of new client acquisition while decreasing closing times").

2. State quickly what's in it for the buyer, e.g., your people will:

   • Master the four steps of the "immediate close."
   • Rebut resistance in the four main objections dimensions.
   • Create larger sales per new customer.
   • Learn to close sales on the telephone.
   • Generate more profit per client.

---

[1] As often as not, they'll either charge you to present or give you "free registration"! But they won't pay you or reimburse your expenses.

3. Have at least two prominent testimonials, preferably video testimonials and/or rotating print testimonials.

4. On succeeding pages, include your position papers, credentials, clients, case studies, speaking topics, whatever. But these are all subordinate to the value to be found immediately on the home page. Think of your home page as the opening two minutes of a speech, during which people decide whether to pay close attention thereafter.

5. It's as simple as that.

Social media platforms, at least as of this writing, are for fun and for looking up old school chums, but not for marketing professional services. (Would you hire a speaker who solicited you on social media? Most high-level buying decisions are made on the basis of peer-to-peer referrals.)

Search engine optimization (SEO) and placing ads on Google and similar sources (or paying for positioning) are wastes of time and money, *because buyers aren't seeking you on the Internet.* Besides, the more you publish, are interviewed, and speak (see the discussion of Market Gravity later in this chapter), the more you'll be automatically elevated on the search engines. Stop worrying about this, and never pay for it.

However, there are some simple actions that can pay dividends. For example, always have a full signature file (including your address—if a stalker wants to kill you, there are other ways to find you), and include a brief promotional statement (e.g., "Cited as the best speaker on global leadership in the manufacturing arena—*Chicago Tribune*") and a reference to your Web site, blog, newsletter, or other source.

If your expertise is in team building, for example, create an electronic newsletter that is provocative and will brand you: *Jim Pay's PAYDAY, the newsletter for high-performing team leadership.*[2]

People complain to me, "There are so many newsletters; won't mine get lost in the crowd?" Yes, if you're dull. There are so many newsletters because people *read them.* (Burger King builds burger joints across the street from McDonald's because it knows that people in the area are buying burgers!) Competition opens markets, it doesn't confine markets.

Pull together a list, no matter how modest at first, and create an online, consistent newsletter. If your list grows, consider a listserv, which will allow automatic subscriptions, cancellations, changes, and so forth, as well as distribution with one simple paste.[3]

While the social media platforms are mostly for informal chats (and can be huge time dumps), blogs are something else. There are 200 million blogs in the world as I write this, and 99 percent of them are awful—self-indulgent, derivative, outright plagiarized, ungrammatical, blatant self-promotion, and so on. Many of them don't even reveal their source, and quite a few are just excuses to sell advertisements.

However, if you are provocative; use text, audio, and video; and post regularly (e.g., at least three times per week—many blogs go months without updating), you can use this as a springboard to refer people to your business and results. Buyers do, on occasion, subscribe to blogs that focus on their areas of interest (e.g., The Strategist Next Door). You can see my very active blog at www.contrarianconsulting.com.

---

[2] You can usually trademark or service mark a newsletter title, and you can get an ISSN (equivalent to a book's ISBN) to protect it and identify it further at http://www.issn.org.

[3] I use databack.com, for example, which costs about $29 per mailing, and I have more than 10,000 subscribers.

Use the Internet as one aspect of your promotion, but don't assume that it's all things to all people. Most of the greatest advocates for Internet marketing make their money by selling Internet marketing services, if you get my drift.

WORKING (OR NOT) WITH BUREAUS AND AVOID BEING A HIRED HAND

The key to riches in the speaking business is working smart, not working hard. That means that you need to examine your own basic beliefs, understandings, assumptions, and implicit approaches to the business, since there's a distinct possibility that some of them are inaccurate and a couple may be plain wrong. That's because there are more people giving advice (and charging for it) in the speaking business than there are good speakers.

The last time anyone looked, coaching was a *leveraging* position, meaning that there are a multitude of excellent players created by a superb coach. When there is mediocre coaching, there is usually a myriad of very average players. But in no circumstances is there a rational reason to have legions of good coaches and a resultant swarm of undistinguished players. There are relatively few excellent speakers in the land (otherwise, fee competition would keep prices low, and my advice in the previous chapter about charging for value would be commonplace), which leads me to believe that the hordes of coaches aren't that hot, either.

One of the worst of the assumptions that even veteran speakers labor under is that a relationship with a speakers' bureau is mandatory and that the parameters of such a relationship are dictated by the bureau, which can be very choosy about whom it represents. Here are some facts about the bureau relationship that apply to all of us, whether we've never been asked, never chosen to work with them, work with them occasionally, or get virtually all of our engagements through them (which is exceedingly rare).

Five Facts to Challenge Your Assumptions about Bureaus

1. Bureaus Cannot Live without Speakers, but the Reverse Is Not True

I worked with an insurance company whose executives warned me that the independent agents were their customers.

"What about the people buying insurance?" I asked.

"Oh, they're our customers, too," the executives quickly conceded.

"Well, if there were no agents, only potential customers, could you still sell insurance?" I pressed.

"Of course, and we sell directly about 30 percent of the time right now."

"If there were no potential customers, only agents, could you still sell insurance?"

"Of course not."

"Well, I think you're confused about who your customers are and what your sales and distribution methods are," said I, as I proceeded to create a long-term relationship with my customer.

I understand who pays me for value, and it's not the bureau. We could speak if there were no such thing as bureaus, but bureaus could not exist if there were no such thing as speakers. Consequently, this has to be a collaborative relationship, wherein the bureau *earns its commission from your client's payment by providing value to you.*

> *Speaking Up: The client is yours, not the bureau's. You are the talent. The bureau is merely a broker, and it had better provide value-added to you.*

I've spoken to scores of bureau principals and owners. About a quarter of them don't bother to hide their belief that speakers are the biggest pain in their lives and that their jobs would be just dandy without them. They treat the speakers that they do represent as hired hands, and they regard speakers who seek to be represented as door-to-door con artists whose phone calls aren't returned and whose submission of materials isn't acknowledged.

Even if you are a neophyte struggling for business—and much more so if you are a veteran to whom buyers come directly—walk away from any bureau that does not treat you as a valuable, talented partner. You shouldn't take rude treatment and lack of respect from a paying client. Why on earth would you accept it from someone you are paying to market you?

2. There's No Magic in a 25 Percent Commission

The standard rate for business is 25 percent from the speaker's fee. Although some speakers increase their fees to accommodate the commission and try to net the same amount as they would otherwise have received, this is a bad practice.[4] Some bureaus try to collect 30 percent or more. For a third of your fee, they'd better be coming to your home and washing the windows.

---

[4] That's because you should never penalize the client for your marketing costs, and your clients (or others who hear of it) will mistrust you if they find that you have essentially two different fees for delivering the same approximate value depending on how the sale is consummated.

Commissions can be negotiable. For example, if a bureau introduces your name to a prospect, works with you to develop a presentation based on the client's unique needs, and closes the sale on your behalf, that's worth a lot of money because the business is probably not a relationship that you otherwise would have secured. Conversely, if the bureau merely gives you a contact's name and suggests that you call him or her and sell a deal directly, the bureau has provided a service, but one of much less value because you had to do the work, and the purpose of bureaus is that *they* do most of the marketing work.

Especially if you're asked to reduce your fee for any reason (e.g., for a nonprofit organization, for a good client who is in a budget squeeze, or for a speech that requires only local travel), ask the bureau how much it will reduce its commission level.

I gave a speech at a reduced fee for a local insurance general agent who employed 20 people. It was an hour's presentation only 10 minutes from my home, and the agent promised to forward my materials and a testimonial to his corporate office, where he served on the committee for the large regional convention. Sure enough, I was later hired at full fee on the basis of his recommendation. His company then asked its exclusive bureau in Washington to send me the paperwork. *The bureau actually wanted 25 percent of my fee for having done nothing but send me the paperwork!*

3. The Bureau's Customer Is the Person Who Pays It: You

I'm sick to death of the malarkey that the bureau's customer is the organization that is seeking the speaker. The buyer isn't paying the bureau (although the deposit check is going in that direction); *you* are paying the bureau out of your fee. The commission comes from the speaker.

Consequently, a bureau's insistence that you conduct no direct conversations with the buyer doesn't serve the buyer well, since you have to explore the buyer's needs and establish a relationship with the person who is responsible for the outcome of the session. That is not done efficiently through an intermediary. Your relationship with the bureaus must be collaborative, not onerous. Your material needn't be entirely "bureau-friendly."[5] But if the bureau believes that your contact with the buyer will result in an unethical deal that excludes the bureau, then the level of trust needed to build a productive collaboration isn't present.

Most bureaus will ask for a 25 percent deposit to hold a date, which becomes their commission. The balance is then due at the presentation and payable to you. However, some bureaus ask for a 50 percent deposit (which is a good idea), but keep the entire amount until your speech (which is a ridiculous idea). Instead of being held, the balance should be forwarded to you immediately. I know of a few bureaus that receive full payment and attempt to hold it until after the speech. While addressing a bureau group one day on the subject of professional ethics, I asked how anyone could tolerate someone else holding his or her money.

"You don't understand," pontificated one bureau owner. "How do we know that the speaker will actually appear? We have to hold some sort of guarantee."

As some of his colleagues murmured approval, I asked, "How do I know that your bureau will be here in six months? What's my guarantee?"

There was no response to that question.

---

[5] This is the practice of providing literature, tapes, workbooks, and other such material to the bureau without your address, phone, or contacts so that the bureau can ensure that all client contacts are exclusively with the bureau. In other words, the bureau doesn't trust either you or the client.

4. If You Allow Them to, Bureaus Will Manage Perception

There is the reality of what buyers really want to see and evaluate, and there is the perception of what bureaus want them to see and evaluate. Remember from our prior discussions that you should try to build relationships with economic buyers and that bureaus tend to build their relationships with meeting planners.

Consequently, there is a developed mythology stating, for example, that speakers must have demo videos if they are to be considered for work. I worked with bureaus for years without such a video, as have many other successful speakers. However, videos are useful to meeting planners for *deselection*. It's easy to watch barely three minutes of tape and decide whether the speaker's "look" or "style" is acceptable to the meeting planner. As the videos become more vanilla and similar—because there are a relatively few "coaches" producing the same look for everyone—the meeting planners are in a position to compare like commodities and make their selections without considering real substance and content. (Which is why the video that I use today is imperfect and of a live two-hour keynote complete with audience reaction. I want people to see me in action, and I don't want to be seen as another slick marketing piece.)

Bureaus also love "showcases," in which they ask speakers to pay for the privilege of auditioning their wares in front of dozens (or even scores) of meeting planners. I find these repugnant because I'd be subsidizing the bureau's marketing expenses, appearing before the wrong kind of buyer, and presenting in juxtaposition to a dozen or more competitors, which creates a commodity—hell, a meat-market—atmosphere.

The audience quickly glazes over. You have eight minutes on the stage, and if you're not among the first few, people are busy texting.

If you don't make enough to pay the bills one month, the bureaus aren't going to send you something to tide you over. Listen to their advice about the market, but then make your own decisions about how you want to be perceived, what your unique value-added is, and how the customer relationship should be established.

5. There Are Terrific Bureaus and Terrible Bureaus

To find the best bureaus to work with (and I've included some on the Web site), ask speakers who work with them regularly. There are some that I direct people to, and others that I divert people from. Don't believe that a bureau's mere interest is synonymous with quality. Even some of the better-known bureaus are run by people who think that speakers should fall on their knees in order to do business with them. One woman said to me that I should change my business card, which has represented me through a practice that creates a hefty seven-figure income, to be more consistent with what she likes to see on a card.

"I'd never do that," I said.

"Then you'll never work with me," she loftily intoned.

"So what?" I asked.

There are, unfortunately, many people calling themselves bureaus who are actually lone wolves working out of a bedroom or off a kitchen table. While there are many speakers who do the same, the difference is that the bureau wants 25 percent of your fee in return for marketing you, which means, unless I've missed something, that the bureau must have marketing resources in addition to a phone and a post-office box. A bureau should have staff to canvass prospects and research organizations, equipment to duplicate tapes and written materials, sophisticated communications media and computers, established business contacts, a stable of successful and happy speakers, and an identifiable and content client base.

There is nothing wrong with asking a bureau for references! Ask it for names of speakers and those speakers' clients gained through the bureau. Don't you provide references when someone is interested in hiring you?

In the early years, my bureau-placed business was 80 percent of my work; in recent years, it's been as little as 5 percent of my work. Bureaus can be a strong market-leverage device or a drain on your time and income. Whatever they are, you can control the dynamic.

To provide both sides of the issue, in the following lists you'll find what you must do to ensure a good relationship and, in all fairness, what the bureau needs to do if it's to represent you professionally.

Alan's Musts for a Successful Bureau Relationship: Speaker Requirements

Here are my personal guidelines for a successful bureau relationship, which can be highly rewarding for all parties concerned. However, if you don't manage the relationship for your best interests, the "default" position will not be very desirable.

1. Establish a relationship with the owner. Others may place you and market you, but you can tell if the bureau's values are compatible with yours only by working with the principal.

2. Request and receive references and examples of the bureau's marketing materials. Don't accept claims at face value. Ask if this quality represents you well.

3. Retain your identity on the materials and literature that you provide for marketing. If the bureau doesn't trust you, then don't get involved with it.

4. Avoid mandatory co-marketing investments. Options to take out listings, showcase, exhibit, and so on are fine and valuable, as long as you can pick and choose. But too many bureaus are trying to earn money *from* speakers and not *for* speakers.

5. Clarify that you will speak to prospects directly and early when this is needed to determine how to help close the business (and if it's right for your skills).

6. Expect a callback on the same business day (or the next morning) when you leave a message with the bureau. You're entitled to professional responsiveness.

7. Require that "holds" (tentative bookings) be managed carefully and removed from your calendar as soon as the bureau determines that the business will not close.

8. Ensure that all fees in excess of the bureau's commission are paid directly to you at the time of receipt and that the client directly reimburses you for your expenses.

9. Request flexibility in commissions for spin-off business, multiple bookings, ancillary consulting work, and related situations that merit reduced commissions.

10. Avoid exclusive arrangements. Only by allowing numerous bureaus to represent you will you ensure your own flexibility and find your own best deals.

Alan's Musts for a Successful Bureau Relationship: Bureau Requirements

The excellent bureaus have legitimate needs that speakers must adhere to, especially if a trusting relationship is to be built. A great deal of this relies on ethical and professional behavior, which, unfortunately, isn't always in great supply.

1. Be honest about your capabilities. Don't accept assignments unless you can serve the client well. Exceed expectations. The bureau's reputation is its main asset.

2. Be original. Don't use others' materials, and don't use shopworn generic stories. Clients who hire speakers can usually spot these instantly.

3. Arrive early and stay late. Let the local coordinator know that you've arrived, and don't rush off during the applause. Avoid tight connections and last-minute arrivals.

4. Be honest about outcomes. If there were problems, whether technical, interpersonal, or logistical, tell the bureau immediately.

5. Keep your materials up to date and professional. Provide contemporary testimonials, quality brochures, and effective handouts.

6. Join in win/win co-marketing. It can make sense for you to appear in a special mailing or create a voice-mail sample of your speaking. You're in this together.

7. Speak to prospects quickly whenever requested. Good bureaus know when a few words from the speaker can close the deal. Don't keep the buyer waiting.

8. Recommend other fine speakers to the bureau. This is not a zero-sum game. The more the bureau succeeds, the more it can invest in your success.

9. Scrupulously forward spin-off business (business leads or closed deals gained during a bureau placement). This is a contractual *and an ethical* requirement.

10. Maintain consistency in your fee structure (although it may be highly diverse), and provide lengthy advance notice if scheduled fees are to be raised.

Having said all that, bureaus should be a minor part of your marketing cosmos.

TRADE ASSOCIATIONS: MAKE MONEY *AND* MARKET CONCURRENTLY

When you speak at a trade association, you are being explicitly or implicitly endorsed by an objective third party—the trade association. In most cases, you're also being paid to be there, which means that you're making money while you market *and* you're seen as highly valuable.

My idea of the hierarchy of highly leveraged marketing through sponsors and third parties follows. The characteristics of the most potentially rewarding third-party sponsors are:

- Full and normal fees are paid to the speaker.
- The audience includes significant buyers for your services.
- The audience is large.
- The event is prestigious, and the sponsor is highly regarded.
- There are other "draws" on the agenda.
- You have a general session, not a concurrent session.
- You can sell products and services at the event.

As you can see, a local nonprofit group is probably looking for some sage advice and professional platform skills, but the audience usually will contain, at best, recommenders. But at a national trade association meeting, all of my conditions can be met.

The Hierarchy of Third-Party Sponsorship

National trade associations

- Health Industries Distributors Association
- International Association for Financial Planners
- American Bankers Association

Local and regional trade associations (or chapters)

- Minneapolis Personnel Association
- Houston Chapter, American Institute of Architects
- Tennessee Recreational Vehicle Association

Management extension programs

- Universities, colleges, junior colleges
- Private programs (The Learning Connection)
- Government support (Small Business Administration)

Local nonprofit business groups

- Rotary
- Chamber of Commerce
- Better Business Bureau

Local nonprofit community groups

- Service clubs
- Youth groups
- Parent-teacher leagues

My hierarchy is not a single, linear climb. I continue to speak at local nonprofits and at every other level in the hierarchy. But I've already been to the top, and I continue to speak there on a regular basis. What are you doing to get there?

Trade associations have a lot of money. They will often have a meeting planner *who is much more powerful than his or her private-sector counterpart* because the trade association's raison d'être is the education of its members, so conferences and conventions are the place to demonstrate to the members that their dues and obligations are quite worthwhile. You will be dealing with either the executive director of the association or a meeting planner who is also an officer of the organization. Don't let anyone kid you; trade associations pay as much as, *if not more than*, private-sector meetings.[6]

Here are 12 tips for successfully marketing to trade associations and successfully delivering a speech to the membership that will result in leveraged business from the attendees.

Alan's 12 Tips to Leverage the Trade Association Marketplace

1. *Talk to members first.* Learn about their concerns and issues. If you are targeting the National Association of Music Merchants, visit some local members' retail stores and talk to the owners.

2. *Demonstrate a unique nonindustry perspective.* These conferences are blanketed with speakers with content

---

[6] I refer you again to an invaluable resource, *NTPA: National Trade and Professional Associations of the United States* (New York: Columbia Books, Inc.). See the Web site for specific contact information. This annual publication contains every trade association, its president, budget, convention sites, conference themes, membership, and other pertinent information, and no speaker's reference library should be without it (https://www.columbiabooks.com).

knowledge, and they're usually deadly dull. Establish conversancy in the field, but introduce your fresh, nonindustry perspective. Your value is in world-class best practices. (I was a huge hit speaking about strategy at the American Feed and Grain Lot convention because everyone else was speaking about the innards of animals.)

3. *Create an intelligence file.* Using your regular business reading, the Internet, and reference resources, generate a "dossier" on the industry's strengths and weaknesses, its past, present, and likely future.

4. *Orient your approach toward the future.* Trade association members are thirsty for help in making sense out of changing times, particularly in volatile industries (e.g., health care, telecommunications, and travel). Don't tell them what they already know.

5. *Be provocative.* Don't be afraid to be contrarian. Give people something to talk about. You want your name mentioned in the halls. (One association executive rushed up to me to tell me, "You were a hit in the ladies room!" You never know about all the private measurement devices that buyers use in this business.)

Speaking Up: Tell people what they need to know to thrive in the future, not to revive the past or to survive the present.

---

6. *Create visual aids and handouts that mention the industry.* You don't have to create an entirely new speech, but you should insert examples, stories, anecdotes, visuals, and aspects of your handouts (if you use them)

that embrace the industry. This helps the learning and greatly increases the likelihood of spin-off business.

7. *Let the audience know that you've done your homework.* I almost always include some segments in which I say, "I polled some of the members at this convention and asked them what advice they'd give someone who was new to your business. Over 80 percent said, 'Save your money!'"

8. *Create a meeting-specific handout.* This could be a single sheet, a copy of your slides, or detailed support for your presentation. Make it something that participants will want to keep. Put the conference date and the title of your speech on the cover. In addition, put your name and every piece of contact information on every page (in case individual pages are photocopied and circulated back home).

9. *Offer to deliver multiple sessions.* Even highly paid veteran speakers will gladly do this. The association likes to provide the keynoter, for example, in the more intimate setting of a concurrent session. The association can save money—and you can earn more—by using you three times instead of using three people one time each.

10. *Parlay your trade association appearances.* Include trade association publicity, testimonials, appearance dates, interviews, and so forth prominently in your media kit. Trade association speaking, as you've seen, is a somewhat specialized skill. If you've mastered it, the accolades can provide ready access to more and more associations.

11. *Record it.* Many large meetings feature projections on screens, and such equipment can automatically record

for you. If that's not the case, ask about the facility or organization recording your presentation. Worst case, consider paying for it yourself. (Get professional advice, for example, using two cameras, avoiding time-sensitive references, wardrobe, and so forth.) You can use this for marketing, product sales, self-improvement, and other purposes.

12. *Meet the board.* Either interview the board members or meet them on site if they're present, because almost every board member of a professional association is a business owner or executive and a prospective buyer of your services. Offer to build in their comments and/or debrief them, but whatever you do, try to make sure that you develop a relationship that you can nurture post-speech.

Trade associations are ideal venues for new and veteran speakers. Go after the executive director with a press kit, a demo video (if you have one), an introduction from a third party (if you can get one), and a follow-up phone call, all emphasizing what you can do to improve the membership's condition. Offer to do interviews for the association's publications and/or contribute articles. These are rich mines of speaking wealth.

WHERE AND HOW TO PUBLISH

If you want to make it big in the speaking profession, you have to publish. Articles in major media will do the following:

- Enhance your visibility and credibility
- Provide solid content for your media kit
- Force you to continually generate new ideas and validate old ones

- Gain entry into more and more publications through repute
- Provide access to other media (radio, TV, Internet)
- Generate leads
- Provide handouts for your sessions
- Form the basis for future books
- Form the basis for future products
- Transform intellectual capital into intellectual property

If you've never published, use the "staircase" technique shown in Figure 5-1. It begins with a local column for the weekly community newspaper and leads to the local daily (*Podunk Pendulum*), the regional daily (*Hartford Courant*), the state magazine (*Rhode Island Monthly*), the national publication (*Bottom Line*), and the "media of record" (*New York Times,*

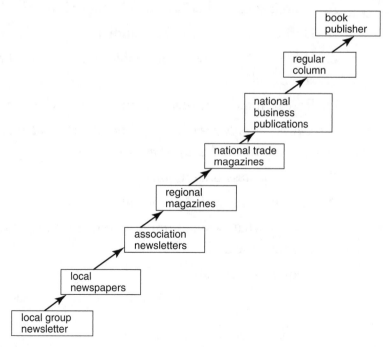

Figure 5-1 The staircase method for publishing.

Wall Street Journal). In other words, parlay what you do, using tear sheets and columns from the first publications to progressively sell editors of larger publications.[7]

How to Get an Article Published

I. Determine what subject you want to write about.

  A. Why are you the person to comment on the topic?

  B. How will this subject enhance your business, repute, or standing?

  C. Why is the subject relevant at this time (and for the next several months)?

    Don't be afraid to be contrarian. The world doesn't need another piece on "left-brain vs. right-brain thinking" or "the seven delta approach to quality."

II. Determine where you want to publish the article.

  A. Who is your audience, and what does it read?

  B. Don't be afraid to ask your audience!

  C. Where is it most reasonable for you to be successful?

  D. Research publications and study their style.

    I was never published in the Times *until I sent it an article that I realized was just what it needed!*

III. Prepare a professional inquiry.

  A. Send it to a specific editor's attention.

  B. Specify what, why, examples, uniqueness, length, and delivery date.

  C. Request specifications.

---

[7] See the Web site for some sources and ideas.

D. Always enclose a SASE[8] if your submission is in hard copy.

E. Cite credentials—yours and the article's.

This step must be more carefully executed than the actual article!

IV. Write it like a pro.

A. Use specific examples, names, and places.

B. Write it yourself, but solicit critiques.

C. Write it to the specifications.

D. Make sure that you include autobiographical data at the end.

E. Request free reprints, reprint permission, or discounted reprints.

F. Don't self-promote; let the substance do it for you.

G. If rejected: resubmit, resubmit, resubmit, resubmit, resubmit.

Use prior articles as credentials to write newer ones.

Some Other Comments

Don't overwrite. Write what's on your mind without worrying about the great American novel. When you edit, you'll find that the piece is amazingly good. Attribute things that you borrow, but don't try to dazzle your reader with superfluous references. Be critical and analytical. Readers respond best to provocation and the opportunity to look at things in a new way. When in doubt, start a new paragraph. Use graphics

---

[8] Self-addressed stamped envelope. Actually, submitting in hard copy can often circumvent the "noise" of e-mail and secure you more attention.

when appropriate, and try to load in the metaphors and similes.

Tell people what they need to know, not everything that you know!

Speaking Up: There's a simple rule for publishing: first, have something to say.

The great debate is about whether or not to self-publish books. I've self-published as well as published commercially. My criteria are simple: self-publish books when

- You want a product to sell with maximum profit.
- You want a handout for your training sessions.
- You have a clearly defined niche market.
- You have a very powerful brand that will draw readers.
- You want to capitalize on a time-sensitive event or window.

But publish only through a known commercial publisher when

- You want maximum credibility with buyers (especially corporate).
- You want to improve your credibility as an authority.
- You want maximum distribution channels.
- You want to maximize your chances for foreign translation.

Sometimes a commercially published book will earn considerable royalties, and sometimes a self-published book will gain you credibility. But not usually. Notice that ego stroking is not on either list. There are a lot of bad books published commercially, and most self-published books are awful. If you need your ego stroked, buy a dog. If you need to tell people that you're an author, yet you have nothing to say that will sell a publisher, use the money you would have invested in the vanity publishing to secure the services of a therapist. You're not a driver unless you can drive a car, and you're not an author unless someone else pays to publish your stuff.

And NEVER invest in a scheme where you have one chapter in a book with famous "names" authoring the others. That is laughably transparent and makes money only for those who organize the "opportunity."

Harsh? Yes. Reality? Also yes.

Here's my route for getting a book published commercially once you've ascended the staircase. Book publishing is slightly easier when you have a long track record of articles and columns to support it, but these are not prerequisites. The most important thing is convincing the publisher (or your agent) that your book will sell, and the way to achieve that is to do your own homework, because the editor hasn't the time or the inclination to do it for you. It is difficult to get your first book published, but with a targeted, systematic approach, it's much easier than most people think.[9] Follow these guidelines.

How to Get a Book Published

I. Determine what it is you have to say.

    A. Your particular expertise from your education, experience, training, or circumstances.

---

[9] Contrary to popular opinion, literary agents can be quite effective for first-time authors. There are some who actually specialize in the speaking field. See the references on the Web site http://www.summit consulting.com.

    B. Your ability to "pull together" disparate things that others haven't.

    C. Your ideas, concepts, theories, and innovations.

    D. Your work with clients.

    If you have nothing constructive to contribute, don't write a word.

 II. Determine which publishers are most likely to agree with you.

    A. Examine their current books in print.

    B. Request their specifications.

    C. Ask people in the business.

    Do not vanity publish or self-publish—it's a waste of time and no one's impressed—unless you apply the previous criteria and they pertain to you.

 III. Prepare a treatment for the publisher's (or agent's) review.

    A. Why you?

    B. Why this topic?

    C. Why this topic handled in this manner?

    D. What competitive works are extant, and why is yours needed?

    E. Who is the audience?

    F. When would the manuscript be ready?

    G. What are its special features (e.g., endorsements, self-tests, etc.)?

    H. Provide at least the introduction and one chapter, a table of contents, and summaries of the other chapters.

    If you can't sell it to the publisher, you'll never sell it to the reader.

IV. Write it like a pro.

    A. Invite clients and/or respected authorities to contribute.

    B. Use sophisticated fonts and formatting.

    C. Don't use a "ghost." If someone else writes your book, why does anyone need you?

    D. Always take the reader's viewpoint.

    E. Schedule your writing sessions just as you would your other responsibilities.

    F. Use trusted others to review, critique, and suggest.

    G. Always attribute anything that's not yours.

    H. Keep it "future-current"—remember, it will be published a year after your submission.

    What is published represents your values. Are you proud of what you've written?

Some Other Comments

Don't become discouraged—keep submitting, and find out why you've been rejected. And remember, a successful business book sells about 7,500 copies! Don't expect to be on *Oprah* the next Monday. Finally, read contracts carefully because they will specify the author's discount, planned promotion, expenses you may incur, and so on. For example, you can often negotiate the indexing costs to be transferred from you to the publisher. Run the whole thing by your attorney.

Publishing will, at first, require a substantial investment of time. However, you can usually find that time on airplanes and in distant hotel rooms. Once you've broken into the field, you'll find it easier and easier to publish, both because your skills are developing and because your credibility is growing.

The staircase method is useful to ensure that you also grow as an author and avoid the success trap of publishing repeatedly for a limited audience.

THE *ZEITGEIST* OF MARKETING: THE MARKET GRAVITY CYCLE

I've found that truly brilliant marketers in this business don't— that is, *do not*—take the proverbial "rifle shot" approach. I don't believe that you should target a specific promotional opportunity and focus solely on it. My experience has been to create a broad-scale visibility that gradually rises, so that after several years you are fairly constantly in the public eye.

Don't fall victim to the numbers approach. People ask me how many "hits" I get on my Web site. I tell them that I don't care, and I mean it. I need only one—the one that's going to lead to my next $25,000 speaking engagement. I don't care how many media interviews my various listings generate because I need only the one that's going to trigger a buyer's call inquiring about a series of regional keynotes.

Perhaps you can't be all things to all people, but I've found that I'm many things to a good many people; just as you shouldn't specialize in your practice, don't specialize in your marketing. Use the print media, pro bono work, the Internet, mailings, speakers' bureaus, newsletters, publishing, trade associations, sponsors, and products, and keep all other methods alive and working for you as your time and resources permit.

> *Speaking Up: When buyers approach you, there is no need to provide credentials or justify your credibility,* **and fees are no longer an issue!**

Beware of the success trap, in which your past success ensnares you in a morass of the repetitive, noncreative status quo. I've sold articles, speeches, books, downloads, and my private mentoring services over the Internet. I've created newsletters, communities, high-end workshops, and diverse experiences that generate over $2 million annually. *Yet 75 percent of last year's income has generally originated with projects that I did not offer three years ago!* I've both commercially published and self-published to meet varying objectives.

Jump into the biggest pond you can find, and intend to become the biggest fish that the environment will accommodate. Avoid the hooks and lures that will attempt to divert you. Watch the larger fish, but don't follow them. Seek what they seek, but in your own way, using your own strokes.

Market Gravity is my metaphor for drawing buyers to you. (See Figure 5-2) Some gravity is active, some passive.

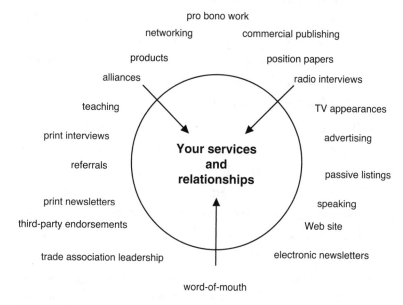

Figure 5-2 Creating Marketing Gravity

Not all may be in your comfort zone. Focus at first on the forms that are the most comfortable behaviorally, since they will be less onerous. (When I was fired and went out on my own, I focused on speaking and writing, which I loved, and eschewed networking, which I loathed.)

Here is a synopsis of Market Gravity. A new speaker should have a minimum of four routes underway. A veteran should have at least a dozen. In no particular order:

- *Referrals.* Referrals are the platinum standard in this business. While it's nice to have your name in the hat when someone requests "a superb speaker on sales excellence," it's far better when they say, "I hear from a good friend over at Acme—get me Joan Martin!"

- *Commercially published books.* The gold standard is a book from a major publisher.[10] Many people who have hired me have never read the book that attracted them to me. That's okay; I don't quiz them on Chapter 8. But they saw "strategy," "HarperCollins," and my name. That was enough. (Excellent source: the work of my agent, Jeff Herman, such as *How to Write a Winning Book Proposal.*)

- *Print interviews.* Every Sunday in the *New York Times* and many days in the *Wall Street Journal*, you will see participants in my Mentor Program cited in articles. They focus on approaching reporters and ensuring that reporters approach them. (Two good sources are Expertclick.com, which also allows a press release to

---

[10] Self-publishing has its uses, as I've noted elsewhere, and I do both. But for *credibility with corporate buyers*, you need a book from a major publisher, not a vanity press, and not a chapter in someone else's work!

be sent daily, and PRLeads.com, where you can tailor the press inquiries that you receive daily. Mention my name with both for personal attention.)

- *Articles.* Determine what publications your buyers may be reading, and try to place your own article there. Sometimes highly targeted newsletters are even better than major but more generic magazines. (Excellent source: *Writer's Market*, which includes every publication with an ISBN or ISSN. You can also find *The Guide to Periodic Literature* in most libraries.)

- *Columns.* Once you have published articles successfully, pursue your contact with the goal of obtaining a regular column.

- *Networking.* Don't simplistically collect business cards. Find key buyers and recommenders, establish the beginnings of a relationship, offer them something of value, and follow up. Remember Alan's Networking Law: *you have to give to get!* (If you've found an executive recruiter who can recommend you to his clients, offer to recommend him to some people who need assistance hiring senior managers.)

- *Pro bono work.* If you find a cause you believe in that is nearby, offer to serve on a committee or task force (or, if it's possible, volunteer for the board). You'll find yourself surrounded by some significant buyers, recommenders, and influencers, who will *perforce* be your peers in the volunteer work. Nurture those relationships while doing good work.

- *Newsletters.* People complain to me that there are too many newsletters, but they don't understand the dynamics of competition. There are so many newsletters because *people are reading them!* (Remember Yogi Berra's dictum: "No one goes there any more, it's too crowded.") Competition *opens* markets. The keys to a newsletter are brevity (one computer screen), consistency (same time each month), and diversity (several short pieces instead of one "take it or leave it" piece).

- *Trade association leadership.* I can trace about a quarter million dollars in business that came my way when I (reluctantly) agreed to become president of the New England Speakers Association. That's because once you're a visible leader, you're the one who is interviewed, requested for panels, coordinating initiatives, and so forth. Assemble a great team so that you can delegate and minimize labor intensity.

- *Blogs.* There are 200 million blogs in the world as of this writing, and most of them are incredibly bad, to the point of being unreadable. However, those that stand out offer provocative ideas, controversy, intellectual property, and pragmatic help for the reader. Get a technical expert to run your blog, and make sure that you use text, audio, and video to maximize the medium. (Make provision for video to go to YouTube, audio to go to iTunes, and so on. Archive everything on your blog.)

- *Reach out.* Contact trade association executive directors regularly, *always offering value for the audience/ membership.* Ideally, provide a demo video. (Excellent source: *National Trade and Professional Associations of the United States.* It is available in hard copy and by electronic subscription. Tell them I sent you and they'll offer a discount—at least they will at this writing!)[11]

- *Broadcast media interviews.* It's easier than ever to be interviewed on radio and TV (particularly if there is other gravity in place, such as a new book). You can record these and create marketing compilations, run them on your Web site, and so on. (Excellent source: *TV and Radio Interview Reporter*, which will help you script your advertisement.)

- *Community service.* This is similar to pro bono, but it means serving on the planning board, school committee, parks commission, and so on. You'll find yourself quoted often in the press, and your background talked about.

Let me conclude by telling you what *doesn't* work and, worse, wastes your time, money, and repute:

- *Paying to host a radio show.* These are scams, appealing to the ego of the speaker, and you're usually paying to drone on to people who could not care less, while also having to bring on advertising! These are beyond stupid. (And paying to be on an infomercial with some doddering ex-C-list celebrity should be enough for your family to arrest you and place you in a home until you come to your senses. Only the people you pay for this travesty make any money from it.)

- *Hosting your own cable TV show.* These generally have the fake plants, tacky backdrop, rickety desk, and

---

[11] See the Web site in the Appendix for a sample letter to a trade association executive director. Also, there are criteria for creating a sample video and estimated costs.

production values of a fourth-grade salute to the history of gerbils. When someone I've never heard of tells me that he or she is a "television show host," I usually begin to taste blood on the inside of my cheek.

- *Speaker "showcases" arranged by bureaus.* No one is a buyer, no one is paying attention, and no one cares except the people who charged you to be at this swamp. These give vaudeville a good name.

- *Direct mail and "cold calling."* For every "expert" who claims that he or she knows how to book business doing this, I'll show you an "expert" who isn't a successful speaker but makes her money trying to teach people how to cold call. Would *you* hire a speaker in this manner? Do *you* buy stocks from the guys who call you with special offers at 8:30 at night? If so, you don't need this book, but you do need to send me all the money in your bank account as soon as you can put this down.

- *Social media platforms.* If you want to look for a job, peddle some offer to individuals, or keep track of old buddies, fine. Otherwise, this is one of the worst time dumps imaginable for true marketing of speaking services to corporate buyers. I've heard advocates say that social media "amplify" your message. The trouble is that they amplify all messages, regardless of their quality or relevance, into an incoherent cacophony.

Marketing is about creating need and emphatically demonstrating that you are the best person to fill that need. And it doesn't require staff, millions, or years.

SUMMARY

The Internet, like cable TV or fast food, can be a boon or a curse. Everything depends on how you utilize it.

Use your Web site as a credibility site, not a sales tool, because only low-level people and gatekeepers troll the Internet to find people. Senior-level buyers use references and referrals from peers, and may then go to your site to learn more about you (determine if you're a thought leader). Stop talking about credentials and initials that no one else understands, and start talking about typical client results.

If you find that you are in a position to work with bureaus, treat them as you would a client. Deal with the bureau principal, expect the bureau to market you in return for its 25 percent commission (don't pay more), require that funds be paid to you as received and not kept in escrow, and don't pay silly fees for "video reviews" or "marketing catalogs." Those are the bureau's cost of doing business, not yours.

You're better off focusing on trade associations, where you can get paid well to speak *and* speak in front of hundreds of buyers and recommenders.

To maximize your chances of success, use my Market Gravity approaches, starting with the ones that are most within your comfort zone, and then moving on to the others. That's how you'll become the center of attraction.

LEAN AND MEAN

YOU DON'T NEED A STAFF, UNLESS IT'S A STICK TO WALK THROUGH THE WOODS

Here's a verbatim conversation I had with a colleague at a speakers' convention:

> Me: How are you? You don't look good.
>
> Him: Not so good. I made 200 speeches over the past 12 months.
>
> Me: Isn't that good, cause for rejoicing?
>
> Him: No; I was never home, *and* I lost my shirt.

You see, it's not what you make, it's what you keep, and minimizing the time it takes to keep it.

WEALTH IS DISCRETIONARY TIME

One of my greatest discoveries is that wealth is about doing what you want when you want to. Wealth is discretionary time.

Time is *not* a resource issue, although many people think it is. We all receive a new 24 hours every day, rich or poor, young or old, sincere or passive-aggressive. We utilize it based on our priorities. Time is about assigning the correct amounts of time to the correct priorities.

Running your speaking practice is about being lean and mean. Despite the somewhat mercenary title of this book, money is merely fuel for your life. If you work so hard and so long that you maximize your income no matter what, you may ironically be getting more money while you're actually eroding your wealth.

I can always make another dollar, but I can't make another minute.

How Do You Leverage Your Time?

Ever since the publication of *Million Dollar Consulting* in 1992, people have asked me if it's really true that I don't have a staff. After all, we hear advice for brand-new speakers about getting administrative help; we're told that we can't possibly market ourselves successfully without someone taking on that accountability; and there's no way, it would seem, to fulfill product orders without dedicated bodies. And then there's all that follow-up . . . and it does get kind of lonely. . . .

So, if even modestly successful speakers need that kind of support, a seven-figure practice must require it, right? *Au contraire.*

Thank the fates that I didn't hear all that advice before I happily discovered that I'd much prefer to keep what I make. Ever since my wife first questioned—25 years ago—why I was considering renting an office for my nascent consulting/ speaking practice, the two of us have rigorously resisted putting anyone else on the payroll other than the chairman, president, and CEO (all of whom happen to be me) and the vice president and treasurer (my wife).

I have this old-fashioned idea about not taking the risks inherent in running one's own business unless commensurate rewards are possible. Consequently, I want to keep what I make, and I've managed to keep between 88 and 90 percent every single year. I don't support other people on my payroll, and that's a large part of the financial success that places me in a tiny fraction of the general population.

How is it done? Here are my major tenets.

Alan's Lean and Mean Speaking Practice

1. *Outsource absolutely everything possible.* I actually have a huge "virtual staff," in that I hire people on a situational basis to do my books, fulfill orders, respond to messages, produce correspondence, and so on. The key point here is that all of them are *paid for performance.* They are compensated only for specific jobs of finite duration. I make certain that I am not their sole customer, so that there is no confusion about their being employees, and there are no benefits or fringes required. Thus, I can afford to pay very well, receive the best help available, and still save money over full-time resources.

2. *Do nothing other than what you must.* Most speakers and consultants I've observed perform too many minor tasks that have nothing to do with the client's need or well-being. (Ironically, this includes many of those who are "organization and time-management experts"!) I make it clear that the client is responsible for a great deal of the administrative and logistical work. I make liberal use of voice mail, fax, and e-mail, which are all quick and simple. And I never perform any task just because someone tells me that "every

good professional does it." I must see a demonstrable return for the client and for me. (For example, I've even stopped using the sacrosanct and overemphasized prespeech questionnaire, substituting the discussions that I normally have with the client for the cumbersome paperwork and follow-up.)

3. *Use leveraged techniques.* For instance (hold on to your seats), I don't follow up on every lead I get. I send out a press kit with a toll-free response number and add the name to my mailing lists. I've found that either people hire me (or at least respond) based upon our initial contact, or they don't. Follow-up virtually never changes the dynamic, so I've stopped doing it (although I make certain that I'm very user-friendly to contact). In addition, I invest in sources that get me all kinds of media attention because I want buyers to come to me, not vice versa. *This does not cost more in the long run because my time is highly valuable—too valuable to spend chasing prospects.* Yeah, I know: blasphemy. But I've been a heretic all the way to the bank.

4. *Exploit technological and nontechnological shortcuts and advantages.* I can touch-type 60 words a minute. I know the language sufficiently to write a letter or report one time—I never create drafts (this chapter went from my head to the keyboard to the editor). My phone automatically dials clients. My computers can do anything but cook me a meal. I carry a phone in my briefcase. I belong to every air club in existence. If you want to reach next door, don't go around the block.

I'd never advise you *not* to have a staff. There are plenty of people who are highly successful explicitly *because* of hard-working, loyal, full-time staffers, and we'll examine those options momentarily. I'm simply suggesting that lean, mean, and green (money) can work quite well also, irrespective of the size of your practice. Give it some thought the next time you have a hiring itch. Don't set "automatic pilot" for the staff destination. Give it some thought because the money you spend on staff must be returned several times over through increased business, or it's money that you'll never see again.

If you already have a staff, think again about its size and even its necessity. I received a panicked e-mail recently from a colleague whose staff accountant had embezzled funds; neglected to pay bills, resulting in credit problems; and failed to follow up on critical leads. His speaking topic is "hiring and retaining good people." I am not making this up.

If you're lonely, get a dog. By the way, you can probably write off part of its expenses as a component of the security system.

In my estimation, less than 15 percent of successful speakers (that is, those who support their desired lifestyle through speaking and related activities) use full-time, paid staffs. So let's eliminate spouses and significant others, and let's place in abeyance for the moment those who are paid solely for performance, such as a marketer who earns a commission only on speeches sold for you. (A little later in the chapter, we'll discuss contract players, who are people hired on a project or situational basis, and whom I don't consider staff.)

ALAN'S FIVE ESSENTIAL AND LEGITIMATE STAFF CHARACTERISTICS

All right, let's assume that you need a staff because of the volume of your existing business or because of your understanding of your own marketing limitations or because all the kids on the block have one and you want one, too. Here are some criteria for staff acquisition.

Marketing Skills

At a minimum, the individual should be able to handle passive marketing, which generally consists of calls made to the office while you're not there. There's a huge difference between saying, "Mr. Weiss will get back to you" and saying, "What dates do you have in mind? What type of audience? It just so happens that Mr. Weiss is available on that date and has worked with those audiences as recently as last month. Would you like me to place a 'hold' on that date, and send you specific information and a sample contract?"

Ideally, the individual should have assertive marketing skills and should be able to find prospects, respond to leads, initiate cold calls, and determine which contacts can be closed without your help, which can be closed with your help, and which should be abandoned (or merely placed on a mailing list). The individual should be able to identify and establish communication with the real buyer. Call these telemarketing skills.

Administrative Skills

The individual should be able to use standard office technology, including the creation of computer data banks; have keyboard skills and a professional phone manner; and handle the assembly of mailings, fulfilling of literature requests, product fulfillment, spreadsheet work, and travel scheduling. Routinely, I reach speakers' offices where the voice-mail recording is more professional and polite than the live administrative help at other offices. If someone's going to answer your phone, he or she should be nothing less than charming.

If you have a staff, "shop" your own office, or have a colleague do it for you. Test to see how rapidly literature is mailed, how quickly leads are followed up and relayed, how a complaint is handled, and what general level of intelligence is conveyed about your practice. I told one highly polished speaker that his administrative assistant didn't have a clue about his speaking topics or background. He was aghast, but he had never educated her or tested her on the topics.

Judgment

This person is representing you to the world, and the world will have much tougher expectations and standards than if they were leaving a message with automated equipment. People are funny that way. Consequently, your office help must return calls received in their absence promptly—within three hours at the outside.[1] Complaints have to be assessed as valid ("You promised a press kit last week, and we haven't received it.") or invalid ("Why won't you send us a free copy of Mr. Weiss's materials so that we can evaluate them?").

Your staff members should be able to schedule your time and travel in full conformance with your preferences, but without your active participation. They should be able to interact with colleagues, vendors, prospects, and clients professionally, articulately (after all, you do run a speaking business), and consistently with regard to your philosophy and

---

[1] I return calls within 90 minutes with no staff whatsoever. If I had a staff, I'd demand that all calls be returned within 20 minutes. Often, merely getting there first is what lands the business, and the competition often doesn't return calls until the next day.

manner. I fall down in amazement every time I meet a speaker's staff member who can't communicate well.

Innovative Ability

One of the primary reasons to have assistance in this lone-wolf profession is to get feedback and to challenge "the way we've always done it." Your staffer(s) should continually be able to recommend new, more efficient, and more productive methods to get results, ranging from mailings and new products to new speech topics and promotional literature. A staff person should know your business intimately, perhaps even better than you do, since he or she is watching it every day from a wide range of perspectives while you're preparing for the next speech and a new audience.

So the staff person should be someone whom you respect and trust, *and to whom you'll listen when new ideas are explored.* If you find that new suggestions aren't regularly forthcoming or that you don't choose to engage in business discussions with the "administrative help," then you have the wrong resource. One of the results you're investing in a staff commitment is innovation and new ways to grow your practice.

Leverage

The investment in staff must result in leveraged growth *on the profit line.* If you're spending $45,000 a year on staff, enhanced revenues of $45,000 are woefully insufficient, and enhanced profit of $45,000 is breakeven. My advice is that your total outlay for staff resources ought to be returned three times over in *profit* or the investment isn't worth it. That's because, in addition to the tangible and measurable outlays, there are the intangible and immeasurable outlays of your time, attention, focus, and energy. Those of you who have managed people know exactly whereof I speak. Even with one person on board, there will be personal issues, training and education time, debate, confusion, and meetings. Multiply that accordingly by the size of the staff.

Hence, staff has to leverage your profit potential in any combination of these types of interventions:

- Acquisition of sales through aggressive cold calling and marketing
- Acquisition of sales through more rapid and effective lead follow-up
- Higher volume of mailings, client contacts, and responses
- Increased speaker sales and delivery time through less office time
- Improved visibility through increased interviews, articles, and so on
- More attractive offerings through new speech and product ideas

Let me state the obvious, in case you've missed it: if you are offsetting the bullet-point advantages through the investment of time required to manage, nurture, and otherwise tend to your staff, you are losing money hand over fist. You should be able to grow a successful practice by 10 to 15 percent a year *simply through your own momentum and referral business,* so a staff has to result in a 20 to 30 percent growth rate to make the investment worthwhile.

If a full-time staff can leverage your success, it's a wise and prudent investment. However, if you're not at that level or, like many of us, have reached that level and don't feel the

> **Speaking Up: A general rule of thumb: you should be able to support your current lifestyle through speaking and related activities, and be growing the business by 10 to 15 percent annually on the basis of your own momentum and repute. At that point, a staff might make sense. Staffs can help leverage the success that you, first, have to create.**

need to invest in full-time resources, then contracting is always a wise choice.

Over the course of a year, I typically contract out for the following help related to my speaking business:

- Web and blog design and improvement
- Graphics creation
- Mailing fulfillment
- Mailing list maintenance
- Handout material creation
- Test and survey creation
- Product fulfillment
- Phone response (especially client "hot lines")
- Visual aids
- Audiovisual editing and dubbing
- Phone interviewing
- Newsletter formatting and proofing
- Material and product storage
- Travel arrangements

Call this "just-in-time support" if you wish, because I pay for performance when I need it and to the degree that I need it. By doing this, I can tightly control my outlays, have strong influence and priority with the contractor (I pay promptly and guarantee future work as long as my quality needs and deadlines are rigorously met), tailor to client need, and create, in effect, a large, talented staff that provides "heft" to my business in the prospect's eyes.[2]

Acquiring the right contract people, I've found, is often a matter of balancing chemistry with talent. A graphics designer might have a bit of an argumentative edge, but I'm not trying to hire a full-time staffer with whom maintaining cordial relations day in and day out is a must. If the talent is there, I can tolerate a wide variety of personality styles and even quirks. (And I have no right to demand conformance to my particular behaviors, since, like me, these people are all running their own businesses as they see fit.) However, I make no such allowances for quality, performance, and talent. No matter how well I might get along with, or even enjoy, someone's company, failure to meet quality requirements or deadlines is anathema. If you don't return my calls, meet my delivery dates, and have it right the first time, you don't work for me.

Most subcontractors I've encountered—and by "most" I'm talking upwards of 90 percent—charge by the hour, not

---

[2] Disclaimer: If you're uncertain, speak to your accountant, but subcontractors who do not rely on you as their sole source of income are not considered employees and do not have to have taxes withheld. However, at the end of the year, you will probably have to issue Form 1099 to those who are not incorporated businesses themselves. If payment is below a certain threshold—at this writing, $600—then no reporting is necessary. This is not meant to be legal or tax advice, and you should consult your CPA for definitive policies for your practice.

by value. Consequently, they represent highly definable and fixed investments, and they generally undercharge for their real worth to you. It's not unusual for me to have a complete publicity piece designed, put through several iterations and edits, and formatted as camera-ready copy *with the first 1,000 copies printed* for under $750. That's a nice payback on my investment, and it's a spectacular return if you consider that doing it myself would have required about $20,000 of my time. (I shoot five episodes of my video series *The Writing on the Wall* at a time, including editing, videographer and assistant, and transfer in the proper formatting to my Web master for a total of under $600 each time.)

It often doesn't matter where subcontract help is located geographically these days, since e-mail, fax, Skype, and FedEx can compensate handily for distance. Consequently, in my experience, the best ways to acquire contract help are

- Ask other speakers whom they use for what purposes.
- Ask *other practitioners* (lawyers, accountants, or consultants) whom they use for similar needs.
- Network through your local printer, Rotary, stationery supplier, or chamber of commerce.
- Place an ad for your needs in the local weekly newspaper.
- Post your need on the appropriate Internet bulletin boards.
- If you see something impressive, ask for the source (which is how I acquired my Web home page designer).
- Watch for ads in association newsletters (or place an ad yourself).

- Chat with neighbors who may be interested.[3]
- Investigate local college work-study and intern offerings.
- Investigate local students seeking research projects.

I've found that subcontractors are a cost-effective, highly leveraged technique to grow your business. The stereotypical test to determine if I'm ahead of the game is when another speaker compliments me on my visuals and asks if I used PowerPoint software.

"No, I have the slides created for me."

"Don't you realize that with the right software, which costs less than $250, you could produce these yourself?"

"The fact is that it would require about $30,000 of my time to learn and use that software, and it still wouldn't produce the creativity I get for a $1,500 investment in their design and creation."

We both walk away scratching our heads, except that my colleague is getting into a Volvo while I'm getting into my Bentley.

The IRS generally considers people to be employees, not subcontractors, for tax purposes if they meet the following criteria:

(continued)

---

[3] Cut me some slack before you call the gender police, but I've found that neighborhood homemakers often have college degrees, are at home raising the kids, and have free time and lots of talent. They are very receptive to the idea of such contract work. I've used these superb resources for mailing, phone work, order fulfillment, and a myriad of other important needs.

(continued)

- *Comply with employer's instructions about the work.*
- *Receive training from or at the direction of the employer.*
- *Provide services that are integrated into the business.*
- *Provide services that must be rendered personally.*
- *Hire, supervise, and pay assistants for the employer.*
- *Have a continuing working relationship with the employer.*
- *Must follow set hours of work.*
- *Work full-time for an employer.*
- *Must do their work on the employer's premises.*
- *Must submit regular reports to the employer.*
- *Receive payments of regular amounts at set intervals.*
- *Receive payments for business and traveling expenses.*
- *Rely on the employer to furnish tools and materials.*
- *Lack a major investment in facilities used to perform the service.*
- *Cannot make a profit or suffer a loss from the services.*
- *Work for one employer at a time.*
- *Do not offer their services to the general public.*

> - *Can be fired by the employer.*
> - *May quit work anytime without incurring liability.*
>
> From the General Accounting Office publication NO. GAO/T-GGD-96-130, "Tax Administration: Issues in Classifying Workers as Employees or Independent Contractors" 5 (1996).

YOU'RE A PROFESSIONAL SPEAKER, NOT A HIRED HAND

I actually heard a speaker at a major convention tell the audience that he was a "hired hand," and that if the organizers wanted him to help move tables or hang decorations or distribute materials, he would do whatever was asked while he was engaged to be on site.

In light of that position, I'd like you to try something for me. The next time you're with your doctor or accountant or attorney (or gardener), say the following near the end of the discussion: "Look, Doc, we've still got a few minutes; would you mind changing the oil in my car?" In about a week, they should allow you a phone call to relatives who may be able to get you out of the asylum.

This proves two things:

1. We are highly skilled professionals with tremendous value to offer within our discipline, and we had better act that way. (Imagine if your doctor *volunteered* to change your oil. Would you return?)
2. You can't believe even half the advice you hear from the purported "experts." That's because they're making their money by giving you advice instead of

doing it themselves. Remember my ski instructor: in front of you, doing what you want to do, and looking back to give you feedback and make sure you're all right, not back in the lodge sipping brandy and giving advice from a lounge chair.

You have the right to require (*demand* has such an authoritarian air) the following from your client:

- First-class travel domestically, business-class overseas.[4]
- An introducer who will read your introduction verbatim and practice it beforehand.
- The type of amplification you desire. (Never let them say, "All we have is this tin can and a string." Tell them in advance that you require a wireless lapel mike, or whatever.)
- Lighting and seating in accordance with your preference, if they're not fixed in place. (You can't change an auditorium, but you can request classroom or theater style or rounds in a convention conference room.)
- A nice room in or near the speaking facility billed to the client's master account. (That way, you won't have to wait for reimbursement.)
- Information about the group (title, responsibilities, geography, gender mix, and so forth).
- A master copy of any recordings IF you approve of them and IF you've reached agreement on remuneration for permitting them.

---

[4] Which you should upgrade to first. It's very important that you arrive fresh and refreshed in this business, especially with the vagaries of air travel these days.

- Transportation from and to the nearest airport.
- Access to the buyer and coordinator prior to the session to review last-minute details.
- A room or private space to wait in if you are on later in the day (e.g., you've done a sound check in the morning, but you aren't on until three hours later).

You get the idea. These aren't wild demands. They are the reasonable requests of a professional who needs certain support to ensure the best possible results for the client.

> *Speaking Up: The client's best interests are best served when your self-interest is best served. Put your own oxygen mask on first.*

This is why you shouldn't deal with powerless meeting planners who are always trying to save money. Deal with the true buyer, who is trying to maximize results. Remember: *the typical business or association convention is costing hundreds of thousands of dollars in travel, fringes, salaries, facilities, insurance, and so forth. Your fee can be created merely by cutting a couple of coffee breaks.* Keep things in perspective.

THE SOURCES OF SOUND, OBJECTIVE, PROFESSIONAL FEEDBACK AND WHY UNSOLICITED FEEDBACK WILL KILL YOU

A man attending my keynote in Birmingham, England (a "speech coach," no less—what else?), asked if he could give me feedback after I walked off the stage.

"Is there anything in what's left of the British Empire that could possibly stop you?" I asked.

Unperturbed, he said, "When you roamed the stage, I couldn't focus on a single point, but when you stood rooted in one spot, I absorbed everything. Do you know what that's called?"

"Yes," I said. "A learning disability."

After a speech in New York City, the usual line had gathered to ask me questions. The fourth person in line gave me her card and said, "I can help you fix your speech impediment."

I ripped her card in half, gave it back, and said, "Can you fix this?"

Unsolicited feedback is ALWAYS for the sender. It's a technique that the inferior use to prove that they're better than you, even if you have the spotlight, have been paid, have been chosen, and have received the accolades and applause. Only *solicited* feedback, sought by you from sources you trust, is worth listening to, but even then you should not automatically act on it.

None of us in the speaking profession ever receives enough feedback. I know that's strange to hear, given the fact that we face audiences on a regular basis who are usually encouraged to fill out the ubiquitous feedback forms. But there are two things wrong with using such responses as your sole—or even main—source of assessment.

First, the audience feedback isn't from the *buyer*. That's like Mercedes asking the family members how they liked the ride, but neglecting to ask the purchaser, who is the person most likely to buy again in the future. Since buyers used both rational and visceral impulses to hire you (logic impels people to think, but emotion galvanizes them into action), it's important that you hear what the buyer's reaction is. Speakers whose feedback loop ends at the "smile sheets" completed before the audience leaves the room seldom have comprehensive information and rarely make improvements based upon the real buyer needs. (You're being compared with the temperature controls and visual aids, not to mention the lousy food.)

Second, with the best of intentions, the audience seldom knows what to look for. The buyer's objectives might have included shocking the audience members or provoking them or driving them to action, not entertaining or comforting them or making them feel safe. Every audience member reacts slightly differently to what he or she hears because unconsciously each is seeking to establish relevance with his or her background. That's why (good) speakers use multiple stories and examples to try to appeal to a gamut of experiences and perspectives.

The advice that we tape all of our speeches and listen to them is among the most simplistic and specious. Our frame of reference is severely limited. Hearing ourselves and trying to decide how to improve is like asking the famous question, "What's different about a duck?" Well, a duck has feathers, but so does a goose. A duck has webbed feet, but so does a frog. A duck can swim, but so can a fish. A duck can quack, but so can a duck hunter. Perhaps there's no such distinct animal as a duck, then? The point is that the question is wrong. It should be, "What's distinct about a duck *as compared to what?*" (It's smaller than a goose, frogs can't fly, fish don't swim on the surface, and duck callers can't mate with another duck, at least not in most states.)

> *Speaking Up: We need independent feedback that includes external frames of reference. Otherwise, we keep getting better at what we already do, and what we already do might be the problem.*

As a business requisite, you need support in the form of qualified, external advice and mentoring if you are to grow as a professional. You trust your finances to the advice of a CPA, your health to your personal physician, your corporate status to your attorney, and your graphics to a designer. Why wouldn't you trust your professional development to equally qualified sources? And why would you ever use people who aren't as good as you are and have very personal agendas?

If you do record your speeches, *send the DVDs and downloads to trusted confidants who you know will give you candid, blunt reactions.* If you want to feel warm and loved, watch exercise infomercials. But if you want to know if you're growing as a speaker, find people who can provide honest feedback and advice and not worry about your sensibilities. These people can be other speakers, but shouldn't be limited to them. Here are some sources for your mentoring and feedback needs.

Techniques for Professional, Honest Feedback

1. *Recruit a mastermind group of people whose judgment you respect and who are familiar with the type of business you are in.* These folks might include your financial planner, a colleague on a civic association, another entrepreneur (e.g., the person who owns one of your supply sources), a local politician or school board member, a business consultant, your attorney, and so on. They needn't be geographically proximate because this can easily be done via e-mail and computer.

   Tell these people that you'll ask their help no more than two or three times a year. On those occasions, send them a tape (or invite them to hear you if you're speaking in their neighborhood) and ask them for their assessment of how you should reach the next level of the profession (larger audiences, larger companies, media work, high-visibility keynotes, and so on). Ask them what you do well, what should be further developed, and what underwhelms them, which might be abandoned. Don't react to stray comments, *but if you see a pattern emerging, take action.* (If one person says, "I didn't like that story," ignore it. But if five people say, "You seem to have no energy in those stories," then you know you've probably told them a few times too many.)

Guideline: Once is an accident, twice is a coincidence, three times is a pattern.

In return for their kindness, take your team out to dinner, offer to reciprocate for them, and/or provide a gift. You don't have to accept their advice, but you won't have it at all if you don't ask for it.

2. *Seek out other speakers who are successful.* Note that I didn't say "whom you like" or "whom you respect," because that leaves the door open for the mutual admiration society. There are a lot of speakers who don't make more than they do because they spend so much of their time telling each other how good they are and bestowing awards on each other.[5]

---

[5] Beware of organizations that provide you with "certifications" and honorifics—and sometimes "guaranteed" leads—after completing their seminar and/or sending in your money. They are a scam and worthless unless there are truly tough criteria to earn your designation and buyers accept the designation as a legitimate indicator of quality. No buyer in my entire speaking career has cared that I'm in the Speakers Hall of Fame, much less for the other 14 initials that groups have bestowed upon me. I don't use them because they make me (or anyone) appear to be overcompensating for some lack!

Find exemplars who represent success with which you can identify. Don't be taken in by the publicity klaxons wailing away. Everyone lives in an "oceanfront home," drives a "foreign car," and is "a prolific writer." (When I was helping someone else in this capacity and was critiquing his promotional literature, I was compelled to remind him that Peter Drucker and John Updike might be among "the world's most prolific writers," but he certainly was not, despite the claims to that effect in his press kit.) Find the time to develop relationships with those whom you see addressing the organizations you want to address in the capacity you want to assume. Or find someone with a platform presence that you admire, a visibility that impresses you, or a business acumen that you'd love to acquire.

Develop a network of several of these people whom you can access just a few times a year. *Don't try to emulate their style or their attributes.* Simply obtain frank feedback on your style, business, and direction that you can use to critically examine your progress. What's good for them might not be good for you, but their insights are from a highly valid frame of reference.

3. *Invest in a formal mentoring relationship.* There are some of us who are called upon so frequently for advice and guidance that the relationships have to take the form of formal consulting. In general, these relationships are focused and directed toward specific growth goals. You can stipulate what you want to tackle: penetrating the corporate market, using more humor, publishing, ancillary products, raising fees, and so on, and you can determine the duration. In my

experience, you need at least six months of regular contacts with a mentor—which, again, needn't be in person—in order to create the follow-through and discipline to reach your goals.

The characteristics of a professional, effective mentor who will provide you with the proper ROI include

- Success as a speaker, *not just as a mentor* (a "doer," not an "expert")
- Unlimited access during the period, not designated days or times
- "Real time" help with actual prospects, fees, presentations, and so on
- Requirements for action and follow-up on those actions
- Contacts provided, such as book agents, speakers' bureau principals, and so on
- Solid references from other speakers

Mentors can be highly effective and well worth the investment if they can focus on your particular needs and offer specific, pragmatic techniques to grow your business and meet your personal objectives. Always eschew a "blanket" approach. This must be an individualized process.

4. *Choose an association of professionals that is geared to provide feedback.* At preliminary levels, Toastmasters International is a good alternative because it offers (predominantly amateur and/or infrequent) speakers the opportunity to hone their skills in front of a supportive audience. There are also contests run by the parent organization on local, regional, and national levels that provide the opportunity to

perform in front of judges. The disadvantages of Toastmasters are that the feedback won't always be crisp and honest (I'm the next one up there, so I'm going to be kind) and that the criteria for speeches are narrow and somewhat inappropriate for corporate speaking.

The National Speakers Association (NSA) has a membership of about 3,000 speakers, ranging from the highly visible, professional keynoters and high-income training professionals to entry-level and aspiring speakers. It's a good vehicle for meeting potential colleagues, advisors, and mentors, and the local chapter meetings provide "spotlight" opportunities to make a brief presentation and receive feedback from the audience. Some chapters provide videotaping and much more personalized feedback, as well. Although (no one uses this construction) NSA considers itself the voice of the profession and provides various levels of accomplishment, its membership represents a minority of actual professional speakers and it's hardly known beyond the meeting-planning industry. Nevertheless, its conventions and meetings can provide camaraderie and an excellent feedback source for those who have the discipline to use them as such.

5. *Seek help on the Internet.* There are numerous speakers' chat rooms, home pages, association listings, and similar sources. Allocate a morning to using the relevant search engines to generate alternatives. The beauty of the Internet is that you can exchange visual aids, speech transcripts, actual recordings, and online discussions if you have the proper equipment and

software. On many sites, mine included, you can actually watch videos of keynotes and training sessions.

You're able, through cyberspace, to access a network of self-selected advisors who can provide you with downloadable examples of promotional literature, critiques of your speeches, advice on your business plans, opportunities internationally, and a host of other potentially useful feedback. If you're technologically able and individually willing, you can find a trove of help sitting right at your desk.

No matter what method you choose, find a source of direct and honest feedback: people who will tell you the truth and not simply stroke your ego. "Care more for the truth than what people think." Aristotle said that, and he wasn't a bad advisor.

SMALL PRINT: INCORPORATION, LEGAL, ACCOUNTING, INSURANCE, TAXES, YADA YADA

There are some random issues that don't belong in Part Two or Three of the book, and that haven't fit in smoothly up to this point. So this final section of Part One will deal with the things that I need to say somewhere. There's a chance that not all of this will apply to you at the moment, so I'll use headings to facilitate your selections and provide for referencing if and when the time comes for their application.

Note, as always, that you should consult the proper insurance, legal, financial, and assorted other experts. However, make sure that they are also experienced in solo practices and

in professional services firms. I'm not kidding; these are specialized fields, and you will otherwise get some awful advice.

Incorporation

By all means, incorporate your business, no matter what its
size. (At this writing, Subchapter S and LLC are better bets
than Chapter C, but the laws can change.) Do not listen to
anyone who tells you that you don't have to incorporate. I
don't care how many degrees these people claim to have; they
don't have any brains.

Incorporation affords the following benefits and
protection:

- A legal entity that can borrow money, sue, or be sued
  (so that your personal assets are safe—this is a litigious
  society)
- A professional status and sometimes a preferred
  status—that is, as a small business—when seeking
  contracts or responding to RFPs (requests for
  proposals)
- Corporate benefits written into your bylaws, which
  may (consult your attorney) include a health plan,
  company car, and retirement plan; board of directors
  meetings; directors' fees; and other corporate
  amenities and perquisites
- Payment of all reasonable business expenses from
  before-tax funds
- Inclusion in certain lists and memberships restricted to
  corporate entities
- Favorable retirement plan options
- Favorable purchasing and health options

Incorporation can be accomplished painlessly by any competent, appropriate attorney for several hundred dollars or so, depending on your state's requirements. (You will probably get a nifty corporate seal, which I've had occasion to use exactly five times in the past 25 years!)

Insurance

Aside from the basic lifestyle insurance that you should carry—health, life, dental, umbrella liability, whatever suits you—there are several other types that you should be absolutely certain to obtain:

1. *Errors and omissions.* This is typically called "E&O" in the insurance industry and "malpractice" by the rest of us. It protects you when you are being sued by a client for purportedly providing bad advice that has injured the client's firm. (Accidents such as someone tripping over your projector wire are covered by general liability insurance, which you should also carry; this is discussed next.) This type of suit has actually become *more* of a likelihood, given the increasing extent to which litigious remedies have replaced discussion and debate. Theoretically, if you gave a speech on strategy that included warnings or opportunities for the audience, and the company acted on them and lost its corporate shirt, some legal beaver on the client's staff might advocate a suit against you. Consulting firms are being sued with increasing vigor, and a speaker's advice can be construed as consulting (and many of you are consultants, as well). Do not proceed in this business without E&O coverage. Do

not pass "go." Do not collect your next fee without investing it in such protection.[6]

2. *Liability insurance.* If someone trips over your laptop power cord, that person will sue the conference facility, the computer manufacturer, the electric company, and YOU. This is the sad state of litigation these days. Liability insurance is cheap, is often provided by the same carrier that provides E&O coverage, and is a must.

3. *Disability insurance.* There is a far, far greater chance of our being disabled than of our dying during the most productive portions of our careers. Yet few speakers comprehend the importance of disability coverage. Choose coverage that pays you for as long as you cannot return *to your full and normal type of work* (some coverage applies only as long as you can't be employed, irrespective of whether it's your normal type of work). The law and insurance company procedures usually dictate that you can carry total coverage equal to some percentage of your normal income, generally about 80 percent. As a speaker, you'll need to work with brokers or companies that are sensitive to the swings in potential income in this profession and can arrive at equitable average earnings in deciding about policy coverage amounts. As with any insurance, group plans are less expensive than individual plans, and a wide variety of trade

---

[6] Fees are usually based on practice volume, but they can be reduced if you join a trade association or similar organization that offers group coverage. On an individual basis, plan to pay anywhere from $1,000 to $3,000 annually, which is easily equal to, or less than, one speaking engagement.

associations—not necessarily speaking associations—offer the former with a variety of options (e.g., the longer the waiting period before the insurance kicks in, the less expensive the premium). You cannot afford not to have disability insurance, even if it means taking less life insurance for the moment.

4. *Long-term care insurance.* Usually referred to as "LTC," this provides for support and assistance at home when you are incapacitated for a long period, either now or in your elderly years. I mention it here because it is *far* cheaper to obtain when you are younger, and it provides the kind of financial support that can mean the difference between having to go to a nursing home and being cared for in your own home. I consider this coverage also to be a "must."

Financial Planning

For many speakers, financial planning means whatever is left after the checks are deposited and the bills are paid. That's not financial planning, but there is a name for it: bankruptcy.

It's silly and irresponsible to take the risks associated with an entrepreneurial business such as this one and not reap the rewards. While some of the rewards may be in instant gratification (especially for those of you from California), and you may feel that you can speak until you drop (and some people are apparently continuing to speak after they've dropped), you should have an intelligent long-term financial security plan.

Consult a first-rate financial planner (*someone who charges a fee for the advice, not someone who earns a commission by selling you securities*), set up a plan appropriate for your circumstances and objectives, and contribute to it faithfully, as though you're paying off the mortgage or the local utility. There are a variety of options and the laws change frequently, so keep abreast of what's best for you. Just one example: a SEP IRA, which is like a personal IRA, at the moment allows up to $47,000 a year to be contributed by your corporation, tax-free, to your retirement account. There are other goodies like this, so invest in professional help. You may also be able to set up 401(k) plans. The benefit of solo practice is that, while these plans often mandate that employees be covered, you have only yourself and perhaps a spouse to worry about.

Banking Relationships

My preference is to have a professional, as well as personal, relationship with a bank. Especially as your business grows and prospers, it makes sense to arrange for credit lines, references, advantageous interest rates, and all the other perquisites that remain hidden until, magically, they appear when you ask about them.

My personal banker is on my mailing list. I meet with her once or twice a year, and I keep her highly informed about my work and its impact. (For example, she gets a copy of every book I publish.) Every so often, a new client's purchasing department will ask for a bank reference, and new vendors request them all the time.

Increasingly in my global practice, I'm paid by wire transfer. This can be tricky and lengthy unless you can work hand-in-hand with your bank. You can also speed foreign checks along and get credit sooner rather than later.

One other perk of this relationship: if you can become a "private banking customer" or whatever the euphemism is in your area, you can shortcut banking lines, obtain easy overdraft protection, and even have the bank cover an inadvertently unsupported check (or allow you to draw on uncollected funds). Banks do a lot for good customers that they obviously don't choose to advertise. If your bank is intractable about affording reasonable benefits, find another bank while saying a silent prayer for the competitive benefits of deregulation.

I personally carry a dozen credit cards, including four different American Express cards. These are of tremendous help in utilizing travel counselors 24 hours a day, having a concierge work for you in a given city, arranging for gifts, and so forth.[7]

Motivational Summary

How many of you couldn't resist this heading? My final point is a simple but often ignored one: you are as successful as you position yourself to be.

As your business takes off, don't continue to regard it (or yourself) as the same enterprise it was when you received your first $500 check for speaking to the local trade association that couldn't find anyone else. The people who reach out to you usually want something—your dollars, your advice, your support, your repute. You have to reach out to make certain

---

[7] I carry the almost mythical Amex Centurion Black Card, which you must be invited to apply for at certain spending levels. When my wife and I found out, while sailing from Naples to Capri, that our daughter had given birth to twins three months prematurely, I made a single 20-minute call to Black Card from our mountaintop hotel when we reached Capri. The next morning we were sent home with private cars, first-class ferries, first-class air, and a hotel suite six blocks from the hospital in New York. I swear by them, and my granddaughters are healthy and a year old as I write this!

things happen *on your terms.* I'm astounded by the people who try to sell securities over the phone, since that seems to me to be the ultimate personal relationship business. But someone must be buying that way. Don't purchase insurance, vendor services, retirement plans, advice, or even pencils from just anyone who offers—and I'm someone who has seen speakers choose their attorney from the Yellow Pages of the phone book or an online experience on Facebook.

You're a success. Act like it. Choose your help carefully, but choose it now. The savvy of this business is in carving out your own route. Only the lead dog ever sees a change in scenery.

SUMMARY

You're a professional speaker, not a corporate manager. Your success is not a factor of how many people you hire; in fact, your success may be undermined by hiring a lot of people.

Lean and mean is the way to the green.

Above all, remember that true wealth is discretionary time. Speaking is a way to improve your life—you don't re-arrange your life to enable your speaking. If you are happy and gratified only when you're in front of an audience, you need to seek help. If standing ovations and high "smile sheet" scores are your validation for occupying space on the planet, you have the depth of lawn clippings.

Be proud of your work, by all means, and be proud of your life, at all costs. Utilize subcontract and "virtual" support before you build infrastructure, which is not only expensive, but also very difficult to *disassemble.* Don't allow a corporate welfare state to build up around you. If you find you need constant adoration, get a dog.

Be careful about your corporate structure, bylaws, financial reporting, insurance, and related business needs. Maximize the use of pretax income. Don't let bureaus or tax authorities needlessly hold your money.

Be cautious about the people to whom you listen. Don't just speak like a pro. Listen like one, too.

STEAK

T HIS PROFESSION is about intellectual firepower. You must become an object of interest to others, which means that your own interests must constantly grow and expand. Too many speakers are giving the same speech they gave 20 years ago, crying at the same place and telling the same story and laughing at it. The problem is that if you ask them a question, they have to start all over again.

ACCELERATING AND ACCENTUATING YOUR APPEAL

BECOMING THE "GO-TO" RESOURCE

I T'S NICE when your name is on a list of excellent speakers on a given topic. But it's far better when the buyer says, "Get me Tom Parsons!" At this writing, people readily identify certain individuals with key business expertise:

Sales: Jeff Gitomer

Coaching: Marshall Goldsmith

Small business: David Maister

Creativity: Seth Godin

Solo consulting: Alan Weiss

People associated strategy with Peter Drucker, and leadership with John Gardner and Warren Bennis. You may have your personal favorites, but no one is going to argue with my examples.

You need to become a "go-to" resource.

THE AMAZING SECRET LEVERAGE OF PROCESS TRUMPING CONTENT

The key to expanding our playing fields and appealing to increasing numbers of potential buyers is to understand that *we build content around process.*

Process is a sequence, system, design, model, or approach that enables the user to achieve a given, desired result. For example, a decision-making process provides the individual with the ability to arrive at an alternative that will meet his or her objectives. A sales process will allow the salesperson to generate new business more quickly and efficiently. Processes are usually about HOW something is done.

Content is the particular environment, surroundings, subject matter, or specifics within which one applies processes. In other words, the sales process at Chrysler involves selling cars, but that at Northwestern Mutual involves selling insurance. The basic process of selling—identifying buyer objectives, demonstrating value versus investment, and so on—is the same, whether one is selling cars, insurance, or lawn fertilizer. The content differs. Content is usually about WHAT is being created, communicated, and/or consumed.

We should identify what processes we are adept at and then build content around them that relates to particular buyers, industries, audiences, and conditions. For example, I deliver a keynote speech called "Capturing Opportunity" that deals with the processes of innovation, empowerment, and relationships. I've achieved great success with this speech in front of everyone from top-level executives to front-line supervisors, from aerospace to newspapers, and from American audiences to Asian audiences. Remember, I believe in huge playing fields.

The following "topics" are really examples of process, applicable to vast arrays of people, places, organizations, and conditions:

- Networking
- Decision making
- Time management
- Spirituality
- Speaking skills
- Team building
- Customer service
- Motivation
- Humor
- Ethics
- Negotiating
- Problem solving
- Planning
- Substance abuse
- Writing skills
- Technology
- Sales skills
- Use of media
- Futurism
- Health/wellness
- Building self-esteem
- Priority setting
- Image building
- Change

- Listening skills
- Creativity
- Productivity
- Leadership
- Diversity
- Career management

Expansion Worksheet: The absolute WORST question in the speaking profession, always from people who don't understand marketing, is, "What do you speak about?" Here is a brief exercise to escape that narrowing trap:

What do you speak about (conventional reply)?

_____

_____

What type of group do you usually speak to?

_____

Fill in each of the lines below with topics that answer each question.

- *What components of your topic could form separate talks (e.g., listening skills are a component of "effective communications")?*

_____

_____

- *What aspects of the talk involve results that are independent of the talk (e.g., higher close rates are a result of a talk on "sales skills")?*

- *What questions usually arise from partici-pants that you have to anticipate and con-stantly answer (e.g., "How do I influence my boss?" is always a question that demands a careful response when delivering a talk on "how to set priorities")?*

- *What visual aids do you use that most in-trigue participants (e.g., your chart on the differing roles we play at home and at work is part of your work on "managing time")?*

- *Now, reviewing your responses in the preced-ing categories, list four kinds of groups that can profit from these topics in addition to the one you listed at the top.*

- *Now let's change the dreadful "What do you speak about?" to "What is your value proposi-tion?" How are those groups better off once they've heard you in terms of professional and/or business improvement?*

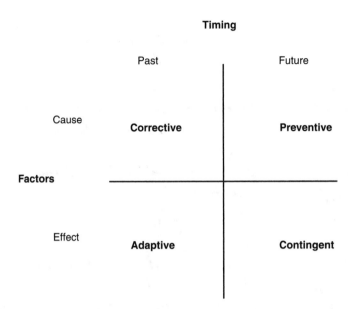

Figure 7-1 Action Sequence

I could go on, but in these 30 topics I've probably covered most of you. The critical issue is that "planning," for example, is the same process whether it is used in a legal firm or a pharmaceutical company, although the content that is plugged into the planning process will be very different. However, I can successfully make these content adjustments as a consultant working on long-term projects, and I can easily make them during the course of a keynote or workshop. So can you.

In Figure 7-1, I've presented an example of mine that is process oriented.

In this example of effective actions, I've used a traditional double-axis chart to show that cause and effect are intertwined with past and future time frames.[1] If you're trying to

[1] I call these "process visuals." For over a hundred examples, see my books *The Great Big Book of Process Visuals* and *The Second Great Big Book of Process Visuals* (East Greenwich, R.I.: Las Brisas Research Press, 2006 and 2007).

remove the cause of a current problem (upper left), corrective action is necessary (e.g., fix the hole in the tire). If you merely want to circumvent the effects of the problem and not fix it (bottom left), then adaptive action is required (e.g., ride with a friend or use another car). If you want to prevent such a problem from occurring (or recurring) in the future, you take preventive action (upper right) intended to avoid it (e.g., check your tires periodically, buy new ones when appropriate, and keep the correct inflation). However, should all your plans fail and you have to deal with the effect of the problem in the future (bottom right), you'd want a contingent action in place to remove the effects (most probably a functioning spare tire in the trunk).

This relationship between cause and effect and the past and the future is applicable to virtually any personal or professional environment. (In manufacturing plants, engineers provide preventive maintenance on the machines; in hospitals, nurses constantly check vital signs to prevent complications; and in newspapers, reporters validate facts from several sources to avoid errors in news stories.)

Choosing your topics as a speaker is a self-limiting and arbitrary exercise based upon what you think you know about your abilities. The real issue is broadening your appeal. Ironically, if you're relatively new to the business, you're in a stronger position to identify broad processes because you probably have less to "unlearn." But if you're a veteran, you should invest time in "deconstructing" what you do to broaden its appeal.

I have a colleague in New England who listened to me speak on the value of processes and later told me that it had been a revelation.

"I had been doing a seminar on customer service for 10 years," he said. "I could do it in my sleep. It was well

> *Speaking Up: All of us can readily describe our content. Sadly, that content is a minuscule portion of the total value we're capable of delivering in our processes.*

received, but I hadn't had the success in my business that I'd hoped, and frankly, my heart wasn't really in that speech anymore. Having heard you, I realized that I had been insisting on delivering it in one format to one kind of business because *I had begun using it in that kind of format and that kind of business when I was first hired a decade ago!"*

People hire you to speak to their circumstances, on their turf, to their people, to meet their objectives. That makes sense. But since those circumstances, turf, people, and objectives differ widely from client to client, refusing to change the content of your talks to better convey your valuable processes makes no sense at all.

THE MYTH OF "SHELF LIFE" AND THE CREATION OF LONG-TERM INTELLECTUAL PROPERTY

I had delivered a highly successful series of engagements around the country for Coldwell Banker on innovation and creative thinking. After the final one, the president of relocation services told me how much his people had benefited from the approaches.

"But tell me," he said, "what kind of shelf life do these speeches have? I imagine you must have to change them fairly frequently to keep them fresh. That's a pretty heavy investment for professional speakers, isn't it?"

I stammered out some reply that glazed his eyes over because I wanted to avoid the cold, harsh truth: I had been delivering that speech in one form or another for 10 years, and I fully expected to continue to deliver it for another 10 years. Oh, my specific examples would change with each client, and my generic examples changed to reflect timeliness (you don't want to use tape cassettes as an analogy when everyone is listening to downloads). *He* had found it fresh and timely. Isn't that the only test?

Processes don't change. There are speakers who make their living doing character portrayals of people such as Mark Twain, Albert Einstein, Abraham Lincoln, and Benjamin Franklin. One of the central reasons for the appeal of such historical figures is that the wisdom, wit, and lessons that they provide are as applicable today—if not more so—as they were the day they were first uttered. There are really relatively few things new under the sun. But the application of traditional ideas in the face of a changing world, new demographics, novel environments, increased stress, and new technologies is a constant challenge for the innovative speaker. Interpersonal sales skills were once a part of the repertoire of the Fuller Brush or Avon door-to-door salespeople, who have disappeared with the rise of dual-career couples and locked doors. But those same skills in varied forms are still applicable for retail salespeople, telemarketers, and assorted others. Conditions and environments change, but basic processes and skills do not.

Shelf life becomes a problem only when topics are inextricably entwined with some fixed event. If one's topic involves quality and is woven around the Haitian earthquake disaster, it's going to suffer from the disinterest caused by distance. However, using the current issues and challenges in the morning *Wall Street Journal* would solve that handily (as would examples from the client's actual environment). We'll talk more about this in terms of specific construction for speeches in the next chapter.

WHY YOU'LL SELDOM GET TOSSED OUT FOR USING COMMON SENSE

For several years early in my career, I was regularly worried that approximately 10 minutes into my speech, someone from the audience would stand up and shout:

"Why, that's totally obvious! Why are you wasting our time with things we know quite well? Don't you have anything new to say??!!"

After a few years of sharing what I came to believe were concepts and principles that everyone should already know, and not having been confronted or pulled physically from the stage, I learned a valuable lesson: most audience members don't always know what you think is obvious, and even if they do, *they don't mind hearing it again.*

In the series of Coldwell Banker keynotes I mentioned earlier, it was inevitable that some people would show up more than once because they carried dual titles, had qualified to attend the conventions several ways, or were changing roles. I tried to keep my material fresh and varied,[2] but there was some unavoidable repetition. Yet no one ever said a word, nor did I or the buyer ever detect the inattention that follows "having heard this song before." Finally, toward the end of my series, participants taught me an invaluable lesson.

[2] More about this later, but every example, story, or anecdote that makes a certain point should have another two or three backups reinforcing it for precisely these circumstances. You should keep a "story catalog," a technique I learned from a wonderful speaker, Jeannie Robertson.

After the keynote, several participants who had heard me before approached me.

"Why didn't you tell the story about how you avoid speaking to people on airplanes?" asked one.

"Yeah, and you skipped the one about the time you couldn't get room service."

"I have to admit," I said, "that I recognized some of you and wanted to eliminate some of the things you'd heard in prior sessions."

"*Don't do that!*" one of them shouted. "Those stories are what really make the points work. Every time we hear them, we get something new from them."

Imagine, people were asking me to repeat stories that they had heard before! In my arrogance, I thought that I knew what was best for their learning and that it did not include repetition. I saw my job as having to be constantly fresh and entertaining. I was working harder than I needed to and achieving less than I wanted to.

When prospects watch videos of my prior speeches, I often expect them to say, "Do the same for us, but make the following adjustments for our industry, audience, and culture." They usually don't. They usually say, "If you can do that exact same thing for us, it will be terrific!" They expect that I have the native intelligence not to open a steel convention by saying, "It's a pleasure to be here with so many accountants" just because that was the group on the video. Clients expect common sense, *both in the content and in the process.*

Of course, everyone knows that you should set objectives before considering alternatives in decision making. Yes, it's obvious that you should handle most items only once if you're trying to be effective at time management. We can all agree that self-esteem is based upon our achieving an accurate view of ourselves and not a distorted picture caused by old "baggage." But apparently, we can't hear any of that too often, particularly if it's integrated into presentations that are unique, energetic, dynamic, and interesting.

Here are my guidelines for avoiding overcomplicating your topic and preventing "fear of shelf-life burnout":

Do Not

- Hitch your topics to the latest fads.
- Depend on highly industry-specific examples.
- Radically rename the topic for each customer (modifications are okay).
- Use convoluted charts and diagrams.
- Portray your topic as the *only* way to achieve the result.
- Assume that the audience doesn't know your topic or doesn't already do it.
- Pretend that you invented it.
- Acknowledge that some of it may not be applicable to this audience.
- Confuse your ego needs with audience learning needs.
- Use others' material, even if it's not original with them.
- Imply that your audience is damaged in some way.

You won't get tossed out on your ear if you're honest about your work and your intent. There is little new under the sun, but you are in a position to help reinforce some important processes for talented, interested participants by presenting these processes in an engaging way that is relevant for the participants' environment and circumstances.

Although I tend to use the corporate world as a frame of reference, note that the premises we're discussing apply to education and youth, volunteer organizations, nonprofits and charities, international audiences, and public seminars as well as in-house groups, short keynotes, lengthy workshops, and virtually all other combinations of speakers' "gumbo."

> *Speaking Up: Common sense is in amazingly short supply. You will rarely get in trouble for suggesting that people ought to use their heads.*

THE USE OF METAPHOR, VISUALS, AND PRAGMATIC CHANGE DEVICES

Sit on your hands. Go ahead. Prop the book open with another book or a stapler or a tire from the car. Okay, good.

Now, describe a spiral staircase. Go on. I'll wait.

Well, I don't have *that* long.

Even if you said, "It's a staircase that climbs while describing a continuing circle around a common axis," I'm still somewhat in the dark. But (you can release your hands now) if you merely made that corkscrew motion with your fingers, we'd all immediately relate.

Visuals—and metaphors are simply conceptual visuals—move conversations along, accelerate understanding, and galvanize interest. They dramatically increase your appeal and drive your point home.

One of my primary tenets is that when you're 80 percent ready, you should move, planning to address the remaining 20 percent only if and when necessary. The final 20 percent,

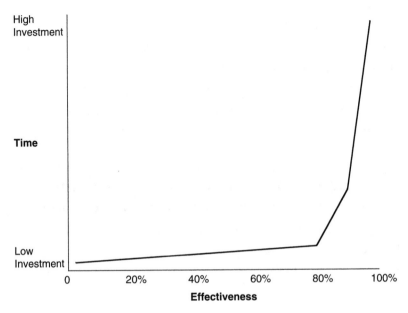

Figure 7-2 The "80 Percent Ready-Move" Dynamic

in your quest for perfection, requires a disproportionate share of your energy and investment. Moreover, the readers don't appreciate that final 20 percent in the book, nor the audience in the speech, nor the observer in the art studio.

That took 69 words. But it looks like Figure 7-2.

You are always better off creating visuals, analogies, metaphor, synecdoche, and metonymy. This applies to your brand ("The Ultimate Driving Machine"—BMW), your marketing ("Bet you can't have just one"—Lay's potato chips), and your delivery ("It was as hot as Georgia asphalt in August"—from *Blue Velvet*).

I was facilitating at a Hewlett-Packard meeting for a small group of internal and external consultants who were struggling with an initiative that just wouldn't get off the ground. They argued about research, and design, and field support, and conflicting priorities. It seemed as if the issue was so complex and ambiguous that it was hopeless.

So I drew a rudimentary rocket ship and said, "What you're lacking is escape velocity. Let's identify the elements holding us back."

In short order I had the navigation devices (strategy), the fuel (management support), the stabilizers (stakeholder support), and the aerodynamics (streamline the mission and jettison lesser priorities). In the next month, people talked about the rocket achieving escape velocity and going into orbit, not the initiative per se or the obstacles. "It's time to release the extra fuel tanks," was an example of the new metaphor. People began putting small rockets on their desks.

If three fully loaded 747 aircraft crashed into the ground every day of the year, what do you think would result? Well, that calamity would equal the number of deaths caused by smoking—direct and indirect smoke—on average over the past few years. Why aren't we equally outraged about that?

That paragraph made you think, as it would your prospects and your audiences. Liven up your speech and enrich your listeners, be they potential buyers or participants.

These devices arise regularly. One of the very newest as of this writing is, "There's an app for that," referring to the myriad applications available for Apple's iPhone. The phrase has entered the vernacular. That's worth a billion dollars in free advertising for Apple, and parallel uses are worth millions for you.

If you're to be an object of interest for your customers, your audiences, your referral sources, and others, you must use colorful language, resonant examples, and crisp visuals. The danger in being a speaker is that we think that everything should be spoken! But the creation of "word pictures" and real pictures is essential to success in our craft.

Set people's hearts racing.

15 IMMEDIATE EXPANSION SOURCES FOR YOUR SPEAKING BUSINESS

Here are some quick ideas to expand your speaking business:

1. Network with successful speakers. Don't ask for business; just act like a peer. My first bureau business came from a speaker who was booked for the date and recommended me.

2. Create six speeches with appropriate benefits for the buyer and audience for each. Provide the buyer with this "choice of yeses."

3. Pursue popular topics. The reason so many people speak about leadership, for example, is that it's so important and so often poorly done. Create your own intellectual property and pursue it.

4. Codify your experience. As you learn things or even dream up things, put them in physical or electronic folders under categories. When you have critical mass in one of these folders, create a new speech or pursue a new market.

5. Speak at local events, chapters, and outlets of much larger organizations, and work your way up through the ranks. The local Red Cross operation may introduce you to the state organization, which might be a springboard to the national organization.

6. Offer pro bono talks to local trade groups that have a variety of businesses and professionals represented in the audience.

7. Volunteer to moderate a panel or facilitate a meeting for your community or a school.

8. If you belong to a club, offer to host an evening after-dinner for members who are interested in a given topic (strategy, marketing, sales, or some other area).

9. Offer yourself as a guest expert to the producers of local radio talk shows. (But do not pay to host one!)

10. Place sample audio and video segments of your speeches on your Web site, blog, and any other Internet outlets to which you have access.

11. Volunteer to be a guest lecturer at community colleges, local universities, trade schools, adult extension courses, and so on.

12. Create a blog and include provocative text, audio, and video postings about topics related to your value proposition, expertise, and speaking interests.

13. Create a free teleconference series—one per month of 45 minutes each—on topics that relate to your expertise. Use the Internet to promote it, and use the downloads for publicity.[3]

14. Let the convention or visitor's bureau in your town and nearby towns know that you're available as a backup if speakers miss their flights, are ill, or cancel for some other reason.

15. Volunteer to be master of ceremonies (emcee) at a public event, fund-raiser, or political debate.

There are a great many ways to become known, and it's all too easy to be forgotten. Keep your name and talent in front of prospective recommenders and buyers.

---

[3] You can do this for as little as $100 per session with services such as those provided by Rebecca Hanson (Rebecca@rebeccahanson.com).

SUMMARY

Content is *what* people do, but process is *how* they do it. Consequently, process is transferable (sales techniques are the same in real estate or auto sales, for example). The more you master processes, the more you will be flexible enough to be a speaker for many organizations and be hired by many buyers.

Because so many processes are constant (e.g., decision making or conflict resolution) and can be used in so many ways (face to face or through technology), there is no expiration date on their effectiveness, demand, or applicability. Therefore, your intellectual property can be lifelong if you focus on the process arena. If you focus on content, you will have obsolescence problems (no one is looking for vacuum tube experts these days).

Accentuate your appeal by using the tools of our trade: metaphor, analogy, and metonymy. Apply process visuals to accelerate understanding and learning. The best speakers speak less, not more. Focus on what the audience and the buyer need to know, not on a "topic" or a "speech."

Expand your business by expanding your thinking.

CHAPTER 8

CREATING GREAT SPEECHES AND WORKSHOPS

THE RULES AND REGULATIONS FOR FORMULATING GREAT CONTENT

MOST PEOPLE who are making serious money in the speaking profession are delivering workshops and seminars. Let's be real about this. That is noble work, and it's tough work. Very few of us noncelebrity speakers can support ourselves any more (in a decent lifestyle) solely by doing keynotes, and even when that's possible, the travel and the wear and tear are ridiculous.

My partner in the annual The Odd Couple® Workshop on marketing for speakers, Patricia Fripp, has been one of the great keynote speakers in the world. But she has stated frequently and candidly that if she had to make her living solely from that source today, she'd be starving. Instead, she has diversified into coaching, consulting, and product sales.[1]

In any case, you need to find, cultivate, and protect your sources of material.

---

[1] For information on The Odd Couple® and our annual program on marketing for professional speakers, go to http://www.fripp.com or http://www.summitconsulting.com.

USING ORIGINAL SOURCES WITH YOUR OWN ORIGINAL MATERIAL

Some people never write a speech. They inherited, stole, purchased, cobbled together, or winged something quite some time ago, and they are still using it. When this is accompanied by poor platform skills, these people are invariably unsuccessful. When it is accompanied by superb platform skills, these people are inevitably not as good (or as successful) as they could be. They're getting by on sizzle without steak.

There are six simple rules for excellent speaking preparation:

> *Rule 1: The Originality/Validity Rule.* The speech should be yours.
>
> *Rule 2: The Relevance Rule.* Stories and anecdotes should be germane.
>
> *Rule 3: The Perspective Rule.* People learn best when they are comfortable.
>
> *Rule 4: The Outcome Rule.* The buyer's condition should be improved.
>
> *Rule 5: The Adult Rule.* People learn in different ways.
>
> *Rule 6: The Timeliness Rule.* Changing conditions must be accommodated.

Rule 1: The Originality/Validity Rule

I once traveled a long way to Lake of the Ozarks, Missouri, to keynote a senior executive conference for corporate giant Unisys. About 70 of the top-level executives were present, and the senior vice president of marketing rose to introduce me. He quickly moved into a story that became alarmingly familiar. *It was one of my real-life experiences, one that I had planned to include that morning!*

At first, I thought he was using the story to introduce me, but it quickly became apparent that he was using it to get some laughs. He merely substituted himself for me and told it verbatim. He had stolen it from one of my CDs and had forgotten the source, creating the Kafkaesque situation of relating it prior to introducing the person he had stolen it from!

This happens all the time, and too often among speakers. I've heard enough variations on a single theme from scores of different speakers to make the various parts of *Bolero* seem like Ravel had an independent thought for each movement.

There are two reasons not to steal from others:

1. Personal stories are just that, and it's unethical to use them unless they're your own.
2. A lot of what you steal simply isn't true.

The first reason shouldn't require a whole lot of explaining. I've occasionally heard my own "stuff" regurgitated by another speaker who had been in one of my audiences previously. Borrowed stories are never as powerful, questions from the audience can't be handled well, and sooner or later, word always gets back to the originator. If we can't act like ethical professionals, then we have no right to call this a profession. If a journalist or writer uses someone else's materials, it's called plagiarism. If a company uses another organization's proprietary creation, it's called patent infringement. If an employee who moves to a competing company uses confidential, classified information from the former employer, it's called theft.

When a speaker takes someone else's materials, it's no less a crime and no less dishonest. Corporate audiences can often spot it, since they're exposed to so many speakers, and they will always react negatively. Buyers will not invite you back and may not even pay you the balance of your fee.

> *Speaking Up: If you have to steal to get material, go into computer hacking or hold up convenience stores. The rewards are more immediate, and at least your comrades will readily admit to what they're doing.*

The second reason not to steal is more subtle, and it's the primary reason for the Originality Rule. A great deal of what you hear from the platform is simply not true. For example, I've heard at least 300 speakers claim during a variety of different presentations that "less than 4 percent of the impact on an audience is based upon what you say." They claim that more than 90 percent of the audience impact is based upon how you say it, and they quote the work of Dr. Albert Mehrabian, who did some sociological studies, as the source of the statistics. The speakers then proceed to make their point, which is that *how* you present something is more important than *what* you present.

There are only a couple of things wrong with this. The first is that Mehrabian did his work more than 40 years ago, far too long to still have credence in a society as turbulent as ours. The second and even more important, however, is that his work (if anyone bothers to actually read it) is based upon social situations and people standing in line, waiting to be served, and so on.[2] About 10 years ago, a speaker at a national

---

[2] For example, he used assistants who attempted to break into lines at a post office, some cordially smiling and others rudely assertive, to see how patrons responded. See A. Mehrabian and J. A. Russell, *An Approach to Environmental Psychology* (Cambridge, Mass.: MIT Press, 1974).

convention cited this work incorrectly, and hundreds of others simply incorporated the nonsense into their "act." Anyone who knows psychology realizes that it's false, and anyone with a decent brain realizes that great, captivating speakers such as Franklin Roosevelt, William F. Buckley, Jr., Peter Drucker, and Henry Kissinger have relied almost exclusively on the beauty of their words, not their platform skills.

Let's end the madness.

It's important to be original for the sake of professional ethics, but also as the basis of your own competence. You can't rely on random "facts" just because they've been spouted by someone holding a microphone. As Casey Stengel used to say, "You can look it up."

Rule 2: The Relevance Rule

Pictures Are Worth, Literally, 1,546 Words

Try opening a conversation with two different sallies:

- How was your vacation?
- Would you like to hear about my vacation?

Now, which do you think will elicit the warmer, more attentive response? If you think it's the second one, then you're Donald Trump.

It's vital that you make your speech as relevant and comfortable for the audience's frame of reference as possible. If that means your discomfort, so be it. It's far better for you to be uncomfortable in alien territory than for your audience to feel that way. The absolutely best way I know to accomplish this is to talk to some of the potential audience members well ahead of time.

Ask the buyer if it would be permissible for you to call a random selection of the audience. So as not to take too much of either their time or your own, tell them that you simply want to ask them three quick questions to help you prepare your remarks, *and be sure to offer the options of a voice mail, e-mail, or faxed response* so that you don't have to play telephone tag with busy people and you can shorten the process.

Ask anything you like to gain relevant input for your speech, but here are my usual three questions, with my permission to steal them:

1. What's the biggest challenge you are facing on the job?
2. If you could change just one thing tomorrow, what would it be?
3. What advice would you give to a new person in your position?

I modify these questions as needed, but they basically stand up well in a wide variety of environments. I use the results at various junctures in my speech, so that perhaps three times during an hour's keynote, I'll refer to "what you've told me." Doing this in advance gives you the luxury of incorporating the feedback into your visual aids if desired. Never mention how many people you spoke to, even though small random samples are generally quite accurate, but merely cite "those of you with whom I've spoken over the past several weeks."

My experience is that virtually no one refuses a request to help a speaker tailor remarks for an individual company if the request is polite and personal, provides choices in the means of response, and is brief.

> **Speaking Up: Don't tell them everything you know. Tell them everything they need to know, and then try not to tell them this too blatantly.**

A "verbal picture" is a story, anecdote, experience, or metaphor that captures a point for the audience prior to beating them to death with it. One of the classics is the college admissions officer who tells new freshmen some variation of, "Look to your left, look to your right, and then consider that two of the three of you will not be here in four years."

A verbal picture is worth 1,546 actual words. So if your keynote is an hour, and that involves about 10,000 words, you can knock that off with just 6.468 stories or anecdotes. How did I come up with these figures? Someone told me that Albert Mehrabian did this study.

Rule 3: The Perspective Rule

There's Nothing Funny about Humor

There is nothing like self-effacing humor to help an audience become comfortable. Comfort is a key aspect of adult learning. If I'm uncomfortable, I'm resisting, not focused, diverted, and looking inward. If I'm comfortable, I'm receptive, open, outward-focused, and "present." The trouble is that most speakers consider comfort to be external, and therefore focus on the room temperature, the seating, refreshment breaks, and a host of other tangential environmental factors. There are actually some self-appointed "coaches" who specialize in external surroundings. I've spoken in rooms with power outages, with failed sound systems, adjacent to gospel meetings, next to street construction, with panoramic views of the Rocky Mountains, with simultaneous translators in the back, with wait staff constantly busing dishes, and with participants hustling in from other late-running events. Such is life, and I've managed to engage almost every one of those audiences (although the bomb scare was difficult).

In fact, comfort is *internal*, and that needs to be our primary focus, not how much water is in the water glasses. People are relaxed by humor, but since most humor is based upon someone's discomfort, it's best to ensure that the humor is self-effacing and directed solely at the speaker. People will tend to commiserate and sympathize ("I've been there!") and identify not merely with your situation, but with the ensuing message.

There are two basic types of humor: generic and specific. Here's a rule of thumb: don't use the former.

Generic humor is embodied in these classic puffballs, one of which I actually used myself early in my career (it didn't occur to me that others had already stumbled on it, even though I read it in a national magazine). I'm presenting both here in the hopes that such exposure will ruin their utility forever.

The Naval Ship Story

The huge naval ship pounded down the coast during a dark and stormy night. Conditions were horrible, with visibility severely limited. Suddenly, there was a light through the haze. Another ship, collision course!

A message was sent: "We're on a collision course. Change your heading 20° north." The reply: "Collision course acknowledged. Change your heading 20° south."

A second message from the massive ship: "This is Rear Admiral Harvey Johnston. Change your heading 20° north." The second reply: "This is Seaman Fourth Class Arnold Jones. Change your heading 20° south."

A third message: "I am standing on the bridge of the largest capital ship in the navy. Every gun and missile is pointed directly at you. Change your heading 20° north."

The final reply: "I am standing in a lighthouse . . . "

The Sand Dollar Story

A little boy was moving down the beach, stopping frequently to toss sand dollars, washed ashore by the tide, back into the ocean. A person approached and asked what the boy was doing.

"I'm saving the sand dollars," said the boy.

"But look at the thousands on the shore," said the adult. "You can't possibly make a difference."

Throwing another back into the ocean, the boy replied, "I certainly made a difference for that one."

After the second story, I'm prompted to say that the sand dollars are being eaten by barracuda stationed just off the beach, which is why the sand dollars had deliberately flung themselves onto the safety of the beach, where they can live quite comfortably and someday build condos, but that's still another story.

Use humor that is specifically yours. Not all of us are comedians or humorists, but that's not what I'm suggesting. Every day we laugh and experience irony. Write it down, make a note, record the occurrence. Then rework it into your material. Here's an example that I use to reinforce my point that there is too much of a "that's not my job" attitude in organizational America. It really happened, and almost exactly as I describe it.

The Hyatt Hot Line

I'm staying at a Hyatt Regency Hotel, and on the end table is a card that says in bold letters *Hyatt Regency Hot Line.* "No

problem too big or too small, available 24 hours a day. Call the Hyatt Hot Line with any request."

I had no room service menu. I said, "This is a job for the Hyatt Hot Line."

I dialed, and a woman answered, "Hyatt Hot Line! How can I help you?"

"This is Alan Weiss, room 734, and I have no room service menu."

She replied, "I'm sorry, we don't handle that."

I go on to relate that I asked if they handled nuclear war, since I needed to know what the criteria were to qualify for Hyatt Hot Line assistance.

All humor is based upon discomfort. In this case, it's my frustration at not being able to get the help I expected.

Here's another tip for adding relevant humor and stories to your work: Always have two in reserve for every one you intend to use. This is because

1. Participants will sometimes ask for additional examples if they didn't get the point. (People learn in varying ways—see Rule 5: The Adult Rule.)

2. You sometimes unexpectedly find past participants sitting in the room who have heard your primary stories.

3. Even a proven story might not work. You can be interrupted by an equipment problem or other distraction. Or a story involving an airplane may be inappropriate if there was a recent air disaster.

4. A story can be inappropriate for a particular audience. I'm not going to tell that Hyatt story to a hotel convention because it would embarrass Hyatt in front of its peers (although I'd readily tell it to a Hyatt in-house meeting).

Three Kinds of Humor

1. *Jokes.* These are the scripted stories that proverbially begin with "Two guys walk into a bar," or "Do you know the difference between . . . ?" These are virtually never effective in speeches because

   - Some members of the audience will invariably have heard some of the jokes.
   - They usually have little to do with your actual topic.
   - Most jokes have the potential to offend, since they deal with someone else's foibles or discomfort.
   - Not everyone "gets" a joke or feels that it's funny.

Save jokes for some fun over drinks or at family gatherings, and then only if you're not that crazy about your family.

2. *Stories.* If stories are original and based on reality, they can be highly effective. Not all stories, of course, are humorous. But those that are should use self-effacing humor. Since a story is yours, it's unlikely to have been heard before (or told as well). Stories are great sources of humor because

   - They are personal and told conversationally.
   - Unless someone has stolen them, they are fresh and new.
   - The audience will usually relate—"I've been there, too!"
   - They can be selected and molded to complement your topic.

Adjust your stories for cadence and timing, and always be on the alert for additions to your collection.

3. *Ad lib.* Ad lib humor is the riskiest and also the outright funniest. It's based on your reaction to a

spontaneous event, and the lack of preparation and use of humor will thrill an audience if it works out. (*Ad libitum* means "freely.") This type of humor works because

- It's "in the moment" and succinct.
- It demonstrates great wit and intelligence.
- It galvanizes people around the incident.

Never use ad lib humor to degrade anyone else individually. Use it to mock a situation so that you're never seen as picking on anyone.

When I keynoted for Toyota Financial one year, I heard a great deal of good-natured banter during the introduction about the discomfort of being in Phoenix in July, where it must have been 114° in the shade. When I walked on stage, I deadpanned: "I know why you're here, it's not surprising. The surface of the sun was already booked." After that, whatever I said was golden.

Build humor into every speech you give. I'm not of the school that says, "Don't try to be funny unless you're a comedian." Adult learning relies on comfort, and properly directed humor creates instant comfort. By using actual occurrences, striving for self-effacing humor, and telling true stories in a practiced, articulate manner, anyone can insert humor into almost any speech (I've seen it excellently done in eulogies and courtrooms).

Rule 4: The Outcome Rule

Now that You've Been There and Gone, So What?

Every valuable speech, training session, workshop, seminar, facilitated meeting, and emceed affair should have an outcome. A humorous after-dinner speech, for example, should leave participants in a positive frame of mind and feeling good about their circumstances at the moment. A training program on time management should leave the audience with tangible organizational skills. A workshop on diversity should leave attendees with an appreciation of cultural distinctions and the harmful effects of inappropriate language.

If you want to be rehired by the current buyer—or at least acquire a golden reference for future buyers—you must provide results *appropriate to the topic and environment* that remain with the client. There's nothing wrong with getting people fired up briefly if that's the buyer's aim, but there's even more power in providing skills, techniques, and approaches that people will be demonstrating to the buyer every day long after you've spoken.

Outcomes originate with the economic buyer. Ask him or her what's to be achieved. If the buyer says, "Well, I'm not certain," or "We just want to have a good time," always ask "*Why?*" The responses will be revelations such as, "The conference was dull last year, and we thought an energetic speaker could liven things up," or "Our people have had a very rough year, but they performed admirably and they deserve to be told how good they are," or "We see our mission as educating the people who come to these meetings, in terms of both their professional and their personal lives." You are then in a position to ask, "If they leave with this (skill, technique, attitude, awareness, or something else), will that contribute toward your goals?" Simply keep this up until the buyer says, "That's exactly what I'd like to see happen."

Even if you're not introduced at the buyer level, find your way to that person. Refer back to Chapter 4 for help in getting there.

I know a great many speakers who don't bother to find the real buyer (they're hired by a meeting planner or placed by a bureau) and/or don't bother to understand what the desired outcomes are. They see their job as delivering a keynote or presenting a workshop. They collect their check and leave. This is equivalent to a salesperson making sales calls and considering the job well done. Salespeople should bring in new business, and speakers should meet the buyer's objectives by achieving agreed-upon outcomes.

How much repeat business do you receive *unsolicited?* How many times does the buyer call you and say, "We've got something coming up that you would be just perfect for"? (Or how often does a new client call and say, "I was referred to you by a colleague who told me I couldn't afford not to hire you for our meeting"?) Most speakers struggle because they labor to make new sales to new buyers under new conditions for far too great a percentage of their available time. They have references, but they don't have *referrals.* They have client lists, but they don't have *relationships.*

Begin your speech preparation with the outcomes to be achieved. If you don't know them, go find the buyer and develop them.

Rule 5: The Adult Rule

People Learn in Different Ways: Not Everyone Is as Smart as You Think You Are

People learn in different ways. Not better or worse ways, just different ways. I'm not talking about esoteric (and highly dubious) right-brain/left-brain codifications, or about labels like "driver" or "INTJ," or any other such nonsense. I'm talking about observable behavior.

Some of us prefer visuals. Some of us like sequences. There are those who rejoice in group learning, but others who prefer solitary absorption. There are as many people who shun volunteering for role-plays and demonstrations as there are people who rush to the stage to take part in them.

Adults make their own decisions. It's always permissible to present options and even to challenge assumptions, but it's never a good idea to assume that your alternative is the best for everyone. Quite a few speakers who really ought to know better demand that audience members touch the people next to them, often in the form of a neck rub or a hug. For many people, this is an intimacy that is completely inappropriate. Some speakers become apoplectic when they ask the audience to sing or dance or otherwise engage in physical activity and then find some holdouts. They see this as a personal affront. It isn't. It's merely a personal choice.

The best speech preparation embraces the philosophy that people are diverse and learn in varying manners. This means at least three things for the speaker and his or her preparation and attitude:

1. Provide varied sources of input. For example, use visuals as well as text; have workbooks as well as slides; provide a summary sheet as well as detailed text; use interaction voluntarily, but also use lecture to summarize key points.

2. Never demand participation in any activity that even one person would find demeaning. If you want to role-play, explain the situation and ask for a volunteer; don't nail someone in the back row (that person, unless he or she is a latecomer, is sitting way back there for a reason). Don't ask people to touch or to

reveal an intimacy: "Tell your partner something you've never told anyone else before." (I've actually been present when this directive was given. My partner said, "It's only 10 minutes into the workshop and I already hate this speaker, and I've never had to say that before this morning.") Never demand that people touch each other, as in rubbing backs or other nonsense.

3. Always give the benefit of the doubt, and never take anything personally. I've had people leave my talks within 90 seconds of my saying, "Good morning." I assume that they had a good reason, such as a sudden call of nature, the realization that they were in the wrong session, or the body odor of the person who sat next to them. I embrace every question as honest and sincere, unless I have incontrovertible proof to the contrary. "I don't agree with you. Can you give me a better example?" is a legitimate and valuable question. "I don't think a woman has any right to address us on a management topic. What do you think you're doing here?" is not.

Speakers are vested with tremendous credibility and support when they ascend the platform. The audience wants to be part of a success. Fewer than 5 percent of your attendees (that's 10 people out of 200, or 1 person in 20) suffer from the kind of personality disorder that impels them to crave someone else's failure. People may slow down to see a traffic wreck, but virtually no one would want to contribute to one.

Give your audience the same respect when you prepare your speech or workshop. Don't insert stories or exercises that merely make you look good and lack any kind of learning point or relevance for the audience. Build in backups and alternatives in case a given segment seems not to work or an example falls flat. Allow time for questions. You can always fill in with support material if there are none, but it's death to cut the audience short because you have too much mandatory material to cram in.

And despite what you'll hear from meeting planners, who seem to feel that they're evaluated by the quantity of time filled, no audience or buyer ever complained because a terrific speech ran 10 minutes short or an intriguing seminar ended 40 minutes early. But once you go even 5 minutes overtime, you'll begin to lose large segments of audience attention, not to mention the damage done to the rest of the agenda.[3]

Rule 6: The Timeliness Rule

That Was This Morning. What about Now?

Finally, keep your stuff current. Everyone is weary of hearing about the Disney Electric Parade and the garbage collectors ("We're part of the show"), the response of J&J to Tylenol tampering, and the fact that shampoo sales were doubled by putting the admonition "rinse and repeat" on the label.

Look for current examples even with traditional processes. Scan the morning paper; chat with client attendees prior to the program; watch the news on TV or the Internet.

---

[3] As a closing plenary speaker for the International Human Resource Information Managers Association, I waited patiently in the wings while an insufferable director of a charity took all of his time and most of mine trying to solicit corporate donations. The meeting planner looked on like a mushroom. I had only 20 minutes left after my introduction. I opened with, "In view of the time, I will be brief," got a thunderous round of applause, finished in 20 minutes, and left, my full fee having been paid six months earlier. I received one of the highest reviews of the entire conference.

I want to know what will work for me tomorrow, not what worked for someone else yesterday. Update your collateral material, your examples, your Web site, and your conversation. Stay in the moment. You'd want the same respect and consideration.

Audiences are no different from you, except that you'll usually be speaking and they'll usually be listening, if you let them.

PEOPLE LEARN IN DIFFERING WAYS: NOT EVERYONE IS AS SMART AS WE THINK WE ARE

This section is for those of you who must have a formula or template for creating a speech from scratch. Fair enough. The previously discussed conceptual part is the tough stuff. The next few pages are easy, but only if you've embraced what preceded them.

There are eight primary steps to building a successful new speech:

Step 1: Outcomes

Step 2: Time Frame and Sequence

Step 3: The Key Learning Points

Step 4: Rough Draft Assembly

Step 5: Supporting Stories, Examples, and Transitions

Step 6: Visual Aids and Handouts

Step 7: Build the Opening and Closing

Step 8: Practice the Speech and Adjust the Cadence and Timing

Let's say that a client has asked you to speak to a management team of 50 people. It is a successful high-tech (or health-care or automotive—it really doesn't matter) organization in a competitive marketplace. The vice president of operations wants to instill formalized techniques that people can use to constantly raise their own standards and outpace the competition. Your speech is the kickoff for the daylong conference. All of the other speakers and activities involve internal people.

Step 1: Outcomes

You ask the vice president to specify the results (the Outcome Rule) he'd like to see in the aftermath of your speech. He says that there are two *short-term and one long-term result.* The short-term results are

- Prepare participants to "open up" their thinking so that the rest of the day can take advantage of innovative and "out of the box" ideas.
- Provide a few simple techniques that participants can use to keep them focused on new and creative ways to get the job done.
  The long-term objective is
- Instill a sense of pride that they, in fact, *have* been very creative, which is why the company is so successful, and that they shouldn't become conservative or defensive just because the company has grown so dramatically.

Step 2: Time Frame and Sequence

You will have 90 minutes, including any question and answer time. You will kick off the session after the vice president's brief welcome and introduction. There will be a 15-minute break after your talk, followed by breakout sessions to discuss the impact of what you provided on several key issues that the company is currently facing. These will be facilitated by mid-level managers.

You believe this timing is adequate and appropriate for the objectives.

Step 3: The Key Learning Points

Ninety minutes is a relatively brief period. At best, you'll want to stress only a few learning points around the three outcomes specified. You might choose different ones, but, for the purposes of my example, I'll choose four:

1. Problem solving is the enemy of innovation and usurps its time and focus unless innovation is formalized as a process.

2. Organizations reward what they truly value, and people's actions are a consequence of those rewards. Since managers are exemplars, they must continue to reward in the future the creativity and innovation that has marked the company's past and current success.

3. We mercilessly examine the reasons for failure, but we seldom examine the causes of our success. This is a successful group. We need to articulate the reasons for our own successes to date so that we can replicate, communicate, and improve upon them.

4. There are generic sources of innovation that exist in most companies. Let's take a look at them and determine how to spot and exploit them in this company.

Note that the learning points combine the short- and long-term outcomes and also combine prescriptive (here are 10 sources) and diagnostic (why have we been so successful?) processes. This is simply another illustration of varied learning—the Adult Rule.

Step 4: Rough Draft Assembly

I'd now place the learning points in the order that makes most sense from a flow and interest standpoint. My choice is to start with point 1 as a source of controversy and then go to point 2 to demonstrate that the managers control their own environment through rewards and examples. Points 3 and 4 will be virtually concurrent and will allow me to end on a "high" with praise for their successes to date.

Step 5: Supporting Stories, Examples, and Transitions

Support your points with stories (remember the Originality/ Validity and Relevance Rules), examples, and transitions from one major point to the next. For my point about problem solving, I'll support it with

- Definitions of problem solving and of innovation
- An audience exercise to test whether its members tend to be problem solvers or innovators (they'll be more innovative than they think, and they'll be pleasantly surprised)
- An assessment of how much time the organization is spending on each pursuit

- Examples of organizations that have problem-solved themselves right out of existence (they fixed old things really well and created new things really poorly)
- A transition to conclude this section that will determine which organizational rewards have supported problem solving and which have supported innovation, and determine whether they should be fine-tuned to further accent the latter

Choose appropriate stories from your personal "catalog." Note that you don't begin with the stories and examples that you always use. Some of them might fit well, but if you begin with them and build the speech around them, you've merely duplicated someone else's presentation for a client who needs his or her own.

Step 6: Visual Aids and Handouts

Given your time frame, environment, major points, and supporting material, what is appropriate for visuals (computer-generated slides, easel sheets, video, and other such material), demonstrations, presession handouts, and postsession leave-behinds? Does the material have its best impact if it is distributed in advance or provided as reinforcement? Vary your audio, visual, and textual material given the Adult Rule.[4]

Note that you do not start by taking handouts or visuals that you happen to have around—even if you've spent a fortune on them—and determining how they fit. Many of them

---

[4] And if any of you use those sophomoric, simplistic, "fill-in-the-blanks" *workbooks* (e.g., "We must ___ the audience to get its attention."), then go back to page 1 and start reading this book more slowly. (The correct answer to my fill-in is "pay.")

might, but if you start with them, you're starting with someone else's outcomes.

In this example, I'll use slides with 50 people if I can ensure that the room will be lighted comfortably but still provide visibility for the screen. I'm going to use a summary handout at the end of my session, but nothing during it, because I don't like having people's attention divided between my message and interaction and their attempts to follow the text in front of them. I'll recommend that people take notes if they so choose, because many people learn better by writing down key points.

If you opt for a separate question and answer session, build it into the latter part of the body of the speech; do not save it for the closing.

Step 7: Build the Opening and Closing

What you've worked on up to this point is the *body* of the speech or workshop. Step 7 is absolutely the most important—and the briefer the presentation, the more important it usually is—but it can't be created effectively until this point. Since the opening and closing are directly related, I find it best to create them at the same time, bearing in mind the Perspective Rule.

Counterintuitively, the opening is created after the body of the speech.

Look at your outcomes and key learning points and ask yourself how you can open your presentation and create this result: *the audience is motivated to listen intently.* This involves the following criteria:

1. There is a "hook" (the Relevance Rule) to gain their enthusiastic commitment (not merely compliance). A

story, humor, a challenging fact about the company, citing your interviews with participants, a contradiction, or a provocation can all be used to set the hook. Use what's comfortable for you and most appropriate for the topic.

2. Apprise the audience members of what's to come. Prepare them for the points you'll be making by *briefly* summarizing your route. This allows people to anticipate and begin to plan their own learning. (If you're using handouts in advance, this is a good time to refer to them.) Now's the time to "tell them what you're going to tell them," albeit with some flair and variety.

3. Make a smooth transition to your first point, and before the members of your audience know it, they're committed to listening, and the process has begun.

For a keynote speech, a good introduction is usually no longer than two or three minutes. For longer presentations, introductions often include people introducing themselves to neighbors or even briefly explaining why they've come to the session. This is "icebreaker" involvement, but it's really about mechanics and comfort, not about learning objectives and motivation. Even with daylong seminars, you'll need an effective opening to the topic, or people may have become comfortable in the environment but still not know why they're in it.

My opening will begin with a funny story about bureaucracy that I encountered with a client who wound up being unable to contact his own office because of the intricacies of his voice-mail system! I'll then talk about how this company's

> *Speaking Up: The opening and closing are the most important parts of any presentation because they inform the audience members why they are there, gain their commitment to learn, and then provide the outcomes in terms of key departure points and calls to action.*

organization has managed to avoid such indignities and some of the reasons for this that I've seen and heard in the phone interviews (which will focus on the outcomes). I'll also plan to refer to one of the vice president's remarks from his brief opening to create a continuity of theme.

The closing (tell them what you've told them) should result from a review of the outcomes and points that have been raised in the body of the speech and should contain two elements:

1. *Key learning points (KLPs).* The KLPs are those points that you want the participants to retain. They are centered on the outcomes. You should formally summarize them at the end, and any supporting handout material or follow-up material should focus on them. There should be relatively few, since people's focus is limited. In my speech, the learning points might include

   - With every new challenge, first try to innovate (not problem-solve).
   - Choose the three sources of innovation that are most relevant to your job.
   - Reinforce and reward those behaviors that are already being done so well.

2. *Call to action.* This step usually isn't necessary in speeches that are meant to entertain or merely inform, but it's too often neglected in all others. What does the buyer want people to do when they leave the session? This is the most immediate of all the outcomes. In my speech, I'll choose only one call to action:

- In the breakout sessions that follow, take an innovative approach to each challenge that your facilitator presents and immediately try to raise the standard, not repair the damage. (Thus, my opening has carried forward a remark from my introducer, and my closing has made the transition into the following agenda item.)

Never end a session with questions and answers. If you don't take questions spontaneously during your talk, then pause just before your conclusion to make the offer. Don't feel obligated to end with a funny story, although humor often works quite well in the closing. Finally, don't let your ego allow you to believe that the closing is about you, standing ovations, and ratings on "smile sheets." The closing is about *implementing the key learning points that will lead to the buyer's desired outcomes.* If you do that, you'll be rehired and referred to others. If you don't do that, your ovation and your 10 rating will get you only a fleeting memory.

Step 8: Practice the Speech and Adjust the Cadence and Timing

Only after you're sure that you have the proper elements and outcomes supported should you adjust the timing. Practice the speech just as you would deliver it at the event, allowing for the introduction, a few questions and brief responses, and a few seconds of laughs where you might expect them. (If you get laughs where you don't expect them, you've got more problems than just poor timing.)

Always provide your own introduction. Never send material and suggest that the introducer select what's appropriate, and never rely on the introducer's having (1) received it or (2) practiced it. Call your introducer ahead of time. Bring an extra copy of the introduction to the event, because the one you sent will have been misplaced. Keep it brief, have it double-spaced in bold type on large paper, and then tell the introducer to be sure to read it as it appears. Sometimes a large-caliber pistol helps.

If your speech is too short, then add examples around each supporting point for the outcomes. A good example takes about two minutes and solidifies learning, so these are your best bet. If you're using visual aids, consider a couple of additional supporting ones. For longer presentations, consider more audience involvement in the form of role-plays, application, small-group work, and/or facilitated discussion.

If your speech is too long, then try to remove any superfluous stories or visuals that you've included for comfort or cosmetic reasons that aren't really essential to the outcomes. If you've included a predetermined question and answer period, shorten it or eliminate it and offer to answer what questions there are as they come up *as time permits*. Consider shortening your opening if it contains icebreakers and logistics. (Most icebreakers are for the speaker's comfort, anyway, not the participants'.[5]

---

[5] I kid you not, I once saw two "professional" speakers run a 90-minute icebreaker for 25 people before allowing the featured speakers to take the stage. Those of us who were waiting to go on roared with laughter, until we had to go up there and fix the mess they had made.

Remember, it's better to be slightly short than slightly long. If you find that you can't reduce the speech to the allotted time without gutting essential elements, then you've probably taken on too much topic for too short a time frame, and it's best to go back to the buyer and suggest either a longer time frame or fewer outcomes.

The practice and timing should also allow you to change stories, sequences, transitions, and other aspects of the presentation for maximum logic and flow. Record your practice and listen to it a day or so later. Ask others to comment. You'll find that you'll have a fine speech if you adhere to the simple criteria from the perspective of buyer outcomes and audience learning.

The Six Rules and Eight Steps for Creating a Speech

The Six Rules

Rule 1: The Originality/Validity Rule—The speech should be yours.

Rule 2: The Relevance Rule—Stories and anecdotes should be germane.

Rule 3: The Perspective Rule—People learn best when they are comfortable.

Rule 4: The Outcome Rule—The buyer's condition should be improved.

Rule 5: The Adult Rule—People learn in different ways.

Rule 6: The Timeliness Rule—Changing conditions must be accommodated.

> ## *The Eight Steps*
>
> ### *Step 1: Outcomes*
> ### *Step 2: Time Frame and Sequence*
> ### *Step 3: The Key Learning Points*
> ### *Step 4: Rough Draft Assembly*
> ### *Step 5: Supporting Stories, Examples, and Transitions*
> ### *Step 6: Visual Aids and Handouts*
> ### *Step 7: Build the Opening and Closing*
> ### *Step 8: Practice the Speech and Adjust the Cadence and Timing*

THE 90-MINUTE RULE

For longer workshops, I'm going to share the secret of creation and efficacy. I've worked with people who simply struggle to either fill up a workshop with high-level content or, more commonly and counterintuitively, agonize over the culling process to reduce the seminar to merely half a lifetime.

First, abide by my rules:

Alan's Rules for Great Workshop Creation

1. Determine the learning objectives. Ask the client what people are supposed to do better as a result of the time they have invested.[6]

2. Evaluate the participants in terms of their experience, sophistication, responsibilities, education, and expectations.

---

[6] And for pity's sake, ignore the "four levels of measurement" that trainers and training magazines love to spout as if it were actually accurate. The only measurement worth a darn is improved performance. People who can perform on a test but can't do the job are worthless, and many people have trouble with tests but perform wonderfully on the job.

3. Create a tentative design of the elements required, keeping in mind point 1. Tell them what they need to know, not everything you know. Include the exercises, visuals, and handouts that you think would be most applicable and effective.

4. Obtain feedback from your buyer.

5. Finalize your design, *including the time requirements.*

Most people start with point 5 rather than point 1. That is, they accede to a request for a "two-day leadership workshop," or a "half day on strategy" without regard for the learning needs. I realize that there are times when an arbitrary time frame is forced on you, but it's far less often than you think *because speakers and trainers seldom, if ever, question the time frames,* which are notoriously arbitrary.

Thus, set your time frame last unless there are strong reasons not to. When you don't, you'll often find that you're either struggling to fill a period of time that is simply too long or desperately trying to remove "essential" elements to fit a reduced time frame. (And this is why you should *never* charge by the day or by the participant. Your value is not based on how long you're there, or you'd be best served by trying to make every workshop last four weeks, meaning that you'd have zero free time, as well!)

Once you've committed to the five rules, apply the 90-minute rule for your design.

A workshop typically runs from 9 to 5 with breaks and lunch. I'm going to suggest that yours run from 9 to 4, because there is serious fatigue in the final hour. (Again, a low-level meeting planner or coordinator who is concerned about "using" the final hour is focused on payment per hour, not value, since learning is maximized before fatigue sets in and seriously undermined thereafter.)

This means that you have two 90-minute segments, less a break, between 9 and noon, and the same arrangement between 1 and 4. Four 90-minute segments less 30 minutes (two 15-minute breaks). That's 5.5 hours of programming per day. And that's about four major points per day, one per 90 minutes. If you have eight major points, that's a two-day program; if you have six, that's 1.5 days. You get the drill.

What's a "major point"? It's a key learning point that can't be omitted if you are to achieve the buyer's desired behavioral change. It may have subordinate points.

Speaking Up: Workshops are boring or successful because of only two components: enthusiasm and pragmatic content. Fortunately, you are eminently capable of providing both.

The typical adult learning sequence in a classroom setting looks like this:

- *Discussion.* The instructor discusses the ideas and approaches that are relevant to that segment.
- *Practice.* The participants try to apply these approaches on case studies or exercises, individually or in small groups.
- *Feedback.* The results of the practice are discussed with self-critique, group critique, and/or instructor critique.
- *Application.* Ideally, the techniques are applied to real job concerns, either in the class or back on the job,

with feedback from colleagues, management, and/or the instructor.[7]

So, back to our design. The early morning will feature a few minutes of greeting and administration, plus the objectives for the day. That should take five minutes. Don't be diverted by dumb "icebreakers" and opening exercises. These are adults whose time is valuable, not children who have been parked by their parents to waste time.

Then, explain your agenda and charge ahead.

Here's an example of the 90-minute rule applied to a day's program.

TOPIC: LEADERSHIP FOR VIRTUAL TEAMS

OBJECTIVES

Participants will be able to

- Interact with and provide personal support for people that they are seldom with physically.
- Ensure that the group acts as a team, supporting one another's work and maximizing group talent.
- Effectively evaluate each person for developmental needs, succession planning, compensation, and promotion.

---

[7] This is why no training program should be an event in isolation, but should involve the superiors of the performers and ongoing feedback after the course.

I've determined, and the buyer has approved, that this can be done in a single day with the following design.

- Use of Technology, 9:10 to 10:30
  - Running "virtual meetings"
  - Time-shifting communications
  - Practicing with virtual meeting technology
  - Chairing a remote meeting
  - Preparing for remote meetings
  - Template for creating agendas using group input
  - Creating a sample agenda
  - Exercise: circulate the sample agenda and call a meeting to order
  - Feedback and debriefing
- Break, 10:30 to 10:45
- Individual Relationships, 10:45 to 12:00
  - Scheduling personal time by phone
  - Uses of phone, e-mail, Skype, hard copy
  - Remote counseling techniques
  - Remote motivation techniques
  - Conducting performance evaluations
  - Determining when personal meetings are required
  - Role-play individual sessions with peers, instructor
  - Use counseling checklist
  - Feedback and debriefing
- Lunch, 12:00 to 1:00
- Dealing with Cultural Distinctions, 1:00 to 2:30
  - The cultures that you may encounter

- Local customer requirements
- Local legal, ethical, and customs distinctions
- Helping others understand colleagues' cultures
- Corporate requirements vs. local requirements
- Thinking globally and acting locally
- Case study of cultural distinctions in customer requests
- Feedback and debriefing
- Break, 2:30 to 2:45
- Action Planning, 2:45 to 4:00
  - Participants identify their specific actions toward subordinates
  - List is created for their superiors for accountability
  - Calendars are adjusted to account for evaluation time, feedback, and so on
  - One subordinate is called from a meeting as a test
  - Accountability partners are created
  - Instructor facilitates report to the class from each individual
  - Group and instructor provide feedback on plan
- Adjourn, 4:00

Note that there isn't a lot of time wasted on evaluations (participants are the worst people to evaluate a learning experience upon completion—ideally, their superiors should do it based on results a month later). Questions are handled "just in time" as they arise, not in segregated periods.

The enthusiasm aspect, of course, is up to you. But read on, and I'll help.

SUMMARY

It's easier than you think to create outstanding workshops, speeches, and presentations. But there are some rules that need to be observed.

Use only your own original material (intellectual capital) except when you are clearly attributing brief passages or models from others, with their permission, or from their published and public work. Someone will *always* find out that you're using others' material if you do so without such attribution, and doing so is the worst sin for a professional speaker. The Internet makes it worse than ever.

Although ad lib humor is the most effective, it's also the riskiest. Make your humor either self-effacing or based on stories that don't denigrate others. Never tell "jokes," no matter how much they break you up. Remember that humor is meant to aid and abet the impact of your points, not the other way around.

People learn in differing ways, so try to provide varying paces of speech and diverse inflection and intonation, and complement this with text, audio, video, demonstrations, metaphor, and so on. Make yourself listener-friendly. That does *not* mean "dumbing down" your approaches, but merely varying them for greatest effect.

Process visuals can help you do that, and can turbocharge understanding and agreement. If you think in 90-minute segments, you can begin to create seminars of any length and also understand how long a given requested workshop should be. Fill each segment with discussion, practice, feedback, and application.

Presentations needn't be perfect (and they seldom are). Just make them very good, and they'll be better than most of what else the participants have experienced!

CHAPTER 9

FROM STEADY, TO SURFER, TO STAR

HEY, AREN'T YOU . . . ? WHY, YES, I AM!

I REMEMBER standing in the lobby of a Cincinnati hotel when a man waiting for an elevator said, "Aren't you Alan Weiss? I heard you speak at my company's conference last year." That was kind of nice. It was even nicer when I was sitting in a boat with a dozen people on Grand Cayman, waiting to go to feed stingrays off the coast, when a man said, "Hey, you're Alan Weiss, right?" (My son moaned, "Here we go again.")

Getting off a plane together in Sydney, I warned Dolly Parton, who was sitting next to me, that there would be a huge crowd of reporters waiting for me when we disembarked. (There was, but obviously not for me.)

You can achieve the kind of semicelebrity that causes people to remember you *because of the value and memorable techniques that you've brought them.*

REFUSING BUSINESS (YES, *REFUSING* BUSINESS)

There is an anchor in the speaking business that drags along the bottom and impedes your progress, at times even leaving you dead in the water. This anchor is called "early success."

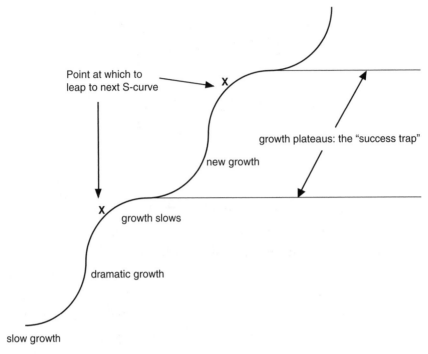

Figure 9-1 The S-curve Phenomenon

All of us can name our first client, our first paid speech, our first opportunity to actually earn a livelihood as a professional speaker. The problem is that it is almost invariably business that we wouldn't accept today. As super coach Marshall Goldsmith writes, "What got you here won't get you there."

Note the S curve in Figure 9-1. The "success trap" occurs when you cease reinventing and improving your material, approaches, and delivery. Because of entropy, all plateaus eventually erode.

Note that you have the greatest acceleration and the least "leap" near the top of the curves, not on the plateaus, where your speed has declined and the leap to the next level is enormous. So, change and the journey upward are critical to "celebrity" status (that's when people call you and you don't have to call them).

Here are 10 dynamics that tend to change as we gain expertise, confidence, and repute in the speaking business:

- *Topics evolve.* As we grow and learn, and as society and business evolve, we move to increasingly relevant and topical themes. We might have begun with "Improving Customer Service Impact" and grown to include "Managing the Customer Service Professional" or created "The Global and Remote Customer." As our skills and learning increase, we might move into entirely new fields as well: "Embracing Diversity as a Sound Business Practice."

- *Fees increase.* This had better be happening regularly. If you don't believe it, start the book again at Chapter 1.

- *Methodology changes.* We might have begun with a heavy accent on lecture and full-group questions and answers, and later incorporated small teams and breakout facilitation. More commonly, we move from the "expert" position of newcomers to the "consensus" position of veterans, allowing key points to emerge from the group. Usually, as a speaker grows, he or she becomes less "scripted" and more spontaneous, appearing to be less of a rehearsed performer and more of an extemporaneous authority. Only confident people can interact freely with audiences and accept questions at any time.

- *Technology changes.* Many of us began with easels and whiteboards. Today, computer-generated graphics are common. Satellite transmission, Webinars, videoconferences, and teleconferences are all common avenues of audience interaction.

- *Duration shortens.* What were once multiday seminars tend to shrink to single days because the client wants less time off the job or wants the work included as part of a larger conference. Speakers with the requisite skills will tend to move toward half-day workshops and keynotes because there are higher fees available for less time on-site. One sure sign of growth as a speaker is that we can make the same points we used to in a third of the time. (Never believe anyone who tells you that a keynote is harder than a full day of training because it's briefer and you have to cram more in. That's hype and baloney, unless it's from someone who doesn't understand the differing objectives of a keynote and a workshop.)

- *Buyers change.* We often begin working through a seminar house that employs us as subcontractors. Or we sell to training directors and meeting planners. But if we're any good, that sale should move to line executives (and be made by bureaus representing us).

- *Industries expand.* Many people enter speaking through an industry that they have been a part of. An insurance agent who is adept at training becomes a speaker focusing on insurance sales. However, once positioned, that speaker can use the same sales expertise to address mortgage lenders, financial planners, and bankers. Eventually, our former agent can address any sales group, regardless of industry, including such areas as telemarketers and call center representatives.

- *Audience level increases.* When we begin, both we and
  the buyer trust us with "safe" groups, usually front-
  line supervisors, new recruits, and/or low-paying
  customers. If we're good, we become comfortable
  addressing anyone, and there is a great need for
  talented, confident people who can address senior
  executives, "grizzled veterans," and tough, skeptical
  groups.
- *Additional services grow.* The lateral moves to group
  facilitator, emcee, after-dinner speaker, panel
  moderator, consultant, speech coach, and related roles
  are relatively easy for highly accomplished, well-
  regarded professionals.
- *Products emerge.* From the first taped session that
  produced a small audio album, the entrepreneurial
  speaker creates books, booklets, videos, performance
  aids, mentoring help, newsletters, hotlines, and a
  myriad of other additional revenue streams.

In view of these inevitable changes that affect good
speakers, we have to be able to "let go" in order to reach out.
This means that old business, no matter how instrumental it
was to your early career (i.e., you would have missed the
mortgage payment without it), will serve as an anchor, snag-
ging you on the bottom, unless you cut it loose. *At least every
other year, you should abandon the bottom 10 to 15 percent of your
business!*[1]

---

[1] Think of those "monkey bars" in the playground when you were a
kid. Counterintuitively, you couldn't reach out to a new bar without let-
ting go of the current one. You had to release one hand in order to make
progress.

> **Speaking Up: Only by removing business that is at the bottom of your priorities can you gain the ability to reach out and embrace business that is at the top of your priorities.**

I've met and mentored hundreds of speakers who don't have the "time" to expand their businesses. Their response is to hire marketers, subcontract business, turn down engagements, and generally tear their hair and rend their garments. The problem, however, is always the same: they treat all business equally, no matter how much it pays or whether it is congruent with their own growth plans, and they cling to old business as though it were still an umbilical cord!

Every December, review your past year's business. Ask yourself these questions:

- Is it at the fee level I want, or even my average fee level?
- Am I growing, or can I do this in my sleep?
- Do they really require my talents, or could anyone do it?
- Is this adding to my image and repute?
- Would I be proud to cite this as a reference of my current talents?
- Have I been doing the exact same thing for more than two years?
- Have I become a habit rather than a resource?
- Would I take on business like this today?
- Am I challenged and joyful to do this, or simply comforted?

If the answers aren't ALL positive, get out now. In fact, if even half of these answers go the wrong way, give the business away. Talk to the customer and explain the reasons, refer a trusted colleague (someone who is where you were a few years ago), or offer to do a few more engagements and then gracefully bow out in a smooth transition. *What's in the client's best interests?* Certainly not your continuing to take the money because you can.

Every day I see people whose literature still reflects the fact that they began in the business 10 years ago as a ventriloquist, a singing bus driver, a car dealer, or a beauty contest winner. But they've changed (one would hope), and they could be proceeding at a much quicker pace if the anchor weren't still dragging behind them.

RISING ABOVE THE CROWD BY AVOIDING MEAT MARKET MENTALITIES

There is a pernicious trend in the profession, almost always abetted by people who should know better, to create speakers in a single image, thereby establishing a commodity that buyers can readily choose among based upon price and, worse, appearance. I have heard meeting planners say that they demand demo videos because they want to make a selection based upon the speaker's "appeal" to the audience. That means, translated, the speaker's gender, ethnicity, race, physical attributes, and other traits that should never enter the decision. When I recommended a colleague for an assignment at a Fortune 100 company that was beneath my fee level, the meeting planner told me flat out: "We don't want a woman for this audience." That, my friends, not only is unethical and moronic, but also happens to be illegal. Welcome to the world of "speaker as commodity."

Fortunately, we control our marketing and our image, *unless we surrender them.* To make a million in this business requires a singularity, not a herd mentality. The following advice might be contrarian and countercultural, but the only people who are making really big money in this business are contrarian and countercultural by definition. Here's how to avoid being displayed in a storefront with the rest of the merchandise, often marked down by the end of the month. (In a classic scene in *Ruthless People*, a character played by Bette Midler was kidnapped, but the abductors had to negotiate their demands because her husband didn't really want her back. Hearing the criminals haggling and their ransom demands plummeting, Midler screams, "Oh my God, I've been kidnapped by Kmart!")

Alan's Stand-Out-in-a-Crowd Techniques

- *Eschew "showcases" and other "auditions" hosted by bureaus and third parties.* Some bureaus will tell you that all successful speakers participate and will drop the names of people you know and respect. The problem is that it's often not true (my name has been used, and I've never gone near one). These events will feature dozens of speakers, each doing eight minutes or so over the course of a full day for "buyers" who usually aren't. Inevitably, low-level recommenders attend, and even legitimate buyers become glazed after the eighth or ninth consecutive spiel. Moreover, there is a charge for appearing (plus your travel expenses), which means that the third parties are profiting, which also means that they accept almost anyone who will pay the freight. These showcases are therefore often filled with novices, neophytes, and people who are new to the profession (or who haven't been able to climb in the profession), which affects the overall quality. I've never viewed appearing in a showcase as a high-value image for the participants and have often used the reverse psychology: "I don't appear in them because I don't have to."

- *Be very selective about bureaus.* I've alluded to this in earlier chapters, but I want to stress here that, while a bureau's interest seems like a sign from the gods when we're starting out, it can become an onerous relationship if it's not collaborative once we're successful. Bureaus that insist that they, not you, own the client, that insist on promotional materials that don't reveal your own contact points, and that present you as simply another horse in their stable aren't bringing you any value, even if they place you a few times a year. You are the one who is paying the bureau *through your commission to it.* You are the one who should make demands, not the bureau. There are some superb bureau principals in the field, all of whom I would trust with my wallet and, more important, my reputation. (I can always replace a wallet.) But there are some that, if you watch carefully, you'll see hiding in the bushes in *Jurassic Park* and *Lost World*, along with the stegosaurs and raptors. The profession has changed, but they haven't.[2]

---

[2] Patricia Fripp, whom I interview in this book and who is my partner in the annual The Odd Couple marketing workshop for speakers, told me that, with one exception, no single bureau placed her more than two or three times a year, and she has been one of the most popular keynoters in the country.

- *Don't create a "canned" video.* Demonstration videos can be quite effective. I've functioned well both with and without them, and contrary to popular industry opinion, my corporate buyers request them only about 25 percent of the time. I find that executive buyers virtually never request them. Meeting planners (and therefore bureaus) require them 80 percent of the time. I recommend that you don't use one of the mass marketers of these services to create one. Several of these production houses are excellent and provide nearly flawless work. But that's the problem. The result is "perfect," and the products all look the same, no matter who is on them. I'd recommend that you hire a high-quality video production group that normally does industrial shows (the ones who provide the projections onto large screens at trade conventions are almost always excellent) or a local operation that shoots advertising and promotion spots. Have them capture a live performance with a client, using one or two cameras on you and another for audience reaction. The key is to show the "live," unadulterated quality of your work. My original demo video was taken from a cassette that was in the camera projecting me on one of those large screens. Neither the lighting nor the sound is perfect, but then neither is any speech I've ever delivered. (You can expect to have a speech recorded with two cameras—one on the audience—edited, and finalized with title screens and voice-overs for less than $3,500. Shop around.)
- *If you're going to advertise or appear in listings, put yourself in the potential buyer's shoes.* Advertising in magazines or "puff pieces" with a quadrillion other speakers isn't

exactly singular. Appearing in a special "speaker's issue" or in the house organ of a speakers' bureau is hardly distinctive. Advertise and promote in unique settings. In what seems like every airline magazine I've ever read, Chester Karrass, the negotiations expert, has a multipage ad. Flying back from Barcelona on Iberia Airlines, sure enough, I found his ad in Spanish in Iberia's in-flight magazine! I'm not advocating this expense (although it reflects what you can do when you make a million in this business), but you might try trade association publications, business periodicals, and educational magazines if you want to stand out in the crowd. Some speakers swear by advertising; others (myself included) largely ignore it. My point is, if you're going to do it, don't do it like everyone else.

- *Beware of coaches.* There are a lot of speaking coaches who are not very good speakers. Okay, I'm willing to buy the fact that great sports coaches don't need to have been superb athletes. But I do want the person who taught my doctor how to operate to have been a hell of a good surgeon. Therein is my problem, and yours. I can generally tell a coached speaker from 100 yards. These speakers exaggerate their platform movements and gestures. They articulate in ways that are not consistent with their meter and rhythm. They insert unnaturally long pauses. They overdo eye contact. They move around so much that they distract from their message. They appear to be delivering a piece from *Macbeth*, not merely a new sales technique. They artificially laugh (or worse, cry) at something that they've obviously rehearsed and performed

4,000 times. Coaches tend to remove the wonderfully imperfect distinctions about us and create smooth, unremarkable performers. I think most coaches are frustrated actors (or unsuccessful speakers). Stay away from most of them. We all need feedback. Buy a tape recorder and get a friend. This is neither rocket science nor Broadway. It's hard to accept, but when we're struggling in this business, the answer is in ourselves, not someone else.

> *Speaking Up: Generally, a little judicious advice will improve anyone and still retain his or her singularity. However, a great deal of paid "expert" advice will transform people into the output from a common cookie-cutter mold.*

THE THREE KINDS OF SPEAKER AND WHY ONLY ONE GETS WEALTHY

There are three speaker "mindsets," each of which will be manifest in a speaker's professional behavior and demeanor. Only one will help create a seven-figure business. The other two will not. Are we clear?

1. The Speaker-Centered Speaker (SCS)

This is the person who talks about him- or herself at dinner for 30 minutes, then says, "Well, enough about me. What do *you* think about me?"

It's all about the SCS. The speaking venue, client, audience, and topic are merely accoutrements that enable the SCS to "perform." This is the person whose photo is on his business card or her stationery. The SCS's name is on everything in sight, not for copyright protection, but for ego fulfillment. The arrangement of the event is for the SCS—the lighting, the music, the promotional material. You haven't lived until you've read an SCS biography or introduction. Two self-published books make the SCS "one of the world's most prolific authors," and he or she has "addressed over a million people over the past decade" (do the math; that's 2,000 people every week).

If the audience evaluations are poor, or if the buyer is unimpressed, the SCS is simply not appreciated, or "over the heads" of the client. The SCS will use jokes and stories that he or she wants to tell, showcasing their delivery, irrespective of their relevance to the proceedings.

Inevitably, the SCS will sing, dance, juggle, or all three.

2. The Audience-Centered Speaker (ACS)

This may seem like a logical choice. What could be better than being audience-focused?

The problem here is that the ACS focuses on "scoring" well with the audience. He or she actually speaks in ways that are aimed at the evaluation forms. The ACS desperately wants high ratings and will pander to the audience to get them. (Have you ever experienced the really lousy comics in small clubs who tell the audience to "give yourselves a hand"?)

The ACS will slap down a ream of audience evaluation sheets and show you that he or she has averaged 4.88 out of 5.0 over the last two decades. (I kid you not; I get a big kick out of replying, "Who cares? Who hasn't?") The ACS lives and breathes for audience love, and anything less than an extended standing ovation will drive him or her into the depths of depression for weeks. (Think of the great Billy Crystal movie *Mr. Saturday Night*, where the crowd goes wild after his comic routine, but he's morose because he spotted a couple of people at table 5 who wouldn't laugh.)

If the ACS is unsuccessful with the audience, the self-doubt and guilt are rather massive, and the speech will be changed and improved and practiced *ad infinitum*. The ACS wants love.

Which means that the ACS needs to get a dog.

3. The Buyer-Centered Speaker (BCS)

This speaker realizes that the buyer is the one who can rehire him or her. It's the buyer's objectives that are important, and the buyer often wants a certain style (meaning that the speaker's preferences aren't as important) and a certain message (meaning that the audience's preferences aren't that important). Many executive buyers want the audience to be discomfited, provoked, and sometimes stunned.

This speaker is focused on the needs of the buyer, not on the evaluation sheets or the desperate need to tell a certain story. The BCS is a businessperson who happens to be a professional speaker and is intent on pleasing the buyer. What could be simpler?

The BCS is dynamic, innovative, and focused, but above all, is intent on creating a long-term relationship with pleased buyers.

You must become a buyer-centered speaker if you are to create serious, well-paid business in the speaking profession. To meeting planners, you're merely an expense that had better not make them look bad. To most bureaus, you're simply the implementer for a client that they believe is "theirs."

Ergo, your focus must be on true economic buyers *sans* middlemen. Your appeal is to the person who can authorize a check and hand it to you, and who personally can tell you if you've helped improve his or her condition.

Million Dollar Speaking is all about creating the right priorities and becoming a "star" with buyers, not a satellite of bureaus and meeting planners.

PARACHUTE EXAMPLES

By "parachute," I mean the skill and ability to "drop" strong buying incentives behind the lines, so to speak (pun intended). If you want to be a star, you have to shine. The sun's energy comes from within, and so must yours. Don't be lulled by false humility.

> *Speaking Up: This is a business for you, not a hobby (or you shouldn't be reading this book). You must have the attitude that you are conveying your value so that people can avail themselves of it. That's a service mentality and a business mindset. If you feel that you're boasting when you try to bring people value, you're in the wrong business.*

Here are examples of subtle, not-so-subtle, and bold alternatives that you can parachute down from any altitude:

- Drop examples into your speaking. Don't simply say, "I've found that 95 percent of leadership is reliant on being a role model"; say, "When I was gathering notes for my new book, *Strategic Leadership*, I found that . . . " or "When I was facilitating a group of senior executives at the American Press Institute, we agreed that . . . "

- Create your own analogies. "I am to health-care consumerism what Jeff Gitomer is to sales, or Marshall Goldsmith is to coaching, or Alan Weiss is to solo consulting . . . "

- At the outset, try to arrange permission from your new clients for any combination of the following: use of their logo, testimonials, referrals, service as a reference, endorsement for a book you're writing, and so on. "Seed" the environment so that it's part of your agreement, and once you cash in enough of these chips, you have a highly impressive brochure, Web site, collateral, and so forth.[3]

- Mention people who have been on other agendas with you, even on different days. "When Colin Powell and I both appeared at the Red Cross International Convention, I heard him say . . . "

- Prime the pump with the media. When I was asked by a *New York Post* reporter who was interviewing me as a source how other consultants would describe me, I said, "They'd likely say I was one of the most highly respected independent consultants in America." He printed that verbatim as his own introduction to me in the story. That quote promptly went into all my publicity material with the source cited as the *New York Post*.

---

[3] This is *de rigueur* when you agree to do *pro bono* work.

- Form reciprocal agreements. My colleague, the aforementioned Patricia Fripp, has a technique of attending a networking event with a trusted colleague whose expertise is somewhat different and noncompetitive. When Fripp (she uses only her last name with friends) meets a potential buyer, she says, "Oh, you must meet someone by the name of Mary Lewis, who is just the expert you would need for that! I think she's here; let me introduce you." Mary Lewis, of course, is doing the same thing for Fripp.[4]

- You've heard of OPM (other people's money)? Well try using OPB (other people's books). Your statement might go something like this: "My views on leaders as avatars are shared by no less than Warren Bennis and John Gardner, and they've made these points in four books between them." (But don't "buy" the right to have a chapter in someone else's book, which is merely a scam that enriches the "publishers.")

- Use both strategic and tactical branding. Strategic branding occurs when Mercedes builds its quality image in the media. Tactical branding occurs when a local Mercedes dealership talks about being open for servicing on Saturday. For you, strategic branding is creating the words and logo that you want to use consistently for your public and personal image. Tactical branding is "Gloria Wilson's Self-Esteem Workshop," which is offered a few times a year. Get your name in front of people so that you're identified with particular services and value.

---

[4] For those of you who are wondering, Fripp's brother, Robert, is the lead singer for the rock group Purple Crimson.

- Create normative pressures. Provide your participants with handouts, cards, framed certificates, desktop job aids—anything that will cause others to say, "Where did you get that?" People don't like to be out of the loop. If your sessions represent popular developments and create their own cachet, then others will want to become adherents. Leave things with people that figuratively adhere to their offices and positions, so that others are constantly seeing an advertisement for your offerings.

You can parachute things at any time. It's always advisable to have a few planes circling, amply stocked, until they are relieved by the next wave.

15 CONDITIONS THAT SUPPORT RAISING FEES

1. A Major Publisher Has Published a Book You've Written

This has to be a known commercial publisher, not a vanity press or a self-published work.[5] Once you have a publication date, raise your fees—*this might be six months in advance of the book's actual release*. Cite yourself as the author of the book by title, to be released in June of next year. Depending upon your existing fee structure, a significant hardcover book

[5] Self-published books are fine as products with high profit margins, but they do nothing for marketing credibility or worth in the buyer's eyes. Ignore claims to the contrary by the vanity press people—only a tiny fraction of self-published books has ever achieved any note in the professional market. Self-publishing and commercial publishing are not mutually exclusive; I do both, with differing objectives for each.

should increase your fees by \$2,500 to \$7,500, and if it's widely reviewed and generates major media appearances, by even more than that.

2. You Obtain Major Media Exposure

I'm not talking about drive-time radio here, but rather a spot on public television or a business talk show, for example. You want to promote this as, "As seen on *Business This Week*" or "As interviewed by ABC's George Stephanopoulos." This is not as difficult as it may appear. A friend of mine, Greg Godek, writes self-published books on how to be romantic (*1001 Ways to Be Romantic*). He's appeared on more major talk shows than Madonna (including a spot on *Good Morning America* with his 40-foot "love bus" tour).

3. You Develop Blue-Chip References

I carry my reference sheet right in my briefcase and include it in every press kit. I've never said to any prospect, "References can be supplied upon request." It sounds too much like I'd have to wake up my cousins and tell them to expect a call from a stranger asking personal questions about my past. I thrust my references into the buyer's lap because they reflect that buyer's peers (or superiors) in analogous organizations. I've placed 15 on a single sheet because they fill up the sheet completely, as if there are plenty more that simply couldn't be squeezed on (which happens to be true for any of us who have made it in this business). Their titles, addresses, and phone numbers are sitting right there, so accessible and so convenient *that the prospect almost never calls them!* After all, who would have the chutzpah to cite these people if they weren't really enthusiastic supporters? The higher level and more known the people on your reference list, the better your position to charge higher fees representing the value you've brought to the buyer's peers.

4. You Provide a Rare Breadth of Talents

Clients have asked me to present the opening keynote and then facilitate breakout groups. They've asked me to modify a presentation so that it can be given briefly to officers, be given in more depth to middle managers, and be integrated into sessions delivered by in-house trainers for supervisors. I've been asked to address boards of directors, to deliver a humorous talk after dinner, and to emcee an awards ceremony. Buyers have asked me to design a brief test so that the audience members can rate themselves against the attributes I'm presenting during the talk and have asked if I'd make the predominant part of my presentation a question and answer format. I've spoken in auditoriums with projection onto large screens, in amphitheaters, in classrooms, over board tables, and in cinder block, bunkerlike, subterranean basements. I've spoken to international groups, people with varying English skills, and people who utilized simultaneous translation. Some of my colleagues have spoken on buses, trains, boats, and planes. The more you can do, and the more different the ways in which you can do it, the more valuable you are.

5. You Write a Monthly Column (or Are Interviewed Regularly)

Many speakers have been able to write monthly (or weekly) syndicated columns that appear in business publications all over the country. I once mentored a fellow who had the monthly last-page humor column in *Management Review*, the former magazine of the American Management Association. He was unhappy about his fees not being higher! It had never occurred to him to leverage his extraordinary monthly visibility. Other people are interviewed frequently because of the nature of their expertise (e.g., negotiating skills) or a set of accomplishments (e.g., writing humor for politicians), or because they have an aggressive public relations firm that is constantly presenting them to national writers. If you can get into the public eye to the point that you can cite the interviews and provide the tear sheets, you can raise your fees because of your repute. (It doesn't matter whether the buyer has read the piece; it only matters that you can show the buyer the piece. A good source for media interviews is PRLeads.com. The cost is about $100 per year at this writing. Contact Dan Janal there and tell him I sent you.)

6. Your Business Has Been Growing and Your Fees Haven't Changed for Two Years

This is an arbitrary measure, but I've found it to be a very powerful one. If your bookings have been increasing over a two-year period (and you're following my earlier advice about eliminating the bottom 10 to 15 percent) at a constant fee level, then you can safely raise your fees in the third year without fear of losing potential customers. (You won't lose current customers because you should never raise fees for current customers for identical work. However, you can ask for concessions: "I'll honor my past fee arrangement even though my fees have increased. However, I would ask that the entire fee be paid in advance to secure the date." If you don't want to honor past fees because they're simply too low, then either raise the fee or abandon the work.) My practice is to raise fees for all new clients, but honor the old fee structure for existing clients (with the exception of those covered by point 7) because existing, valued clients shouldn't subsidize new ones by paying higher fees than they are (which is why I'm outraged when publications provide better subscription deals for new customers than for their renewal customers).

7. Your Existing Clients Ask You to Do Something New and Different

The one exception—and opportunity—concerning raising fees with existing clients is when they ask you to do something novel. For example, I've been asked to provide feedback to management on the results of speeches across the country, to design programs specific to a given organization, and to learn the technical aspects of a company's operations in order to create relevant applications. Others have asked for a transfer of copyright for the program or have wanted to create audio- and videotapes to incorporate into their training programs after I've concluded the assignment. All of these "one-off" requests allow you to structure a proposal above and beyond what you've normally provided in return for the clearly enhanced value that the client is requesting. If you feel that you have to do these things merely to retain the customer, and therefore cannot charge for their value, then there is something seriously wrong either with the relationship or, more likely, with your perception of how much value you're providing.

8. You May Be Asked to Do Something You Can Do, but Don't Like to Do

I despise full-day sessions. I find them labor-intensive, long, and uninteresting (for me). However, some clients rightfully demand them to take advantage of the expense of bringing their people together off-site (and others demand them incorrectly because they equate length with worth). My response has been to develop a tiered fee structure in which the full-day rate is extraordinarily expensive. However, occasionally a client says, "Just do it. The value far exceeds the cost." And you know what? I find I really enjoy doing it at that rate of pay! Whether it's the length, as in my case, or the type of audience (salespeople) or the environment (after dinner) or the geography (more than a two-hour plane ride) or the circumstances (three identical concurrent sessions in a row), you have the right to charge very high fees for things that you're capable of doing but don't like to do.

9. You're Asked to Do International Work

My feeling is that you should always charge a premium for international work (and, no offense meant to anyone in the United States, you can easily include Alaska and Hawaii in this category, but rarely Canada). From an American perspective, trips to Europe, Africa, and Asia are especially grueling because of time changes, and South America is little better, even though the clocks don't change as radically. I've found that I need a full day of acclimation, on the ground, prior to the session and, for my own health, an intelligent return, which isn't always the first flight out after the applause ends. In addition, logistics are difficult: paper size is often different, electric current varies, words and phrases must be altered, examples changed, delivery modified to accommodate language requirements, customs paid on materials shipped, visas secured, money exchanged, and so on. Even for existing clients, and certainly for new ones, a significant premium is appropriate for international assignments. My suggestion is that you take your existing fee structure and charge a 50 to 100 percent premium for international assignments, depending on your confidence level and the other factors noted here.[6] (Beware of people offering you a "tour" of multiple bookings in their countries as a package deal. You'll lose your shirt. Once you board the airplane, they've got you, unless their check has already cleared your bank.)

10. You Are in a Nondifferentiated Fee Range

Let's say you're charging $3,500, working frequently, and growing your business. However, you know that you're in a fee band ($2,500 to $4,000) that contains 90 percent of your competitors at your level of expertise and success. My suggestion is that you get out of there because you have to become more distinct. *Buyers believe that they get what they pay for.* Their expectations (and their egos—"I hired a $10,000 speaker for our conference") are greater for a $5,000 speaker than for a $2,500 speaker. No buyer I've ever met said *before the speech*, "This is $5,000 worth of talent, and we're getting it for only $2,000!" I believe that you can increase business by increasing your fees. Yes, you read that sentence correctly.[7]

---

[6] By the way, always get paid in U.S. dollars drawn on U.S. banks, preferably in advance. There are laws against taking too much currency into and out of some countries (including the United States), and exchange rates will often kill you. In addition, U.S. banks charge a premium to cash and convert checks drawn on foreign banks, sometimes as high as 25 percent of the total. Attend to this contractually in your proposal. Accept wired funds. And fly *at least* business class on the client's dime, and first class if you can (or upgrade yourself to it).

[7] You can easily increase your margins. Speaking 10 times for $7,500 is much more lucrative than speaking 20 times for $2,500. But I'm also talking about increasing your *business*, that is, speaking 20 times for $7,500.

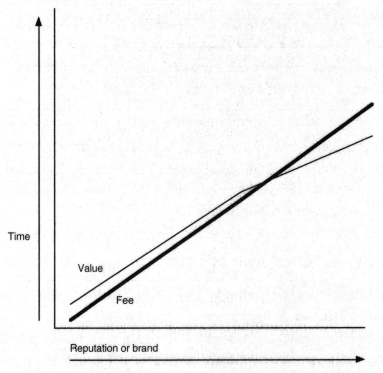

Figure 9-2 When Value Follows Fee

(I don't believe, by the way, that you create differentiation by doing bizarre things like charging $4,800, which some "experts" advise, as if the buyer is too stupid to know that it's an attempt to be sneaky—close to $5,000.) If you're good at what you do and in the midst of a crowd, step out by raising fees to escape the masses. The only people who follow will be the buyers. As you'll see in Figure 9-2, once you develop a brand and repute (where the lines cross), fee ceases to follow value and value follows fee, *because people expect to get what they pay for!*

11. You Become an Internet Star

When you have a popular blog, you are constantly "retweeted" on Twitter, and people quote you throughout

> *Speaking Up: Make no mistake. Buyers believe that they get what they pay for. Your fee actually creates an expectation range and ties into the buyer's ego as well.*

cyberspace, you can use this attention to further publicize yourself and raise your fees. Copy the plaudits and accolades onto your blog, and keep telling people about the numbers following you on a daily basis.

12. Your Newsletter Is a Hit

People ask why they should enter a crowded field like newsletters. Because Yogi Berra was right: no one goes there anymore because it's so crowded. There are a lot of newsletters because people are reading them. If you can establish a strong niche following, you can parlay that into higher fees because of your publishing repute. Anything that can make those lines in the graph cross helps you to increase fees.

13. You Are Popular with Trade and Professional Associations

In most cases, appearing on the agenda, especially as a keynoter, at these associations is an instant marketing boost because the audience is usually seeded with buyers and key recommenders. When you have that kind of captive audience, make sure that your fees are as high as you can bear without getting a nosebleed. Once you're hired, people talk, so you can't go up from a low initial fee. (You can explain a lower fee for the nonprofit on the basis that you charge less for nonprofits, but I wouldn't suggest that, either.)

14. A Bureau Is Recommending You Repeatedly

This means a couple of things. First, even if you're not ultimately hired every time, the bureau thinks that you're a prime candidate to bring it commissions. Second, the higher your fee, the more the bureau makes. Third, bureaus are lazy and scared, and often don't put upward pressure on fees for fear of losing clients. Therefore, when you're booked a great deal by the same bureaus, or even offered frequently, raise your fees. That's your decision, not the bureau's.

15. Every Two Years, If None of the Other Factors Prompt You

If you're not raising your fees every two years, then either you're underestimating yourself, you're scared and have low self-esteem, or you're not very good. I'm sorry, but that's as candid and honest as I can make it.

How many of these conditions are you actively managing? No one grows by correcting weaknesses. We grow by building on strengths. If you've reached the levels of success in this business that this book is meant to engender and support, it's remiss not to "turbocharge" your continued growth and prosperity.

How and when do you raise fees? Boldly and often. No one else, you see, is looking to do it for you.

SUMMARY

You may not become an international celebrity, but you can gain attention and even be recognized in this business. Parts of that route are counterintuitive.

Learn to turn down business. You can't have a poverty mentality and feel that every offer is likely to be your last! Some business doesn't pay enough, some hurts your brand, and some hurts your head.

Eschew the mass auditions and cattle calls. "Showcases" are never worth it. Bureaus should be placing you, not exhibiting you. Don't respond to fishing expeditions from low-level people. Talk only to true economic buyers.

Only the buyer-centered speaker is likely to maximize repeat and referral business. Don't worry about ovations and "smile sheets." And don't try to validate yourself on the platform.

If you want to create ongoing business with the buyer and with members of the audience who may be buyers, use "parachute stories": drop in statements about your prior work, experiences, and clients to prove your points ("When I was working for a major insurer, we found that . . . "). It's never bragging to cite your own experiences as actual examples of how something is accomplished.

There are many conditions that support raising your fees. Keep in mind that the more you increase your value, the more you can charge, but that increased value must be *manifest* to the buyer. Determine what you will use (newsletters, interviews, blogs, books, and so forth) to manifest continued value growth. No one else—not the economy, technology, or competition—controls this.

Only you do.

SIZZLE

T HERE ARE a great many terrific speakers, and sizzle is taken for granted by the buyer. What do you have to do to stand out in this crowd? You need to ignore the crazy myths and focus on the tools of our craft. You'll then be in a position to exploit the life and wealth that this great profession has to offer.

STAGE WORK

THE SPEECH WAS FIVE MINUTES ... THERE WERE DULL STRETCHES

U NFORTUNATELY, THERE are as many myths surrounding speaking and success in this profession as there are around some strange air force hangar with dead aliens out in the western desert somewhere. Except that there is more likelihood of finding aliens there than there is of finding that we can move an audience mostly by our shrugs and gestures instead of our words!

THE MYTH OF BODY LANGUAGE, GESTURES, AND MOVEMENT

First, a definition: "platform skills" are those techniques that you employ as a speaker during your delivery to enhance the receptivity of your message. Most of the books on speaking and many of the "authorities" will attempt to convince you that these techniques are the most important part of the profession and that their mastery is essential to becoming a successful speaker.

They are wrong. It's akin to saying that a dancer's outfit is more important than the choreography, which happens to be true only if the choreography involves a solitary pole.

We've already discussed the errors in citing Mehrabian's work in support of this view. The key to successful speaking is *to be able to make a living at it,* which means that marketing and content are the two most important aspects. You do not improve the client's condition with delivery techniques; you mostly improve your own, and even then only temporarily.

Then why do so many people advocate and focus on the acquisition and development of platform skills as the key to success? The answer is simple: that's the area where money is to be made as a coach. There aren't many people who are adept at coaching in marketing (although there are some very good ones), and there are even fewer who are skilled in advising on content and developing presentations. Those are tough areas, but they are the critical ones, which is why the prior nine chapters of this book have focused on them. Platform skills, however, can be taught by anyone, partly because they're relatively simple and partly because they're highly subjective. A great many unsuccessful speakers, bureau principals, consultants, and sundry others have found that it can be lucrative to teach people speaking mechanics.

But the medium is not the message in this business, Marshall McLuhan notwithstanding. No one has ever walked away from a speech saying, "Get that speaker back next month. Did you see how well she used hand gestures?" or "That was the most important speech I've ever heard. Did you notice how often he asked us to raise our hands?" People remember a speech by commenting, "I'm still using that planning technique he showed us a year ago," or "I refer to her notes on reducing stress at least once a month."

> *Speaking Up: Content is audience-centered; platform skills are speaker-centered. The only function of the latter is to enhance the former.*

The techniques used on the platform are important insofar as they augment the content of one's presentation, thereby enhancing the client's condition. This applies whether the presentation is an hour or a day, a keynote or a seminar, upbeat or serious. Even for humorists, the nature of the story is everything, although it can be augmented through physical techniques. Yet, I've seen humorists who had me rolling in the aisle while they never moved from a fixed microphone.

Having said all that, there is a place for the development of platform skills, but my belief is that it demands a chapter, not a book. I had to put it someplace, and it seemed most appropriate here, in the "sizzle" part of the book. Here, then, are a relatively few pages on those techniques that require attention in order to enhance the client's receptivity to your message.

ALAN'S 10 INTERPERSONAL TECHNIQUES (AND EXPERT DEVICES) TO ENGAGE THE AUDIENCE

1. Eye Contact

Look audience members in the eye. Even in large halls and auditoriums, you'll find that you can establish eye contact with people seated at quite a distance.[1] The more intimate the group—for instance, 20 people seated around a U-shaped table—the more important it is to establish personal eye contact.

---

[1] The exception occurs when you are spotlighted, making it impossible for you to see the audience. In this case, look at the room from the stage prior to your presentation and remember the seating layout. During your talk, keep your eyes moving to the seating arrangement as you recall it.

In general, hold eye contact for two to five seconds. Less than that creates distracting movement, and more than that can make people uncomfortable. If someone doesn't return the contact, move on, but return to that person later. If someone continues to look away after two or three "invitations," then respect that person's discomfort and don't look at him or her directly again.

Eye contact is not merely to create a more direct link with the listener. It is also a primary source of nonverbal feedback for the speaker. If people are eager to return your glance, including smiles, head nodding, and similar reinforcers, you know you're striking a chord. But if people are reluctant to return your glance and are sitting dead still, then you are making them intensely uncomfortable.

> *Expert Device: If possible, chat informally with some participants prior to the speech, particularly with smaller groups. Use these people as your "friendlies" and first establish eye contact (and a smile) with them. Their nonverbal behavior (return smile, nod) will quickly increase your comfort level.*

2. Gestures

I once watched a speaker deliver a 90-minute speech on the distinctions between men and women with the sole aid of moving her hands to illustrate the differences between how men and women viewed life. It was extraordinarily effective.

Avoid the overly dramatic (and banal). There's seldom, if ever, a need to sink down to one knee or rend one's garments. If you use a lavaliere or earpiece mike, you'll have both hands free to use for illustration and support. With a hand mike, you usually can use just one. Specify which type you'd prefer, but be prepared for either. The larger the group, the more you can exaggerate your gestures, since they need to be seen in the back of the hall. The smaller the group, the more you can get away with nuance and subtlety. But avoid most drama coaches' advice to make every gesture into a sweeping, panoramic ballet movement. It's terribly artificial and detracts from the message.

A highly effective technique is to acknowledge the gesture itself. For example, when using your hands or arms to portray a grand event—an airplane's takeoff, bridge building, or tidal waves—you can also state, "We spare no expense on visual aids for the Acme Company."

> *Expert Device: always try to practice your speech, and the gestures and movements that you intend to use, dressed exactly as you'll be during the speech, complete with anything that will be on stage with you. I've seen otherwise carefully prepared speakers get ties caught in mike cords and high heels caught on projector wires.*

3. Inflection, Intonation, and . . . Pauses

There are actually approaches that stipulate that there are nine different types of pauses and indicate the conditions under which each should be used. Maybe that's true for Al Pacino playing Hamlet, but for speakers, there's simply one type of pause, and it occurs when they are not speaking. The only question is: how long should it be?

There are only three reasons I know of to pause, two of them deliberate and one accidental. In the case of the first two, you want to either dramatize a point or allow people some time to think. Pauses are wonderful for people who need some self-correction in their pacing because they tend to speak at full tilt. (One participant told me once that I was speaking faster than he could think, which is not exactly a condition that's going to thrill my buyer.) The third reason is that you've forgotten where you are, and at that moment, you literally have nothing to say. That's all right. Take a moment to think or return to your notes (or say to the audience, "Where was I?"). Don't fill the silence with "ums," "ahs," and grunts. I know a fine speaker who includes a great deal of extemporaneous material in his presentation, but who fills every silence, while he thinks, with a loud "ummmm." I think he loses 20 percent of his effectiveness when he does this. Pauses should be brief, in any case, unless you're waiting for laughter to subside. For dramatic purposes, 3 to 10 seconds should do it.

Inflection and intonation concern emphasis and volume. Varying your pitch and speed are important techniques to keep the audience involved. Lowering your voice to a whisper or raising it to a shout can be very effective if you do so judiciously. Even high-volume, dynamic speakers need to learn this lesson. A colleague told me that a speaker he had invited was so fast, so dynamic, and so high-octane that no one really understood him or retained his message. "It was like a Midwesterner trying to understand someone speaking Cajun," he explained. "It took so much energy just to try to listen and sort out the facts that we were too exhausted to learn anything." The best practice is with a tape recorder. Listen to your speech devoid of any visual accompaniment. Are you interesting and easy to listen to orally, or are you monotone, too fast, too slow, and/or too consistent? The "tape test" is an excellent self-assessment.

> **Expert Device: When you are introduced to the audience, try beginning your talk with a pause. Simply establish eye contact and smile. The room will settle down, people will be interested in what you're up to, and you'll quickly establish a locus of attention. Hold the pause for about as long as one deep breath. You'll find that it focuses both you and the audience.**

4. Audience Participation

Participation (not "involvement," since every audience had better be involved) has been transmogrified from a rarely used device in an era of "podium lectures" to a trite affectation in an era of "feel good" speeches. It makes sense to include the audience members only if it enhances their receptivity and acceptance of the message, and not as some ego device for the speaker.

The very worst technique I've seen over the past several years is that of repeatedly asking the audience members to raise their hands if they've shared a certain experience or if they agree with the speaker. It's one thing to say, "How many of you work directly with the customer?" in order to get a sense of the audience's disposition if you don't already know it, but it's another to say, "Raise your hands if you think I'm right," and "Raise your hands if you've been to Texas, if you like fried chicken, or if you breathe oxygen." After a second or third request, only about 10 percent of an audience will respond to this stuff, and small wonder. Unless you're trying to get some legitimate feedback or information to help guide your comments, don't do this—it's the sign of an ego-centered speaker. (Right next to it in amateurville is the instruction to the audience, "Give yourselves a nice round of applause.")

Occasionally, a presentation requires a volunteer or direct input from the audience. For example, in training sessions and workshops, it's much more common for participants to present their work, raise interactive issues, and take a significant role in the proceedings. But it's relatively rare in keynotes (and should probably be outlawed).

Depending on the nature of the presentation, the audience can be embraced through the use of handouts, brief exercises (either completed alone or, preferably, with a colleague or small group), question and answer periods, and similar exchanges. As a rule, the longer the presentation, the more critical the audience participation.

> *Expert Device: The rhetorical question is an ideal way to increase the psychological participation of an audience. Ask a general question such as, "Think about it—how many of you have actually wanted to tell a customer to take his business elsewhere?" Or you can present a model and ask, "Where would you place your department in this grid, and where do you think it should be?" These challenges create active, individual emotional participation and can be used repeatedly during even brief speeches. And what I call "rhetorical permissions" ("May I stop you here and ask that you consider this?") are also extremely useful.*

5. Visual Aids

Some speakers are superb with just a mike. Others are superb with a sound and light show rivaling Disney World. The criteria are twofold: (1) what will be most effective for the audience and the conditions, and (2) what is most effective for your personal style?

There's a speaker who goes around claiming, "In 5 years you won't be hired if you don't have extensive, state-of-the-art visual aids." He's been saying that for 15 years, and I think most people may finally be wise to him. I've delivered the exact same speech with visual aids and without (because the conditions wouldn't permit them), and the result was virtually identical. The 10 percent effectiveness that I lost without some of the visuals was regained as a result of the poor conditions in which they would have been shown (low ceiling and a virtual blackout to create visibility).

Everyone knows how impressive computer-generated graphics can be, but only if they make sense for the topic. (One client told me, "Don't use them. They're too distracting.") I've seen videos that show a person using an easel and marker *on the video!* (Hardly a state-of-the-art usage.) I've seen slides that are simply copies of memos and reports that people already have in their materials. I've seen slides that don't relate to the topic, but were obviously included and tap-danced into the presentation because the speaker had them in her "kit." At one meeting, we had to pay to rent a projector so that the speaker could show three slides for a total of less than 2 minutes during a 90-minute presentation.

We are not facing nonvisual Armageddon, no matter who claims it. Use those visuals that help make your point, are friendly to the environment, and are comfortable for your style. They are not a prerequisite, particularly in shorter presentations. As a rule, try not to use visual aids in an after-dinner speech. The full meal (and sometimes alcohol), the end of the day, and the presentations and conversations that no doubt have preceded you will have created high fatigue levels. Focusing on visuals, especially if lights have to be dimmed, is the equivalent of taking sleeping pills.

Hear this: PowerPoint slides are WAY, WAY overdone, and generally constitute a crutch for poor speakers.

> *Expert Device: If you don't like to memorize your speech (which is fine), don't like to read from notes (which is fine), and are afraid of forgetting your material (which would not be fine), use a few visuals as your frame of reference and outline. In 90-minute presentations, I frequently use slides that serve as my total outline. I simply speak from each visual, incorporating the current group's dynamic and relevant examples about that client.*

> *Speaking Up: If you have to explain a visual aid, you're working backward. A picture is supposed to be worth a thousand words, not generate another thousand words.*

6. Handling Questions

There are three elements to effective question and answer sessions, whether they are formal ("I'll now take questions") or informal ("I see you have a question in the back").

1. *Repeat the question.* This allows everyone to hear it, any taping to pick it up (since you have the mike), the audience to reflect upon it, validation that you heard it correctly, and time for you to think about a logical response.

2. *Respond.* Provide your answer. Don't be afraid to say, "I don't know" or "What do the rest of you think?" Never view a question as a sign of hostility. Even an objection, after all, is a sign of interest. Treat every question with respect. Don't be afraid to disagree. Don't begin with, "That's a good question" every single time, because it gets hackneyed (although using that phrase occasionally, contrary to conventional wisdom, can be effective to highlight a crucial point raised by a participant). Don't think you have to play baseball (hit a home run every time). Play volleyball and throw the question back (over the net) to the audience. "Would someone like to comment on that from a sales perspective?"

3. *Review the response with the questioner.* Ask, "Did I answer your question?" "Does that address your point?" or "Is that something that may be useful?" Don't assume that you've answered satisfactorily. More times than I care to admit, a participant has said to me, "That was an interesting response, but it wasn't what I was asking you." Oh.

When you solicit questions, wait in silence for at least 20 or 30 seconds if none is immediately forthcoming. Don't worry; people won't get up and leave. Allow time for people to think and to gather their nerve. It's better to wait in brief silence than to continually badger the audience with, "Come on, *somebody* has to have a question!"

Never end a presentation with a question and answer session. It's not appropriate in terms of participants leaving with a call to action or an uplift. If you do take questions near the end, make it clear that you'll then have a brief summary after the question period. This will keep people in their seats and create the right expectations. And don't offer a question period until such time as you've given them enough to know what to ask!

> *Expert Device: If you get a clearly hostile question and you want to avoid confrontation and/or a prolonged debate with the questioner, use only elements 1 and 2 from the list. Repeat the question and respond to it, but then move your eye contact elsewhere in the room and ask, "What other questions do you have?" or state, "I saw someone's hand up over here." That will enable you to move away gracefully and also allow the group to help change the focus.*

7. Errors

If you make an error, admit it and move on. Neither try to ignore it nor fall on your knees begging forgiveness for it. If it's a modest error, humor often helps. I was once referring to the hostess of a party when I realized in mid-sentence during the story I was relating that the term "hostess" might not be *au courant* in terms of gender equality. So I wound up stammering, "The hostess, er, wife of the host, er, person who . . . well . . . the woman who owned the place . . . " The audience laughed, a woman said, "We get the point!" and I moved on. I've since included the "error" as a standard part of that particular story.

There are stock phrases that you can use to cover generic errors. If a slide is upside down, you can always say, "I've changed my view on this point." If a bulb blows, you can comment, "Well, now you're in the dark along with me." However, if someone points out that you've confused return on investment with return on equity, you should immediately correct the point, apologize for the error, and ask if there are any further questions or comments.

I once spelled a client's name wrong on handouts that had already been distributed prior to my speech. I apologized at the outset, told people that a corrected set would be sent to everyone, and said that I was waiving my expenses for the trip as a gesture of my regret over our own inattention to detail. The audience immediately forgave the error, and I went on with my normal presentation. As in the "hostess" dilemma, we can often turn an error into an opportunity.

Expert Device: If you're comfortable, use the error to point out that we live in an imperfect world and that the point isn't to be flawless but to be accountable. Tell the audience that, as in their professions and jobs, you'd rather be able to correct an error than be unaware of it, and anyone who points out an error is always exhibiting an interest in your work. Customers who complain should always receive a polite and careful hearing because not only might they be correct, but they are invariably potential long-term customers.

8. Disruptions

Let's call a disruption an error that's outside of your control. These range from a wait staff clearing dishes to participants talking to each other loudly enough to interfere with your communication. There are two kinds: major and minor.

Major disruptions are fire alarms, blizzards, loud noises, and so on. Every speaker eventually experiences the room next door with a sound system that overwhelms his or her own. Or the snowstorm that causes participants to begin worrying about getting home. I've been in two sessions, as an observer, in which medical emergencies occurred.

In the case of a major disruption, stop what you're doing. Confer with the buyer or coordinator. *Inform the audience about what's going on.* "I see the snow accumulating steadily outside, and I'm going to pause to allow Charley and Joan to decide what we should do. Let's take a five-minute break." "We've had a medical problem occur here in the first row, and if all of you would please keep your seats, we'll be able to help the individual with a minimum of commotion. Could I ask that you chat with your colleagues for just a few minutes?"

Remember, you have the microphone and the attention. You cannot ignore your surroundings, and you should never assume that an alarm is anything less than it is. It's better to evacuate for a false fire alarm and lose 20 minutes of your presentation than it is to suffer a single injury during a real fire.

Here is the ultimate approach to minor disruptions: *never make them into major ones.* Ignore the wait staff. If its members become overly noisy, don't pick on them. Ask a coordinator or manager from the platform, "Could we ask whoever is responsible for the staff, who are only doing their jobs, if the rest of the work could wait until we're through here?"

Don't blame anyone; simply try to enlist help in correcting the situation. If another meeting's noise level is interfering, raise your own volume and ask someone if he or she can work out an accommodation. If it's so loud that you can't be heard easily, then take a short break while you work out the problem.

Never embarrass a participant. If two people are talking, try walking in their direction while talking to the group. That will often squelch it. If it's chronic, ask them during a scheduled break if they would stop, since it's tough for you to concentrate. You might ask them if there's a question you can respond to in the room, but don't use that technique more than once. The onus is on you to overcome disruptions. They are not a personal affront.

Never assume that someone leaving the room is making a statement about your presentation. This person may be visiting the restroom, making a critical call, or taking a breather, or maybe he or she really has no interest in what you're saying. None of this matters. Your obligation is to those who are still sitting there. This is about them, not about you. If everyone gets up and leaves, you're in the wrong business.

Expert Device: When you are speaking in conjunction with a meal, work either with your client or directly with the banquet manager to arrange for tables not to be cleared after the final course if you will already have been introduced. It's the busing of tables that creates the worst noise and most movement. Have the dishes cleared either before you speak or after you speak, but not during your speech.

9. Use of Humor (Assuming You're Not a Humorist)

There are two kinds of humor: planned and unplanned. In my opinion, everyone should build some planned humor into their talks. Unplanned humor—ad libbing—is much more problematic because it can backfire.

I've touched on this in an earlier chapter, so let's simply cover the basic rationale for using humor:

- Make the audience comfortable.
- Create a congenial learning environment.
- Make a point.
- Take yourself off the "pedestal" (self-effacing humor).
- Break tension.
- Put an error or disruption into perspective.
- Begin or end on an upbeat note.

The safest humor involves personal stories, because they are guaranteed to be original and unheard, they can be practiced and perfected, and they are highly personalized to your style. Unplanned humor can be safe if it's aimed at you—for example, when you can't get the computer to work and comment, "I'm in the breakdown lane of the information superhighway." If you're quick and very good, unplanned humor can create bonding with the audience that is invaluable. A participant who was an avid fisherman once said to me that, when I was asked a question, my face seemed to go through all the expressions that a fish does when he pulls it toward the boat. "Yeah," I replied, "but I always get off the hook." I told a group of unhappy people baking in Phoenix in July that the only reason they were there was because the surface of the sun was already booked.

Expert Device: Talk to the client in advance and find out something that you can safely use that the group would find funny. For example, there's usually a story about a golf outing, a trip, a sales meeting, a retirement, or some other company legend that can be incorporated. I found that one participant, in a prior session, had actually gone onto the stage to draw a picture of his point. I began my speech by introducing myself and then asking if I could just turn my segment over to Joe, as I pulled an easel forward.

Speaking Up: Don't laugh at your own jokes. Everyone knows that you've told them and heard them 10,000 times. People will wonder if you think that little of their intelligence.

10. Theatrics, Music, and Effects

To each his or her own, I guess, but I'm underwhelmed by attempts to create a "mood" in the room. I know a speaker who specifies that certain music be played as people enter and depart. He is certain that it adds to their receptivity as they enter and their memory as they leave. In my observation, it just makes them speak a little louder as they converse on the way in and out.

Music can set moods and make dramatic points, as can various theatrical effects, such as lighting, sound, and multimedia. But the basic question remains: how are we improving the client's condition? We are not in the entertainment business; we're in the learning business. I'd never suggest to a singer that he or she refrain from using music, but I have suggested to several that they stop giving speeches. Their skills are in entertainment, not in learning.

If you do use existing music, you must have permission to do so, usually from ASCAP, the licensing body. All commercial music and lyrics belong to someone. You must pay a royalty to use them in public, no matter how briefly.[2] You can purchase "generic" music, especially created to be sold or leased for these purposes. Or you can have your own original music created, which is then your property. The same rules pertain if you use tapes or slides that are proprietary, such as a segment of a television news broadcast or a clip from the Super Bowl.

Do not ask people to touch other people. Sound elemental? Well, this seems to be an increasing affectation among speakers, who must mistake themselves for therapists or masseuses. Many people do not like to touch or be touched, gender issues aside. Asking people to rub each other's shoulders, hug, or even hold hands is a very basic infringement on their personal comfort and is totally inappropriate for any speaker to request.

I've seen speakers cry on stage, as if they'd never done it before. Yet everyone in the audience knows full well that the speaker cries at precisely that point in every speech on that topic. It's phony and manipulative. (As one participant remarked during stirring music and the speaker's tears, "Ah,

---

[2] This is the law, and it's enforced. If you want to play even a short segment of Billy Joel at a local trade association chapter meeting, you need permission, which almost always requires a fee. In the same way, no one can record your speeches and use them without your permission. It's just that Billy Joel has wider play than you do.

it's the obligatory, emotionally manipulative call to patriotism and false tears.")

Finally, never, ever sing unless you're a trained musician and it's an integral part of your act. Singing is virtually *never* done to improve the client's condition. It's always done out of the speaker's ego. No one pays to hear a speaker sing, just as no one pays to hear the Rolling Stones or Madonna give a speech. Sing in the shower if you must, but keep the door closed and the shades drawn.

> *Expert Device: The client will often have a theme for the conference, a logo, or even music that has been rented for the event. With moderate advance planning, you can place this logo on your materials and incorporate it into your slides, use the music in your opening, cite the theme in your points, and so on. This creates a highly customized approach that buyers truly appreciate.*

Finally, if you're speaking "remotely," via Webinar, virtual offices, and similar technologies, you'll have to make some adjustments. Look into the camera, unless you also have a live audience. Arrange to have visuals superimposed as you speak. Keep your gestures and movements within the range of the camera's limits. Wear clothing that doesn't distract (e.g., plaids and stripes are often exaggerated on video). Humor doesn't usually work as well without a live audience.

You get the idea. Adjust to your actual environment. If it's the first time, rehearse.

20 GREAT WAYS TO ENGAGE ALMOST ANY AUDIENCE

1. Handouts

There are three options to use in distributing handouts:

- *Prior to the presentation.* This enables participants to arrive at a common level of understanding about your topic and to prepare themselves to learn by determining what aspects appeal to them. Participants can use your handouts to track your presentation. Downside: People often lose them, they aren't distributed correctly, or, if they're not clear and concise, they can be a turn-off. If you change your sequencing, people can become confused and unfocused.

- *During the presentation.* This is a dynamic method to enable people to reinforce what they've just learned. People will use them to make additional notes in the margins. You can also use them as an interactive tool, asking people to complete certain portions. Downside: Passing things out is often time-consuming and disruptive, especially during briefer presentations. Not everyone likes to complete questions or write in personal responses.

- *After the presentation.* This can serve as a powerful reinforcer and provides a rationale to contact participants again. The materials in this case will reflect exactly what was discussed in the proper sequence, since alterations can be made. Downside: Many participants don't like to take notes anymore and prefer to use handouts as a "crutch" during the presentation.

2. Room Setup

There are actually people who make their living trying to coach speakers on how to establish the room environment. But the fact is that poor speakers will die in Carnegie Hall and terrific speakers will knock the audience's socks off in a dungeon. Having said that, here are some safety tips.

Try to arrange for a center aisle so that you can walk down it, if appropriate. Don't shoot a projector down a center aisle, which will put you in the line of fire. Shoot it at an angle or use rear projection.

Visit the room far enough in advance (usually 45 minutes to an hour) to make changes, if necessary. If someone is using the room prior to you or if you're following other speakers without a break, make sure that whatever you need has been provided prior to the program's start (e.g., have yourself "wired" with a lavaliere mike well before you're introduced). Test the mike for dead spots and feedback. There is sometimes unavoidable feedback below ceiling speakers. Practice your movements to avoid those spots in advance, not while you're delivering your key learning points.

3. Pre-presentation Participation

While this is highly interpersonal, I've included it here, since it's not something that occurs during your presentation.

Many clients will offer you the opportunity to participate in a dinner or social event the day or evening prior to your presentation. Unless your schedule prohibits it, such participation is always a good idea. You'll be able to meet participants and become a known entity. You'll be able to pick up recent developments about the client that you can include in your talk ("I understand that your field force has just expanded by 50 percent, which makes my talk today on retaining good people more important than ever!"). And you'll be able to chat with company officers and prospective future buyers on a casual, unhurried basis.

4. Product Sales

There is not a thing wrong with selling products in conjunction with a speaking engagement. Here are some tips that I've found effective:

- Give one of your products away while you're on the platform. I ask for a volunteer, reward him or her with "any book on my table over there," and move on. You can also hold up the book or tape and present it at the moment.

- Have the introducer mention your products and how to acquire them while at the conference. It's a good idea to include that "Ms. Jones has kindly provided a 15 percent discount to conference participants while she is here."

- If there is a convention bookstore, arrange to have your products displayed with you advertised as a featured speaker.

- Have someone staff your table. Never do this yourself. I try never to exchange products for money personally. If you need someone from the association, facility, or client, make arrangements to provide that person with a commission or a flat fee.

- Accept all major credit cards. This can be arranged easily through your local bank or American Express.

- Create a "package" price, for which someone can purchase every product on the table at a discount. If it's not there, no one can take advantage of it. If it is there, someone will almost always do so, and you'll get a several-hundred-dollar sale from one person.

- Give every visitor to the table a catalog of your products, whether that visitor purchases or not. You may want to stamp the conference or client name on them and indicate that there is an XX percent discount in effect for 30 days.
- Present one set of your products as a gift to the trade association library, client library, or a charity supported by the client.
- Offer to stay and sign books.

5. Personal Preparation

You have to be in the "right place at the right time" if you're to be effective for a client. An audience can sense uncertainty and/or distraction, and people get restless if a speaker is tentative or scared.

- Focus on the speech in front of you. Don't worry about the one next week or next month (or even tomorrow morning).
- Practice not to be *perfect*, but to be *comfortable*. Audiences don't care if you're perfect, but they will be comfortable only if you are.
- Understand that this is not a turning point in Western civilization. The world will continue unimpeded tomorrow, no matter what happens today on the platform.
- View the audience members as mature, intelligent, constructive adults who want to see you succeed.

- Your job is to please the buyer and meet the buyer's objectives, not to receive a standing ovation or perfect scores on rating sheets.

- Don't try to outdo the prior speaker or to latch on to something that seems to be working for everyone else. You are unique. Use only your strengths.

- Be provocative. No one is roused to action by platitudes and repetition. Force your audience to think, and make it feel an urgency. Logic makes people think; emotion makes them act.

6. Do Not Accept the Myth of the Butterflies

Myth: You should always get nervous "butterflies" before you speak. I don't know about you, but if you're still nervous about speaking after scores, hundreds, or thousands of talks, you ought to get some Valium. I get an adrenaline rush, and I can't wait to go on, but I don't get nervous. Anxiety will kill your timing, deaden your reflexes, and paralyze your movements. Athletes who perform well under pressure don't get nervous. They get good. Get some DDT for the insects.

7. Do Not Overprepare

Myth: You should always prepare for a talk for at least three times as long as the speech itself will take, no matter how many times you've given it. Well, perhaps you should do this if you're a fish, since fish have a measured attention span of 4 seconds (which is why the same fish keeps getting hooked—it forgets everything it ever learned 15 times a minute). This is utter malarkey. Prepare, perhaps, for the nature of the new audience, a new environment, and some contemporary delivery, but if you still need to rehearse your signature speech for three hours every time, better check for gills around your throat.

8. Don't Create a Speech with a Book in Mind

Myth: If you have a speech, you have a book. This should be restated as follows: if you have a speech, you have an excruciatingly tiny book. Speaking and writing are discrete skills, sometimes synergistic but not at all equal. Don't give the published work short shrift: books require extensive research; tight, Jesuit-like logic; brilliant metaphors; and immaculate construction. If that sounds like it doesn't resemble a lot of books out there, that's because most books are not very good. (Maybe they *ought to* be speeches.) Focus on each audience and each buyer, not your literary future or T-shirt sales.

9. Don't Trip over Your Mechanics or Your Underwear

Myth: Study your platform skills carefully and get coaching. A speaking colleague, Jeff Slutsky, has observed that nothing has ruined more good speakers than speech coaches. Content and knowledge are what carry the day, and if you have those, decent platform skills will get you through nicely. If you don't have those, superb platform skills simply put the icing on a house of cards. I find that speakers spend inordinate amounts of time on delivery mechanics and not nearly enough time on research, new ideas, client familiarization, and spontaneity.

10. Never Worry about Your Ratings

Myth: Track your audience evaluations more carefully than you check your stock listings. Dr. Albert Bandura, whom I had the good fortune to meet and work with at one point in my career, is one of the preeminent psychologists of our time. His work on self-efficacy raises an interesting issue for speakers: people with low self-perceptions of their knowledge and abilities put a premium on external performance standards to reassure themselves of their accomplishment. People with high self-perceptions of their knowledge and abilities place the emphasis on personally established learning goals and—his words—self-mastery. Think about that.

11. Don't Try to Validate Yourself on Stage

Myth: Our self-worth is based on our success and our accomplishments on the platform. I don't think so. Our self-worth ought to be based on our contributions to the environment and society around us, to our families and friends, and to our own vision for our futures. Speaking is simply a means—one of a great many—toward that end. People who tell me that all of their friends are speakers frighten me. We need a broad perspective, big gulps out of life, and a diverse variety of experiences. Those are what make us vital people, and better speakers in the bargain.

12. Create Exercises That Involve the Audience in Its Own Diagnostics

People love to assess where they are against others, their own expectations, your suggested guidelines, and so forth. Whether you're talking to senior groups (i.e., on strategy) or front-line groups (e.g., on customer service), try to create an environment in which people are learning about themselves and their colleagues thanks to your intellectual property.

13. Always Include Questions

Even in keynotes and in large groups, try to provide a question and answer session so that you can address specifics and enable people to feel that their personal issues are being addressed. You can arrange for people with handheld mikes to roam the audience, you can have standing mike stations, or you can take shouted questions and repeat them (which you should do anyway, of course). The longer your session, the more critical this is.

> *Speaking Up: The advice that you "dumb down" your speech, attire, and other aspects of your abilities for an audience is among the worst advice you can possibly receive. Ignore the dummy giving it to you.*

14. Use Small Teams

Even if you ask a huge audience to turn to the people around them, or if you use separate breakout rooms for smaller groups, this kind of interaction produces excellent learning and attempts to actually apply the skills you're providing. When you're dealing with smaller groups, keep in mind that a group of 20, for example, will provide teams of 2, 4, or 5 (or even two teams of 10).

15. Arrive Early and Schmooze

I wander around or sit at a table and casually listen in and chat with participants before my speech without revealing who I am at first. (I always do so before we're done.) I inevitably learn fresh and current issues that are going to help me in my examples and focus. If I want to use specifics, I ask the permission of the people who provided them.

16. Study the Client's History

If you're working in-house for a client, read its background on the Web or in its collateral material. You'll surely find examples of things that the client has done that reinforce your points, and you can make your client organization a "hero" and demonstrate to the members of your audience that you're simply reinforcing what they have already done well but may not always realize, being so close to the issues.[3]

17. Play Volleyball

Throw some questions back to the audience. Don't try to be the fount of all knowledge. This will help if you really don't know the answer (!), but it will also help to demonstrate that the intelligence and talent required for what you're talking about are resident right in that room.

18. Adhere to Your Time Frames

No audience will ever become upset at a speaker's ending ten minutes early (and if a meeting planner does, just ignore him or her), but it will immediately become restless if you're two minutes late and you're still droning on. People are thinking about phone calls, appointments, and a variety of other issues, while forgetting everything you've previously said. Hit your marks.

[3] When my veterinarian told me that Merck had done more for the health of animals than any organization in history, I relayed this to its animal health division during a speech. You could have heard a pin drop anywhere in the room. "We hear the complaints," said one manager, "but rarely news like this."

19. Use a Recurring Theme or Signature Reminder

I talk about Tools for Change: The 1% Solution, which means that if you improve by 1 percent a day, in 70 days you'll be twice as good. (Do the math.) I periodically foreshadow a point by saying, "Perhaps this will be the 1 percent for some of you." Not only do you rivet attention, but people start using your phrase ("I just received my 1 percent.").

20. Never Assume that Your Audience Is Damaged

I've seen big-name speakers talk to the audience as if they were addressing a remedial reading class. One woman puts up huge, simplistic easel sheets with a single word on them. Assume that the members of your audience are intelligent and successful—that's why they're sitting in front of you. Your job is to help them become still better, given the buyer's objectives. Never pander or "dumb down." Speak and teach to the top third of the group. The rest will run along to catch up as needed.

BIDING YOUR TIME

Here is an amazing fact that you may scoff at, but only at your peril: *your timing is as important as your content.*

People expect you to start on time if you're leading your own session. If you're part of someone else's session (a keynoter, concurrent presenter, and so forth), you're somewhat at that person's mercy with regard to your starting time. But that mercy ends there.

Hit your marks. Take breaks when you've promised AND end the breaks when you've promised. (You can often cue people back with music a minute or so before you're about to begin. I've seen this done effectively with audiences of more than a thousand people.) Pace yourself. Don't start cramming 40 minutes of content into your remaining 10 minutes (which is called a *blivet* by the cognoscenti), and never, never, never go over your allotted time.

No audience in the history of speaking, beginning with those listening to the grunts of the landlord giving house-keeping instructions to those renting the cave in prelapsarian times, ever objected to a speaker's ending early. Oh, yes, there are those who wanted more than the time allowed (always leave them wanting more) and those who regretted that the speaker did not use the final five minutes for more questions (never end a session with a question and answer period), but they were nonetheless happy to leave as planned. The train was departing the station.

However, for every minute you go *over* your allotted time, the audience will forget the prior 10 minutes of your talk, so if you go about 10 minutes beyond your designated ending time, your audience will pretty much have discarded the entire preceding 90-minute keynote. (There are nonapocryphal stories of academics with their omnipresent computer slides who arrive at an hour's presentation with 120 slides. Do the math. Every one is an ego-centered speaker, or, as we nonacademics say, "clueless.")

About 30 seconds past your "stop" time, people will begin thinking of the following:

- How am I going to get to the next presentation?
- Will I have time to make those phone calls?
- I need to recharge my recorder.
- There are six e-mails I must send.

- I'm behind on my Twitter account.
- I'm supposed to be (making reservations, sending flowers, checking in with my parole officer).
- Will I make the restroom in time?
- I've got to do something with my hair.
- I desperately need a drink.
- I'm supposed to meet my friend.
- This will ruin my timing for "accidentally" running into Justin, Brittany, or whoever.
- Lord, I need a cigarette.
- I must change this seat; the person next to me has an unusual odor and a surfeit of body hair.
- I need to call my office and use what the speaker just recommended.

You get the idea. Move people out. Most of them have at least four of the above concerns simultaneously creating pressure just behind the right eye.

> **Speaking Up: Knowing when to stop speaking is as important as knowing how to speak.**

Of course, the major point is that you cover the powerful points in your presentation proportionally and do not waste time on 40-minute icebreakers, 30-minute exercises, and useless visual aids.

Worst case example: as the closing general session speaker at a poorly run human resources conference (there's a surprise), I waited in vain while the preceding speaker went 30 minutes over time proselytizing for his favorite charity.

When I was introduced, I had about 20 minutes of conference time left, but, of course, 60 minutes of material.

I took one look at the worried faces in the audience and said, "I'm ending at 4 as advertised, and I'll make up for our lateness by abbreviating my talk to the three most important points. All I ask is that you listen to them attentively!" The audience cheered. The coordinator frowned. (He wasn't getting his full 60 minutes of blood, but that's why you should always be paid in advance.)

Here's how you carefully bide your time:

- Practice and rehearse with a recorder. Note that you'll be *at least* 10 percent faster this way, and that you're not compensating for laughter, applause, or questions. So this will probably represent about 75 percent of your actual length.

- In shorter speeches, limit questions to the period you designate, and adjust that time based on whether you are on time or not. You can shorten it, extend it, or eliminate it entirely (which is easy to do if you don't announce earlier that you're going to save time for it).

- Keep a clock or watch clearly in view on the podium, hidden from the audience. It's not good form to keep looking at your watch. Some facilities actually have a computer or TelePrompTer with a clock in front of the stage.

- Minimize your ad libs. You may think of an interesting story or fascinating example as you're talking, but if you go too far down those roads, you'll get lost in the wilderness.

- Keep your answers to those questions that you do accept very brief. Don't show off. Answer the question in a succinct matter, and refrain from proving how smart you are by reciting all of your undergraduate notes on the subject.

- Ask for a front-row timer who holds up a sign at designated times (e.g., ten minutes to go, five minutes to go, one minute to go). Always have a system whereby the timer holds up the card *until you've clearly acknowledged it.*

- Put "PACE" on the top of each page of your notes so that you see it whenever you glance down. (Most of you will go too fast, not too slowly, meaning that you may finish very early).

- If you are "short," extend the question session and/or use reserve material that you've prepared for this purpose.

- Adjust your future timing and material based on your past experiences delivering the speech or workshop.

How many plays have you enjoyed until the end, when you said to your companion, "This would have been better if it had been 20 minutes shorter"? In that case, the psychological ending point had long passed. In your case, there is always an actual ending point that you dare not allow to pass.

ADJUSTING FOR TROUBLE

Occasionally you'll hit some trouble. Here are the most common problems and their resolution.

- Improper equipment. You asked for a wireless lapel mike, but all they have is a handheld version. You asked for projection into a corner, but it's up the center aisle.

Preventive: Send a checklist to your client and then call the day prior to ensure that all is as requested.

Adaptive: You can travel with your own lapel mike, or you can observe the setup the day before or early that morning and request the changes you need.

Worst case: Live with it.

- The prior speaker or the entire conference is running late.

  Preventive: If you are intending to leave that same day, let your client know in advance of your mandatory departure time. Suggest that the client move you up in the agenda if things are late. End at your assigned time, even if you shorten your program. (Always get paid in advance, so that you have leverage. The client's sloth is not your problem.)

  Adaptive: Take a later flight or change your travel plans. Ask your client if he or she wants the original length or a shortened version. (Remember that your audience will tend to be fatigued and somewhat ornery in these circumstances.)

- Major interruption for a fire alarm, illness, or something similar.

  Adaptive: Ask people to follow the appropriate instructions (leave the hall, allow EMT people to get down the aisle) and serve as an avatar. During the break, ask your client how best to continue, depending on the length of the disruption.

Preventive: Have a plan that allows you to remove up to a third of your material or add a third, just in case of emergencies.

- You can't get there.

  Adaptive: Always have colleagues who are willing to fill in, and have quite a few, because most of them will be busy. Always have your client's home phone or cell number. Offer a substitute or a refund.

  Preventive: Watch weather reports and be cognizant of conditions at your destination and en route. Never plan to arrive the morning of an event. Allow an extra day if you're concerned, and always do so overseas. Never schedule activities immediately before an assignment.

- Ambient noise.

  Adaptive: Take a short break and ask the client's people to find a hotel or conference manager to take care of it. (It's often a "bleed" from the sound system in the next room, although I once had a 40-person Baptist choir in the next room—they were quite good!)

- *Preventive:* Find out who or what will be in adjoining rooms. Always perform a sound check on the day of your presentation.

- Disruption by casual client actions.

  Adaptive: Ask people to quiet down so that everyone can be heard. Ask people with private agendas and conversations to take them outside the room. Do not tolerate anyone openly chatting about other business.

  Preventive: Stress your brief time together and ask for attention over that limited period. My favorite line: "You'll have those PDAs and cell phones forever, but you have me for just the next 59 minutes. How about you take advantage of the more limited opportunity?!" Finally, be outstanding, especially in your opening two minutes, which determines the attention span for what follows.[4]

- You lose power or have a technical problem.

  Adaptive: Use the handouts instead of the projected slides. Ask people to move closer and project your voice rather than rely on the mike. Take a quick break if you believe the problem can be fixed quickly.

  Preventive: Test your equipment that same day. Always have hard copies of projected visuals. Use two mikes (you can use one to record your presentation, as well).

- You lose your place.

  Adaptive: Ask, "Where was I?" (I've seen Broadway stars do this.) Go back to your notes and ask for a moment. Just resume with a logical next step.

  Preventive: Never memorize your presentation. Have notes on a lectern or table. Use your visuals as an outline.

- Something unexpected and uproarious occurs.

  Adaptive: Go with the flow. Get a good laugh and gradually segue back into your topic and point. Be a partner in the fun. But don't join in embarrassing anyone else.

  Preventive: See the next section!

---

[4] Note that many people take notes on small devices, so don't jump to the conclusion that they are texting or doing their e-mail. And if they are, don't take it personally.

TURNING ERRORS AND/OR TROUBLES INTO THE EXTRAORDINARY

I thought it would be fun to end this chapter with some of the best turnarounds, twists, recoveries, and "saves" I have seen, can remember, or perpetrated! You need to land on your feet and not take yourself too seriously.

- Someone says, "I don't agree with your points; they conflict with everything I know that makes sense, and you're just wrong about this!" You say, "Don't repress, tell me how you really feel."
- You trip when you're walking onto the stage (I've done this a dozen times). You say, "We'll start with my new book on coordination."
- Someone's cell phone goes off. You say, "I asked you to hold my calls."
- You repeatedly stumble on a word or phrase. You say, "Easy for me to say."
- You call someone by the wrong name, e.g., Sally instead of Jane. You say, "I bet you think I just called you Sally, right?"
- You can't get people back from breaks or lunch on time. Assign a "room captain" every day and give him or her a whistle.
- You have a hard time getting volunteers. Give the first volunteer you get a prize (e.g., someone's book) for no work other than volunteering.
- You can't get rid of the interfering noise (remember that Baptist choir?). Sway with the

rhythm and tell people they have to ask questions that rhyme.

- Your visuals are in the wrong order, or are marred, upside down, or something else. Ask everyone to look at them sideways or on their heads.

- Two people get into their own debate or simply don't stop reinforcing each other vocally and frequently. You say: "Do you two need a few moments?"

- Lunch isn't ready on time, and you've arrived at the assigned area. Don't worry; find the right authorities and ask them to get you out in time for your regular starting time.

- Someone from the client organization tells you that he or she would like you to change something or add something, or that something isn't working well. Go to your buyer. Ignore random feedback unless your buyer requests something. If the feedback IS abundant and consistent, then do something about it.

- People keep asking you to change the temperature. Refuse, unless it's overwhelming or you can see people's breath. One person's request to change the temperature is simply self-absorption if no one else is requesting it.

- The client asks you to do something additional or as a substitution at the last minute, when you are there. If you don't want to do it, say, "I'm sorry, I'm not prepared for that, and it will not be the quality that you deserve." If you want to do it, say, "I'm happy to do so; it may be a tad rough, but we'll make it work, and I hope you'll accept this as my flexibility in wanting to work with you long term!"

SUMMARY

Words are the tools of our trade. Ignore those who tell you that nonverbal behavior is critical. People care about your *words*. You can't dazzle them with footwork. (Or music or slide shows. My favorite audience reaction to a former beauty queen who had lighting effects, mood music, and Power-Point: "Well, still another emotionally manipulative presentation.")

You can, however, engage an audience using a variety of techniques described in this chapter. Be patient. Build your presentation to gain interest, commitment, and fascination. Don't be afraid to be provocative, challenging, or even contrarian. Some of us have been asked to be solely that by some of the best-paying clients around!

Trouble is like rain. No matter how long the drought, it eventually falls on our heads. Be prepared preventively to minimize the likelihood, but also contingently to minimize the effects. Whatever happens won't be the first time and won't be the last time.

In fact, you can turn errors and the unexpected into extraordinary opportunities to delight and educate. Remember that the audience is basically with you, strongly desiring a success, unless you lose that trust. Why not join them in having a good time and learning as much as possible?

CHAPTER 11

YAWN: PASSIVE INCOME

HOW MUCH DID WE MAKE OVERNIGHT?

NEVER VIEW products as "sales items." View them as value extensions. You're not trying to make money; you're attempting to provide your value in a variety of forms and configurations that allow diverse people to learn in varied ways.

Make that your mindset.

My partner in The Odd Couple, Patricia Fripp, whom I've alluded to earlier, has a shopping bag available at many of her events where the full array of her products are present. On the side of the bag it says, "Take Fripp home with you."

Exactly.

10 IDEAS FOR PRODUCT AND SERVICE REVENUE GENERATION

Every morning, including holidays and weekends, my e-mail, voice mail, and/or post office box will contain orders for books, booklets, downloads, and newsletters. Sometimes I'm more productive when I'm sleeping than I am when I'm ambulatory.

For a long time, I was not a supporter of product sales. I felt that hawking products from the platform was sleazy, and that even the speakers who were most adept at it couldn't hide what they were doing. Holding up your own book and quoting it or announcing that you'll be happy to stay after the presentation to "personalize" books had all the subtlety of a train wreck. If you were perceived as a huckster, it had to detract from your message.

I still feel that way, and I never, ever, promote products in front of a corporate audience. However, I've learned that the objective is quite legitimate and that there are means with which I am quite comfortable. I've also come to realize that I was ignoring my own message: first and foremost, *help to improve the client's condition.*

Whether you're speaking to a corporate, educational, nonprofit, civic, general public, or pro bono audience, some of its members will want to continue their growth and education beyond your session. The best way to provide for that need is through personalized learning options. My awakening came when I realized that we're not in the "speaking" business or the "seminar" business or the "training" business or the "keynote" business. *We're in the information business, and information can take many forms.*

The good news is that providing additional information in varied forms is an extremely natural aspect of our business. The bad news is that too many speakers see it as having a primary, not a secondary (follow-up), role and create products that are arbitrary, of low quality, and/or obviously nothing more than revenue generators. The more a product possesses inherent value and perpetuates the learning experience that you began on the platform, the more likely it is to be seen as a natural—even required—continuation of the improvement process.

I've said frequently that not everyone has a book merely because he or she has a speech. But I do believe that everyone should have products if he or she is a speaker. A book simply may or may not be the right alternative, and fortunately, there are a great many alternatives to choose among. There are at least 12 pragmatic reasons for creating and marketing products:

1. They enable the participants to continue the development begun at your session.

2. They provide the buyer with the opportunity to supply additional value to the audience.

3. They create a lingering presence and visibility that can lead to additional business.

4. They provide revenues from people who have never attended (or are unable to attend) your sessions.

5. They provide promotional opportunities among the media.

6. They provide (in the right context) credibility.

7. They help to differentiate and distinguish you from your competitors, including those in similar geographies, topic areas, or industries.

8. They generate income, which can be vitally important during arid periods in your speaking schedule.

9. They build brands.

10. They are manifestations of thought leadership.

11. They take advantage of the multimedia available today.

12. They are instantly global (and translatable).

There are also downsides to products that can't be ignored:

- If they are promoted crassly, they detract from your professionalism.
- If they are poorly created, they detract from your credibility and professional image.
- If they are created in isolation without a marketing strategy, they will result in a net loss on the bottom line.
- If they are overly specialized or dated, they will become obsolete rapidly, requiring either their abandonment before they realize their full potential profit or more investment for updating.
- If they are overpromoted or overdelivered, they may cause the perception that more intimate and effective experiences with you are not necessary. (See the discussion of the Accelerant Curve in the section that follows.)

The benefits clearly outweigh the risks if the products are carefully developed, intelligently marketed, and professionally sold. So if you have the inclination at all, products are a natural and lucrative offshoot of your involvement in the information business. The driving force of your business is your speaking, however, and products ought to remain in a secondary position. That means that speakers must first focus on developing a successful speaking career. A premature

Speaking Up: As a rule of thumb, it's probably wise for you to have been supporting your current lifestyle solely through your speaking activities for at least a year before you try to develop products as a separate pursuit.

investment of time and money into product will cripple the locomotive, even as you're perfecting the observation car.

I know speakers who are struggling to make a living, working a day job, and delivering most of their work pro bono or at very modest fees, but who are also busy churning out self-published books and creating videos. This is not an innovative business strategy. It's egregious ego. If you want to tell the world that you have a book or audio album because it makes you feel better, I can guarantee that there's at least one organization that won't be interested: the bank that supplied your mortgage.

Here, then, are 10 sources of the most lucrative products and services. The list isn't meant to be exhaustive, but I believe it does represent the most propitious areas for any speaker, whether that speaker has been on the platform for 2 years or 20 years.

1. Books

The moneymaker here is self-published books, and we'll focus on them. (For those who also publish commercially, as I do, see the footnote.[1]) There are two flavors of self-published book:

- Make an arrangement with a publisher/distributor, who might or might not share some of the production

[1] There are three primary ways to make money with a book from a major publisher. One is through the royalties gained on book sales, as specified in your contract. A second is by buying your own book through a major discounter, such as Ingram, at better than 40 percent off and reselling it at retail price (or at a more modest discount). Finally, you can print the book yourself when it goes out of print (under a standard contractual term called "reversion of rights") and sell it as a self-published book, which leads you back to the text of this section.

costs, and who will publicize and distribute the book in return for a (sometimes substantial) share of the revenues. I don't favor this approach, although it has proved successful for some people, because it involves many of the disadvantages of a commercial publisher (shared revenue; concessions on titles, covers, and even text) and few of the advantages (promotional campaigns, major bookstore chain sales, cachet of the major publisher's name).

- Locate a good graphic designer and printer who will work specifically to your specifications on a book, which you totally control. The advantage is that you'll reap far more net profit and produce exactly what you intend with flexibility and timeliness. The disadvantage is that *all* of the marketing and promotion is in your lap. People do not knock your door down as soon as word leaks out that you've published something. In fact, word doesn't even leak out. (Just-in-time printing and print on demand also lower production costs.)

You can self-publish hardcover or softcover, lengthy tomes or booklets. I've found that a booklet of about 60 pages covering any one of my speaking topics (or even a portion of a topic) is a very good investment. Of the 60 pages, there are only about 30 pages of text. There are another 20 pages or so of highlighted points, quotes, and learning aids. The remainder is autobiographical materials, information about other products, and order forms. I invest a lot in the cover art and the quality of the paper. The cost is about $2 per book for a 2,000-copy initial run (including the one-time costs of the artwork, typesetting, and so on), and $1 per book for each successive 2,000. I keep the runs limited, even though larger amounts would generate additional savings, for two reasons:

1. Inventory requires both room and expense.
2. I want the freedom to update easily without worrying about 10,000 books stored in someone's basement.

On the initial sales of 4,000 booklets, for example, at $6.95 each, I'll net $21,800. At the moment, I have five booklets in my catalog. If I sell one press run of each every year (2,000 × 5 × $6.95), the net is $59,500. That pays the mortgage.

Create books or booklets that are easy to read, contain a multitude of graphics and models, and are *attractive* to the eye. That's why you'll need both a professional designer and a printer, but those costs are minimal in today's competitive marketplace. Use a sliding scale for multiple purchases—it's common for clients to buy hundreds of copies of my leadership or innovation booklets at a time for distribution well beyond the immediate audience.

Books and booklets can be produced during "downtime" and can be used as value-added for the presentation (purchased in conjunction with the speech), as follow-up sales either in the back of the room or by mail, and/or as opportunities for others who haven't been able to hear you personally.

One final note that applies to all product sales: if you're going to sell products at the presentation site, have someone other than yourself staff the table and handle the transactions. You can always sign books for people off to the side, but it's a better idea to remain aloof from the actual purchase. And it's far, far superior to have your *introducer* and the program's written publicity stipulate that your books have been made specially available for the audience than for you to do it from the platform.

At this writing, my newest book, *Thrive! Stop Wishing Your Life Away* is a hardcover, 230-page book, printed by a printer that also prints for major publishers. It's self-published and is in the top 20,000 on Amazon, a number that includes both fiction and nonfiction. (*Million Dollar Consulting*, published by this book's publisher, McGraw-Hill, is at about 14,000, by way of comparison.)

2. Downloads and CDs

These are very popular because they can be used in iPods, iPhones, computers, cars, and so on, where a large number of people do their learning and self-development. You can sell these singly or in albums and series. There is a plethora of production houses that specialize in everything from the artwork to the album configuration and from the tape editing to the duplication.

Teleconference series are perfect to create in these forms to leverage the expense and effort into additional products and learning alternatives.

All of my audio works are the result of either recorded platform deliveries, teleconferences, or radio interviews, where there is audience participation or where the interaction with the interviewer compensates for the lack of audience participation. I try to keep them under one hour. I sell some singly, some in sets of three, and some in large series or albums with textual material.

Have your work edited by a professional. If the introducer at the event did a poor job (not at all an uncommon phenomenon), have a new one dubbed in. Remove extraneous noise and dead spots, such as the five minutes of an audience exercise.

You can obtain tape editing, duplication, labels, boxes, and ancillary services for extremely good prices in what's become a hugely competitive industry. Shop around and ask other speakers what their experience has been. Despite economies of scale, I recommend that you create and maintain relatively limited inventories until you can project sales reliably. That might mean an initial run from a few hundred to 1,000, and reorders of 2,500 for hard-copy duplicates. Downloads, of course, don't have these drawbacks.

My approach is to have my technical experts put all of my recorded work and downloads on iTunes. I also place them on my blog and my Web site, where they are archived.

Self-published tapes face the same challenge as self-published books: marketing. We'll talk about that in more detail later in the chapter.

3. Videos

Videos must be done professionally. I'll never forget the guy I saw standing in front of a camera, drawing on an easel sheet. His video price was only $10. It wasn't worth it.

The best alternative for video as a product is to collaborate with a client to help produce one. That means that the client allows a production crew to shoot both you and the audience, and to light and mike the venue as required for top quality. In return, you provide the client with the option of free copies of the video, a reduced fee, and/or a video of the remainder of the conference for the buyer's purposes. Many clients will graciously consent to such a quid pro quo, which is more than worth it in terms of the live audience and professionally equipped environment.

You must adapt your presentation to your video product intent. That probably means refraining from citing the client or specific client examples during the talk, avoiding time-related examples, including devices (humor, questions, requests) that generate audience involvement and responsiveness, and using only those visuals that will tape well. *You'll need a signed release from anyone who appears on camera, or one from the organization that covers everyone.*

In my experience, videos for sale as products should be no longer than an hour and can be as brief as 30 minutes. Retail sales prices vary from about $15 to $95, depending on the factors we cited earlier. The production expense, however, can be substantial (unless you're crafty enough to work out some reciprocal arrangement with the production house, such as internal training, references to other speakers or clients, or something similar). A professional two-camera production, with all the related equipment and editing, could cost anywhere from $5,000 to $10,000. The good news is that DVD duplication, like audio duplication, is very inexpensive and can be as little as $5 to $10, depending on quantities.

A taping that costs $5,000 to produce and 100 copies at $10 apiece results in an initial investment of $6,000. If the product sold for $60, that would create a first run that broke even, and I'm being kind in the cost and the price. Video products are best created either with a producer/distributor who will underwrite the costs and pay a royalty *or* when your name and repute will produce enough momentum to drive sales. Typically, videos are a product that makes sense for established speakers who can rely on past book and/or tape sales for repeat business for new products.

You can run video excerpts on your Web site to whet the appetite of prospective buyers. You may also be able to use this as a "demo" video for buyers who demand one.

4. Newsletters

I'm not talking about the blatantly self-promoting, mostly free fliers that many speakers distribute. I'm talking about a monthly, bimonthly, or quarterly publication of from 4 to 12 pages that people actually buy, or an electronic version of one or more "screens" on the computer.

This is a tough market, but also a lucrative one. The ability to create periodic contact with constantly new information *and be paid for it* meets every criterion mentioned earlier for the success of a product. If you're in a position in which you constantly receive new ideas and information or are crafting new approaches and techniques or have responses and resolutions to ongoing issues of interest, then you might want to consider publishing a newsletter.

One of the great disadvantages is the pressure on people's time to read a myriad of sources related to their work and interests. One of the great advantages is the nature of renewal subscriptions: if people like the product, then the original sale will result in annual business, which is a powerful revenue generator.

An eight-page, two-color, professionally designed and printed newsletter can be produced for about $500 an issue, with postage dependent on circulation size (after an initial, one-time cost of perhaps $2,000 for design, plates, artwork, and so on). If your newsletter is a quarterly that sells for $45, and you attract 300 initial subscribers, then your first-year profit is $9,500 (300 × $45 − $4,000). If you grow to 500 subscribers in your second year, your profit is then $20,500, less postage ($45 × 500 − $2,000).

You need to have the organizational skills, inclination, writing ability, and time. Most of all, however, you need the readership. Newsletters are ideal when they are highly targeted toward specific markets, are backed by a credible name in that area, and contain high content. Newsletters of this kind are not the place to promote your latest book, your speaking schedule, or your awards and honors. Focus on bringing value to the buyer. No one wants to pay to read your promotional propaganda. They can do that for free.

Electronic versions are harder to charge for and are more likely to be free vehicles that promote your brand and repute.

I think that newsletters are highly specialized products that are probably best for speakers who have a customer base that has purchased other products. However, they are also often overlooked products that are the perfect vehicles to both generate annual revenues and softly promote your credibility and stature. By sending the newsletters to publications such as *Bottom Line Business*, *Training Magazine*, or the local newspaper, you'll find that excerpts will be printed citing the source.

People complain that there are "too many" newsletters. That's because people are subscribing to them and reading them! *Competition opens markets; it doesn't narrow them.*

5. Advice and Counsel

Most speakers' most valuable asset is their intellectual property. Unless they are simply parroting someone else's ideas, they provide expertise and a unique source of improvement. Those qualities are salable beyond the platform.

Several years ago, I appeared at a series of presentations for Coldwell Banker. The buyer found that my approaches to consulting were of far more than merely informational value to the firm's internal service people and wanted to provide "real-time" help for those people around the country. As a result, a toll-free number called "Ask Alan" was established, and those service people were encouraged to call at any time to leave a question about a client situation that they were currently facing. They were guaranteed a response within 24 hours. In return, I received a retainer for the three months that the program was in effect. The next year, I appeared on interactive television *originating from my home* and administered completely by a third party. Who knows what happens the year after that?

I don't refer to postplatform advice as "consulting" because the objective from an income standpoint is that it be remote and *not* dependent upon your being on-site.[2] It's passive in the sense that it can be recorded, requests can be received but not answered until later, and/or it provides access to you. Some clients will want their executives to be able to talk to you prior to their own presentations to obtain some presentation tips, some humor to insert, or some techniques to involve the audience.

6. Teleconferences

You can conduct teleconferences from your home with your feet up on a desk for less than $100 a session these days, and you can charge anywhere from $29 to well over $100, depending on your brand, value, and timeliness.

I run 10 teleconferences a year (I don't work on them in January and February) and charge by the series or by the individual session, all obtainable on my secure Web site shopping area. There are more than 70 available at this writing, which include interviews, case studies, role-plays, straight presentations, and so on. They are all recorded, were originally sold as CDs and in albums, and are now solely downloads. The

[2] And besides, too many speakers call themselves "consultants" when in fact they are not, and they shouldn't be confusing the issue. Speaking, training, and facilitating are noble callings in their own right.

downloads are provided free to subscribers, but cost more than the original teleconference for those who order after the fact.

These also establish you as a thought leader, can easily accommodate question and answer sessions, and can go directly to venues such as iTunes if you so desire. They are typically an hour in length.

7. Podcasts

Working with software such as GarageBand on a Mac and any good microphone, you can record podcasts (with music and sound effects already licensed for use). These are typically brief (10 to 30 minutes) but can be longer. You can create a series or independent sessions.

It's harder to charge for podcasts, but you can easily set up subscriptions and circulate them to selected audiences. They are more informal than teleconferences and they usually can't accommodate question and answer sessions, but they are excellent devices to provide very timely and provocative information.

8. Manuals and Guidelines

One of the members of my Mentor Program was an expert in heat loss and energy costs in plants and buildings. He developed a simple, nonelectronic little cross between a slide rule and a Rubik's Cube that enabled a maintenance engineer or site manager to determine energy waste quickly. He soon converted this to an item for sale.

An attorney in my Mentor Program found himself developing simple guidelines, manuals, charts, and checklists for small businesses (which rarely had their own legal or human resource experts) to handle hiring, termination, evaluations, benefit administration, and so forth. He gave up his formal law practice to sell these items on his Web site, including annual memberships that permitted unlimited downloads.

9. Devices

You might consider the energy indicator just mentioned a "device," so I've included the category here, as well. Some image consultants provide illustrated charts (often with movable, matchable indicators) that enable you to tell which colors go best with which skin type, which accessories best match outfits, and what the proper attire is for varying occasions.

What value do you have that lends itself to this type of self-learning and personal use?

10. Chat Rooms and Forums

When you create communities, value accrues to you for having brought the component parts together, irrespective of whether you are actually involved in every transaction. If you go to AlansForums.com, for example, you'll find a membership-only chat room (the general public can read parts of it) that offers conversations, case studies, referrals, and advice on a 24/7 basis, globally.

The members value the experience (we have 70,000+ posts at this writing), for which credit accrues to me by dint of my creating it and being there frequently. People who "own" certain niches, as I do solo consulting, form vibrant, long-term communities: for example, Jeff Gitomer in sales, Seth Godin in creativity, and Marshall Goldsmith in coaching.

THE ACCELERANT CURVE

I've organized an annual gathering of the Million Dollar Club, which is a small group of entrepreneurs who generate seven figures of revenue on an annual basis. At our first meeting, one of our members, Mark Smith, shared a diagram with a right angle and a curved line from the top left to the bottom right. He explained that the vertical axis had low barrier to entry for clients at the top, and the horizontal had high fee and high intimacy at the bottom right.

I dubbed this the "Accelerant Curve," because as people purchased your products and services through varying offerings, they moved toward higher fees and higher intimacy. Trust—and/or a brand—speeded people down the curve, and the idea was not to allow for "chasms" where there was no easy next step in the progression.

As we began applying this to businesses, however, I became increasingly uneasy with it because so many of my clients would purchase a book—exactly like the one you're reading—and "bounce" to a point much farther right on the curve. In addition, word of mouth and branding often brought people directly into offerings on the extreme right without ever sampling the left.

What you see in Figure 11-1 is the revised Accelerant Curve:

- From left to right, products and services usually migrate from merely competitive, to distinct, to breakthrough.
- From left to right, offerings are usually higher fee, higher intimacy, *but also less labor intensive*.
- "Bounce factors" enable you to propel clients forward dramatically (e.g., a teleconference that creates an appeal for hiring you for a series of keynotes).

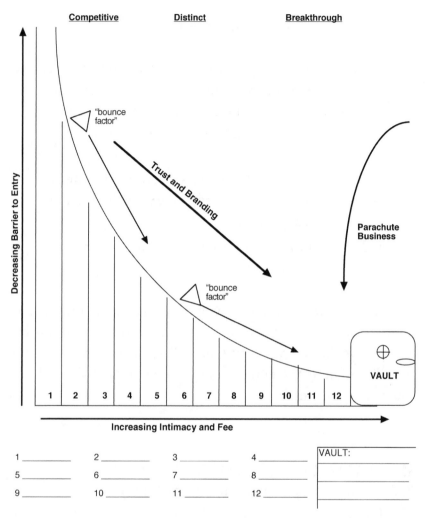

Figure 11-1 The Million Dollar Consulting® Accelerant Curve

- "Parachute business" is that business that "drops in" directly on the right.
- Your "vault" comprises those offerings that are unique to you and on your terms, for example, retainers, licensing, guaranteed appearances, and so forth.

My advice to you, therefore, is to

1. Make sure that you have at least three competitive (e.g., booklets), six distinctive (e.g., topical keynotes or training sessions), and three breakthrough (e.g., proprietary training the trainer or "boot camp") offerings.
2. Fill your vault with retainers, licensed programs, franchised intellectual property, video and remote offerings, and so on.
3. Build your brand and viral marketing so that parachute business increases.

If you want to increase your success exponentially and climb to the top of this profession, you need a cogent, evolving, personalized Accelerant Curve. Use the illustration to fill in your intent. (Or feel free to engage me to help you! That's the "bounce factor"!)

BUILDING COMMUNITIES: REV—CREATING EVERGREEN CLIENTS

The iPhone has apps. Everyone knows this. At this writing, it has about 150,000, and by the time you read this, it may have twice that many.

Apple creates an iPhone, and people buy it; others create applications for those people, and still more people are attracted to the apps; the iPhone creates more advanced versions of itself, and more apps are created, attracting still more sophisticated users. You get this never-ending picture.

This is what I call reciprocating, exponential value, or REV. It is a community that builds value continually, attracting more and more people who provide still more value, thereby making it yet more attractive to others. It is a perpetual motion machine.

My communities act the same way. I referred to chat rooms in my examples of passive income. People who commune in my chat room are deriving value from me irrespective of whether I am present or not, because I'm the one who is responsible for the medium they are using. As their own quality and contributions attract still other valued people, my value grows, even though I personally may have had nothing to do with the entry of those newer people.

Now multiply that by a dozen communities that I've created that overlap in numerous ways, and you can begin to see the perpetual motion machine of attraction and value providing clients for life and referrals for life. For instance, people in my Mentor Community meet at least once a year in a free Mentor Summit, during which smaller communities form and reform around my workshops (the Million Dollar Consulting College graduates have actually staged their own reunion), experiences, and groups.

Similarly, you can form communities within your client network that reinforce and continually revisit your value. As a speaker, trainer, facilitator, or any related expert, your communities might include

- Buyers at certain levels (e.g., sales vice presidents)
- Participants
- Venue management
- Those interested in your topics and expertise
- Aspirants in your specialty

- "Graduates" of some of your specialized programs
- Trainers you've trained in-house
- Subcontractors
- People who read your blog
- People who subscribe to your newsletter
- Teleconference audiences
- Podcast listeners
- YouTube viewers
- Social media platform groups
- Readers of your books

You get the idea. I could easily triple this list. What are you doing to create, nurture, and grow these specialized communities so that they are exchanging information, forming subgroups, and attracting others, *all under your aegis and within your purview?*

Speaking Up: Frequently, your value multiplies without your speaking at all!

With technology at our fingertips, we can organize, monitor, and develop these communities by judiciously providing intellectual property, making introductions, creating new experiences, and exploiting our brands. As I said earlier, you may not agree with us, but if you're in sales and you don't know of Jeff Gitomer, or you're in coaching and you don't know of Marshall Goldsmith, or you're in solo consulting and you don't know of me, then you're simply not in the mainstream and are an amateur.

At this advanced stage, you create clients for life by raising your profile as an object of interest, and enabling people to profit and improve from the company you keep.

SUMMARY

This can be a risky business. It can also be a hugely profitable one. How can one endure the former without capitalizing on the latter?

Create passive income through products, remote coaching, teleconferences, and so forth. (If you use a definition like mine, passive income can include workshops and "live" experiences close to your home.) Use the Accelerant Curve to ensure that you have no "chasms" in your product and service offerings, and to propel clients toward more lucrative and less labor-intensive relationships. Bear in mind that the greater your clients' trust in you and the more you have a powerful brand, the more this will occur.

When your "sizzle" is sufficiently loud and clear, you can build communities in which reciprocating value enables more and more people to join in a variety of ways on the curve, making the community still more valuable to others. You're then able to demonstrate value merely by dint of allowing people to come together under your auspices.

If you do this continually and intensively, you'll develop clients and loyalty for life. Referral business will explode, viral marketing will take hold, and you may become a well-known name within your field of expertise.

Ironically, the more you produce passive income opportunities, the more power accrues to your brand, and the more powerful the brand, the more people will flock to your passive income options.

That's not a bad cycle to get into.

PREPARING FOR SUCCESS

GO AHEAD, TREAT YOURSELF

WE PREPARE ourselves for failure, but we seldom prepare for success. If you follow the advice in this book, and you have the requisite talent and discipline, you will be successful. Therefore, you must adopt an abundance mentality, not a poverty mentality.

TIAABB: THERE IS ALWAYS A BIGGER BOAT

Earlier in my career, I was speaking in Philadelphia, which is about 90 minutes from where I was born and raised in northern New Jersey (just across the Hudson River from Manhattan). During the 90-minute keynote, I had related to the audience that I was raised in the most densely populated city in the United States and had grown up playing stickball on the streets amidst the traffic, for which the prerequisites were to steal a broom and to fish old balls out of the sewers.

"A couple of the stronger kids would prise up the sewer grate," I explained, "and then we'd hold the lightest, a kid called Berger, by the ankles and dangle him down the duct until his head was just above the horrors and he could reach the balls. We'd wash them in some rainwater and get on with the game until the cops chased us."

I was speaking on the subject of entrepreneurial success and establishing one's own business. Afterward, while I was signing some books, a man approached and asked if he could speak to me privately. He told me that his name was Henry Johnson and that he had been talked into attending by a friend. He was very slim, somewhat shy, inexpensively but neatly dressed, and missing a front tooth. Henry, it turned out, was 29 years old.

"In two hours, you've changed my world," he stated simply.

Being a middleweight cynic, I replied, "I don't think I can change your world, but if you received a few useful ideas today, then it was probably worth it."

"No, you've done more than that. I've had a string of bad breaks, and I'd given up. My plan had been to work with young people in the inner city, to help them to get jobs, to stay in school, to take pride in who they are. I felt that way until I got out of the army and couldn't get work myself. Friends have been pushing me to start something on my own and not rely on the city agencies. They want me to shape up, get my teeth fixed, develop a business plan, and go after private money. I've decided this morning to do it."

I had a feeling he was putting me on, or maybe repeating something that he said after hearing anyone speak.

"Henry," I pointed out, "you're black and I'm white. I've been speaking to corporations for 20 years, and you're thinking about beginning to speak to youth groups. I live in a suburban New England town, and you live in the heart of Philly. If I've helped, I'm honored to have done so, but what on earth did I do or say to cause you to feel this way?"

"I was Berger," he said. "I was the kid who had to go down the sewer and under cars and into yards patrolled by huge dogs to find the lost balls. I know exactly what you were talking about, because I was there. And if you could leave that behind and succeed to the point where you're invited to speak to us today, then I can surely get my act together for my dream and for these kids. There are kids out there like us, and I'm going to help them. You helped me understand that I can."

Like us. That was an amazing moment. Henry shook hands and walked off before I could even offer him my card. I never found out what became of him. But I do know what became of me.

I learned again—and perhaps most profoundly—that what we do as speakers has impact far beyond our understanding. Henry happened to choose to talk to me that day, but he might not have done so if there had been more people in the group milling around, and he could not have done so if I had made one of my customary dashes to the airport after I had finished my talk. It's not critical to talk to the Henry Johnsons each time, but it is essential to know that they are there. Our behavior, our words, our examples, and our *presence* provide a powerful model to people.

What Is the Model You Are Creating?

You'll hear many speakers talk about their successes and their lifestyles. Most of them are lying. Keep this in mind: there is *always* a bigger boat (TIAABB). I've seen $25 million yachts lined up like Volkswagens in St. Bart's harbor. I've been in McMansions and private jets. And I've been in rooms with people who could buy and sell me in a half-hour.

So what? If you agree that real wealth is discretionary time, then the key is to provide the time you need to enjoy your loved ones and your life while helping others in the process of your career, which fuels your life.

> ***Speaking Up: Many speakers are so busy running around making money that they are eroding their wealth.***

What is the example you're providing for people? That example is the sum total of what they see on the platform, in front of the room, behind the lectern, on the stage. It's a combination of your words, actions, attitude, spontaneity, examples, humor, materials, ideas, and emphasis. Are you extemporaneous, "in the moment," interactive, and honestly enthusiastic? Or are you rehearsed, choreographed, superficial, unoriginal, and "falsely authentic," shedding phony tears and sharing contrived laughs? (Ask some speakers a question during their "act" and they have to go back and start all over at the beginning.)

No one believes what they read or what they hear. They believe what they *see*. When people watch you, what are they seeing? Ironically, and wonderfully, the road to success in this business is paved with honesty, not subterfuge. All of the coaching and specialized platform skills in the world can only dress up a shallow message and an insincere delivery. They are contrivances that cannot lend weight, depth, or meaning. Superficiality and dishonesty will eventually collapse under the weight of the camouflage.

This profession is not like selling ice cream or televisions. The audience doesn't decide on the flavor. Its members can't test the picture before buying or call for repairs after they've bought. Our responsibility is immense. Our account-ability doesn't always measure up.

Don't worry about how much you *have*; focus on how much you *help*.

ETHICAL CONSIDERATIONS: A SPEAKER'S CREED

There is no government agency, trade association, or consumer group that monitors what we do. While a given client can make the decision to rehire us or never to set eyes on us again, that is after the fact, and there are always other potential clients who have never heard of us. We have to be self-governing. After all, anyone can hang out a shingle that says, "Professional Speaker, Inquire Within." In fact, most of us have done exactly that. Let's not kid ourselves—we didn't pass any rigid qualifying tests to enter or remain in this profession.

But my contention is that the more ethically you act, the more successful you are. "Doing the right thing" is not so much an abstract nicety as it is a pragmatic business need. In-tegrity, in this business, outshines glossy marketing bro-chures. Honesty counts for more than slick graphics. Your word is more important than your résumé.

Speakers gather frequently for formal conventions and in-formal meetings. I virtually never hear discussions about the ethics of our business. I know of no other professional group that so consistently ignores this aspect of its profession, and that often tolerates plagiarism and charlatanism in its midst.

Here, then, is my nomination for a speaker's guidelines for correct conduct. I think it's a pretty good test for any of us and an excellent way to comport ourselves in a profession that demands high values and self-discipline.

A Speaker's Creed

- I will use predominantly my own ideas and experiences, and will credit others when I refer to theirs in support of my own.
- I will be honest on the platform and never make a statement that I know to be untrue.
- I will approach my work with the intent of meeting the client's objectives through my involvement with the audience.
- My fee structure will reflect the value that I bring to the client, and that client will feel that the investment was exceeded by the results.
- My intent is to help people learn, think, change, and act, and my real impact occurs well after the audience has left the room.
- I will never deliberately manipulate emotions through stories or actions that are unrelated to the client's objectives.
- I will never use material or actions with the intent of building my own ego or image without regard for my topic and the audience's needs.
- I will refrain from proselytizing and respect the diversity, varied beliefs, and private spirituality of the audience, no matter how strong my personal beliefs.
- I will keep feedback in perspective, knowing that I'm never as good as the highest rating or as poor as the lowest; my self-esteem comes from within.
- My materials and publicity will accurately reflect who I am, and I will never take credit or make claims that are undeserved or unsupported.

- I will help other speakers through sharing experiences, providing ideas, referring business, and mentoring, because as we all grow, so does the profession.

- I will make a contribution to my community and my environment through pro bono work, financial contributions, and volunteer activities.

- I will never make claims that I cannot support, nor claim accomplishments that I have not experienced.

- I will have made a difference in that my presence will have been felt.

PERSONAL AND PROFESSIONAL REWARDS

The subtitle of this book is not inconsistent with this section. The fact is, if you don't help yourself, you can't help others effectively. Think of the oft-cited oxygen mask rule on airplanes: first your own, then others'.

A sophomore at a high school youth conference asked me, in front of a hundred students and teachers, "What's the shortcut to success? You're here as an example of success, so save us the trouble. What's the quickest route?"

After the laughter died down, I responded without hesitation, "Find something that you love to do and throw yourself into it, body and soul. Don't try to find something that pays a lot and learn to love it. If you do the former, you'll become wealthy, however you define it, and you'll have a great life. If you do the latter, you'll be miserable."

Our lifestyles and our aspirations reflect very personal belief systems. I would never hold mine up as the avatar to which all others should aspire. I've found that the extraordinary financial rewards available in this profession can provide me with the ability to help others through the luxury of pro bono work, contributions, volunteerism, and flexible terms with clients. I've also found that the better I'm able to take care of my family and personal responsibilities, the better I'm able to handle the inevitable stress and pressures of dealing with diverse clients in different settings on a routine basis.

As I've become more and more successful in the profession, I've been able to become more selective about my work. I've referred lower-paying and lower-learning assignments to others who can use them; I've stopped doing the full-day programs that I never enjoyed and found to be exhausting; I've reduced my travel from 85 percent at one point to under 15 percent today, and I am able to draw people to me from all over the globe. I've been able to travel the world with my wife, send two kids to the finest private universities in the country, and pursue the hobbies and interests that help maintain my energy, *all out of cash flow*. Don't forget, I was one of the kids hovering over a sewer, holding on to Berger's ankles.

Speakers tend to overemphasize what they do and underemphasize what they *contribute*. Their focus is on the task (a training session) as opposed to the result (increased profits). Consequently, for all the ego and self-centeredness in this business, *most speakers consistently undervalue what they contribute and undercharge their clients*. Ironically, only by understanding the internal measures that I've alluded to in this chapter, and only by moving away from the ephemeral external measures, can we achieve a real appreciation of our contribution and our results.

I've heard of speakers aligning their fees with the evaluation sheets. The higher the rating, the higher the fee. That's the equivalent of a doctor being paid based upon his or her bedside manner and not whether your health has been protected or improved. I've heard speakers say, "I knocked 'em dead," in response to "How'd you do?" But I hear others say, "I made a difference. They just don't know how much, yet."

> **Speaking Up: If you can't evaluate your own contributions, no audience's evaluation sheets will do you any good at all. If you need to be loved, get a dog.**

Mounting a lonely platform to speak the truth isn't a profession for the timid, the irresolute, or the uninspired. Nor is it the proper setting for someone who needs adulation, validation, or congratulation.

We, each of us, are engaged in a most noble calling, one whose roots are millennia old and whose future is assured despite globalization, technological change, and political strife. We are professional speakers, capable of affecting the hearts and minds of millions, who can in turn influence millions of others. That is a unique and profound accountability. In so doing, we can enrich ourselves, thereby enhancing our ability to continue to enrich others.

We might as well get good at it.

PAYING BACK

In the movie *Mr. Saturday Night*, Billy Crystal plays a comic who, in one memorable scene, has just knocked the socks off a crowd in a Catskills resort. As he leaves the stage while 500 people are on their feet applauding, his manager is shouting in the wings, "You were a smash! They want a *long-term contract!* We can write our own terms!"

But Crystal is only half listening and appears troubled. He's glancing back toward the crowd, which is still screaming.

"Didn't you hear me?" yells the manager. "What's wrong with you? You were the biggest hit they've ever had here!"

"Yeah," says Crystal, "but did you see that guy near the front at table 5? I couldn't get him to laugh all night."

That's the story of our profession. Unless every person is on his or her feet telling us how good we are, we're a failure. (My feeling has always been that a successful engagement means that no one has thrown anything and the check has cleared.)

I cannot make someone else learn. I can't even motivate someone else. I deal with adults. They are responsible for their own learning, and motivation is an intrinsic aspect of human behavior—it can come only from within.

So what good am I? What can I do? Well, I can establish an environment that is conducive to learning and motivation. I can provide content that is relevant, delivered in an interesting and entertaining manner. I can answer questions honestly to the best of my ability and relate the answers to the questioner's circumstances. I can provide personal examples to demonstrate my points. I can involve the audience, actually or rhetorically, to enable its members to relate my points to their issues. I can prepare carefully for a particular group's needs and can adapt suddenly when the unexpected occurs. I can keep the audience's learning needs superior to my own ego needs.

You know what? That's a lot. I'm successful if I've managed to deliver on what I'm capable of doing. Then the audience probably will learn, will change, will take action, will be motivated. But I can't guarantee it. I can guarantee only my part.

The problem is that we can get the standing ovations, the superb ratings, and the outstanding comments without really having contributed a thing to the audience or the client except a temporary view of our dexterity on stage. I know how to get the audience members to laugh. I know how to get them to applaud. If I wanted to, I even know how to make them cry. So what? The question is, can I get them to want to learn?

There is a great deal in our arsenal that rarely needs to be used. But too often, we haul out every weapon and fire it simply because it's there, creating a lot of sound and light, and never failing to get a reaction. I can get any audience on its feet. My measure, though, is, can I get it out of its lassitude?

Earlier in the book, I mentioned Albert Bandura, one of the most renowned psychologists of our time, who has done extensive work on self-efficacy. He says that people with low self-esteem and low belief in their abilities tend to place great weight on external measures of their performance. They incessantly want to know how they performed in the eyes of others, and they rely on instruments and evaluations that assess their performance.

However, those with high self-esteem and an intrinsic belief in their abilities and talents tend to use internal measures to gauge their success. Bandura's work suggests that these measures are usually clustered around learning and self-development. He calls this "self-mastery."

In our profession, we have the potential to grow more than any client, any audience, or any sponsor. We have the capacity to learn from each engagement, from each diverse client, and from each new environment. Some of us do, and we are different speakers from the ones we were two years ago. Some of us don't, and we continue with the same hackneyed approaches and old stories that we were telling a decade ago. What's the difference?

If we're not growing, we're simply not increasing the value that we bring to our clients and our audiences. We need to have the perspective—and the courage—to move away from the external measures of our often temporary successes and move toward the internal measures that indicate self-mastery. Just as there is a runner's "wall" and a test pilot's "envelope," there is a transcendent place where speakers can move from hearing the applause and being concerned about the guy at table 5 to listening to themselves and being concerned about the degree to which they are fulfilling their own potential. That transcendence has arrived when you can walk out of a room reverberating with applause for you knowing that the session wasn't as good as it could have been, and when you can walk out of a room to a tepid reaction knowing that no one could have achieved more with that group under those circumstances.

We are not triumphant, nor do we "bomb." Some groups, some days, some places are better than others, perhaps, but what we do is put forth our best effort each time. It is the quality of the effort, not the quantity of the hoorahs, that matters. Helping 10 people out of 30 in a cynical, resistant group to acquire skills and techniques to improve their situation is a far better result than emphasizing to 100 motivated high performers how good they already are. We'll all wind up doing both, but let's not become confused about relative worth.

I'll preach to the choir any time, but burly sinners run the world. It's the latter who are tougher, but ultimately more important, to change.

SUMMARY

There is *always* a bigger boat!

Stop judging your progress and your status by others' standards, either those imposed upon you or those that are merely visible to you. Understand what is important for your life, since work is merely fuel for our lives and real wealth is discretionary time. The only boat I've ever owned is the rowboat on my pond. But I've been known to rent a few when the spirit moved me.

Do right and you'll do well. Always act ethically. You'll stand out in this profession and in life by so doing. And that way you can enjoy the personal and professional rewards that will accrue from your behavior and your success.

Being a professional speaker is only one small part of your persona. It should not be how you are defined. It is one way you express yourself and influence your environment. Do so in a way that makes you proud.

It's incumbent upon us to give back. I hope you'll find ways to do that.

This book is one of mine.

EPILOGUE

Now that you've read the book (few people start with or skip to the Epilogue), I thought it would be useful to reflect on some major factors in building a seven-figure practice. Because if this book is dog-eared, heavily highlighted, and carrying self-stick tabs on most pages, where do you begin?!

If everything is a priority, nothing is a priority.

If you're a beginning speaker, consider the following major elements and actions. (If you're a veteran, then move on to the next section, though this one may still be of value to you!)

ALAN'S ACCELERATORS FOR NEW SPEAKERS

1. *Determine your basic value proposition.* That is, how will the buyer and his or her organization be improved once you walk away?

2. *Identify your buyer.* Who can write a check for that value? It is never a meeting planner or a speakers' bureau; these are merely middlemen. (If you're running public workshops, the buyers are audience members, but this is not recommended for new speakers with no brand or following.)

3. *Create gravity that attracts buyers to you.* Become a center of expertise and a thought leader. Options include

- Publishing articles
- Being interviewed
- Blogging
- Speaking at events with buyers and recommenders, even for free
- Creating a newsletter (electronic or hard copy)
- Teaching part-time at a local college
- Creating teleconferences and podcasts
- Participating on panels
- Creating position papers on your key subjects

4. *Reach out to key buyers.* Options include

- Tell everyone you know of the value that you're providing, and ask for referrals.
- Network at events such as fund-raisers, awards ceremonies, and political events.
- Do pro bono work for nonprofits to meet people and get references.
- Assume leadership positions in trade and professional associations.

5. *Create three or four speeches within your area of expertise that are about 60 percent complete.* Save another 30 percent to be tailored to a prospect's individual needs, and use the final 10 percent as the mood strikes you on the day of the session.

6. *Adopt a pricing strategy of a minimum of $3,500 to $5,000 for a keynote of up to 90 minutes (including anything shorter).*

7. *Build a Web site that is a* credibility site, *not a sales site.* Use it for your value proposition, typical client results, testimonials, biography, position papers,

products, and so forth. Web sites are organic, in that you can start with something simple and build from there. Never have anything "under construction."

8. *Use e-mail with a domain name* (e.g., alan@summitconsulting.com), not a generic server (AOL, Yahoo!, gmail, and so on). Use a complete signature file, with name, all contact information, and your value proposition.

9. *Create high-quality letterhead, envelopes, labels, and business cards.* Leave your photo off them!

10. *Adopt power language.* Shamelessly promote. Develop and manifest the mental set that says, "I have tremendous value, and I'd be remiss if I didn't provide you with the opportunity to avail yourself of that value."

11. *If you listen to anyone for advice, make absolutely sure that this person has done what you intend to do* (e.g., has been delivering keynotes to the corporate market for several years for significant fees). Otherwise, move along. Quickly.

12. *Treat bureaus as gravy if they're interested, but never pay them to market you.* They should make their money only from their commission for *having placed you.* Treat meeting planners as leverage points to get you to the real economic buyers. Never waste your time with intermediaries.

13. *Never despair.* This business is about rejection. Those who succeed are resilient.

14. *Ignore audience feedback, "smile sheets," and dreadful, tepid standing ovations.* Focus on your buyer's objectives and his or her satisfaction.

ALAN'S ACCELERATORS FOR VETERAN SPEAKERS

1. *Reexamine your brand and your value proposition for contemporary impact and differentiation.* (What? You don't have a brand? Then develop one. Remember, if you've developed effective intellectual property, the ultimate brand is your name.)

2. *Create processes, not events.* Include pre- and post-speech value, so that instead of a $10,000 talk, you have a $35,000 project.

3. *Utilize advanced technology.* Take your capabilities to Webcasts, forums, chat rooms, and remote help.

4. *Write a commercially published book.* The gold standard in this profession is a major publisher agreeing that you are, indeed, a center of expertise. If you already have one or more, it's time to write another.

5. *Periodically and intensively mine your referral sources.* This is a chronic shortcoming of veteran speakers, even though they should have a great contact list. Three times a year, at least, ask your contacts to introduce you to new buyers. This is the platinum standard in the profession.

6. *If you haven't done so in the past two years, update your Web site and your blog.* Technology is changing too fast not to be current.

7. *Create more sophisticated products.* Use combinations of text, video, audio, and Web access to educate and improve your clients, independent of whether or not you appear on-site.

8. *Adopt a "wholesale/retail" philosophy.* If you've been successful in corporate settings with a single buyer

(wholesale), and you have a strong brand and word-of-mouth support, begin offering sessions directly to the public (retail).

9. *Go global.* Create alliances in other countries where you can bring insights and ideas that will be valuable locally.

10. *Raise your fees.* Your keynote fee should be a minimum of $12,000 if you're simply doing single events. You should be able to charge up to $25,000 as a noncelebrity expert.

11. *Reassess your relationships with bureaus.* Demand a commission maximum of 25 percent, cease paying for any marketing, and demand that you be paid in advance, with nothing held in escrow.

12. *Improve your payment terms.* Require full payment from clients to hold the date, and make the money nonrefundable, although the date may be postponed and rescheduled with no penalty.

ALAN'S ADVICE FOR BUREAUS

1. *Make your income from booking speakers, not from charging them for your marketing or advice.* That should be part of your commission charges.

2. *Abandon arbitrary fee ranges and allow the speaker to negotiate based on client needs.* You'll both be getting larger pieces of the larger pie.

3. *STOP dealing with meeting planners,* who are paid to conserve funds and have no clue about strategy or additional value. Deal directly with executive buyers.

4. *Understand that the speaker is the talent and that the business is the speaker's client, not yours.* Clients and speakers can readily exist without bureaus, but bureaus can't exist without both. Treat speakers as talent, not as "hired hands."

5. *End "meat markets" such as "showcases"* that generate money for you but don't attract real buyers and that position speakers as performing seals.

6. *Take on fewer speakers and focus more on promoting top talent* instead of creating huge "used car lots." There are speakers who are not good enough to be represented. Why would you represent anyone whose fee is under $5,000?

7. *Be reasonable about "spin-off" business.* If you want ethical conduct, practice ethical conduct. Expect to get additional business that develops from an engagement at which you've placed a speaker, but with a declining commission each year thereafter.

8. *Exhibit some trust.* Telling speakers that they can provide only materials that have been scrubbed of their own contact information is tantamount to saying, "We'll represent you, but we don't trust you." Then why should you be trusted?

9. *Stop watching "demo videos" for 60 seconds to determine whether a speaker is good or not.* How would you like to be judged that way? (And stop charging to "review" demo videos.)

10. *End escrow accounts.* The statement, "We're keeping your money until you deliver, because otherwise how can we be sure you'll be there?" is classically stupid. How do we know YOU'LL be there?

ALAN WEISS INTERVIEWS
PATRICIA FRIPP

PATRICIA FRIPP is one of the most successful keynote speakers in the world. She has dramatically and successfully expanded her business into coaching, products, consulting, and other areas. She was the first female president of the National Speakers Association, and she is my partner in The Odd Couple workshops on marketing techniques for professional speakers, which we conduct every year.

Her progress and her reinvention of herself, beginning as a hairstylist, is a great example for every one of us.

When and how did you begin speaking professionally (for a fee)?

In 1975, a hairstyling company called Markham paid me $350 a day for hairstyling demonstrations. What set me apart from other stylists was the fact that I could cut hair for four hours and talk the entire time! I realized that the people in the back could not really see what I was doing. Therefore, I had to describe what I was doing in a way that let them think that they could see. To keep their attention, I also told them how to sell more, interview potential employees, and promote and market. The speaking part of the program was so successful that Markham extended the training to a second day on management and motivation. Since I was the star of my Dale Carnegie class and attended Toastmasters, I knew how to organize my remarks without notes.

At the same time, my executive clients invited me to speak to their service clubs, staff meetings, and small conferences. Because of my personality and my expertise at cutting their hair, my clients thought I would be a pretty good speaker. However, without exception, they were amazed at how good I was! Many of my first free or low-fee talks to their companies eventually led to major long-term relationships.

For example, the first time I spoke to Bob Kessler's team at the San Francisco office of Moore Business Forms, he paid me $75 in Moore business forms. Throughout the years, as he got promoted, he hired me multiple times in many cities. The last time was to keynote a convention in Hawaii to sales professionals from 16 countries with name entertainment. It's a shame he retired!

In 1984, when I finally retired from hairstyling and became a full-time professional speaker, I was hired to speak to AT&T National Account managers. I was referred by Gary Hickox, who, at age 27, impressed his boss by bringing in a top motivational speaker to speak at a small team meeting—his hairstylist! In 2010, 26 years later, we still keep in touch.

At a Rotary Club speech marketing my salon, I was asked, "What would you charge to say that to the Oakland Appliance Dealers?" "$50!" The next request was to speak on goal setting to the San Mateo School Administrators. I replied, "$50 an hour and travel time." He offered me $125! Incidentally, the next time the same gentleman asked, "What would you charge to say that to the Oakland Appliance Dealers?" he paid me $5,000.

In 1977, I attended my first NSA convention and realized that I could one day be a speaker.

How did you choose your early topics, since your prior career was as a hairdresser?

Alan, we teach speakers that you get paid for what you know. You get paid well when you deliver what you know with impact. I realized that I was an expert on building a small or medium-size business.

My early topics were the result of what I did on a daily basis: "How to Get, Keep, and Deserve Customers" and "How to Promote Business."

As a hairstylist, I learned important business-building advice from my successful entrepreneurial dad. Good fortune led me to always work with brilliant bosses, such as Jay Sebring, the Hollywood hairstylist, and I maximized my 45-minute haircutting sessions with my executive clients as an education. I would ask, "What made you the top salesperson in your company?" and "What did you do to your small company that made a big one want to pay you millions of dollars for it?"

In the early days of my speaking career, audience members would sometimes ask, "Where did you get your MBA?" or "Are you an industrial physiologist?" I would reply, "No, I just spent 24 years behind a hairstyling chair . . . taking advantage of opportunity."

Was it difficult at first for you to prove your credibility to buyers and the audience? Why or why not?

Actually, no.

In the middle 1970s and early 1980s, there were fewer speakers and fewer requests to customize. I met Mike Frank at my first National Speakers Association convention, where he "discovered" me. Mike promoted big sales rallies and ran a speakers' bureau. He was an early supporter and recommended me to some of his clients. In those days, he would ask, "Would you consider a woman speaker?" Often the answer was, "No." Then after a few years, it was, "We must have a female speaker."

At the time, there were few women speakers who fit into several categories, as I did. I was entertaining, yet I was not a humorist. I had been successful in a male-dominated industry. Plus, my energy and personality were a match for the business, just as they had been in hairstyling. Mike reported, "Men and women like you, and so do young and mature audiences."

Most of my early engagements came through recommendations from speakers' bureaus or people who had heard me and knew what they were getting.

What are the biggest changes in your career while in the profession?

The Internet and technology. A Web site is a salesperson who works seven days a week, twenty-four hours a day, and knows what you do, whom you do it for, and what they say about your service.

My business was built with me as a keynote speaker. In my heyday, I presented 100 to 130 keynote speeches a year. By listening to my clients, I realized that my passion—speaking about speaking—was something that they desperately wanted and would pay handsomely for. Also by listening to my clients, I developed a very profitable and actually more satisfying part of my business: teaching executives and sales professionals to deliver their messages more powerfully and persuasively.

My business is now three-fourths sales presentation skills training and executive speech coaching.

If you were to start again, knowing what you now know, would you do anything differently?

Technology did not exist when I started. That would have made a difference. On reflection, I wish I had embraced technology, hired the speech coaches, and collaborated with others earlier. Nothing differently—just embraced sooner.

What's the most important advice for a beginning speaker?

You may not lack the talent it takes to be successful, but you may lack the patience. You need a superb speech or seminar, you have to market effectively, and you have to understand the speaking business. Don't reinvent the wheel. Learn from others who are where you want to be.

What's the most important advice that you have for a veteran speaker?

Value your wisdom and experience, partner with younger professionals, stay relevant, and let your long-time clients know that you are still in business and how you have expanded and adapted your expertise. Revisit, rediscover, and refine what you are doing. This will help you fall in love with your content again.

Where do you see the profession going during the rest of this decade?

That's tough to answer for a whole industry. However, from my own experience and point of view:

More business leaders will enter the professional speaking ranks as the "boomers" retire and enter their next career. Humorists and celebrity speakers will always have an important place at conventions. However, experts who deliver their message in various formats will be the most successful. More companies are going to question the value and contribution of outside speakers and consultants. The ability to customize and personalize your message is mandatory. The ability to deliver in Webinars, as well as in person, will give a speaker an advantage.

After experiencing the last couple of years of "the new normal," clients will continue to look for value; however, more meetings and conventions will return.

What's the most astounding or incredible thing that has occurred while you were speaking?

Personally:

Getting out of a spaceship in a Wonder Woman costume.

Looking out at my audience of 150 $350,000-a-year sophisticated sales professionals and not believing that they could all be that drunk.

Early in my career, when I was speaking at an enthusiastic direct sales company, I paused for effect before my review; they leapt to their feet in a standing ovation—so I walked off without finishing the presentation. After all, I thought, "How many standing ovations of that magnitude does a speaker deserve?"

Corporately:

I never cease to be amazed that companies spend $6 million for conferences, especially for their valued clients, and then key executives frequently walk on stage with a few scribbled notes that they just put together and deliver very poor speeches.

Celebrity:

The weather was bad, and nationwide all planes were delayed. A celebrity speaker refused to even go to the airport. I told the client I would deliver two speeches, my own and one in her place. He stood up and said, "I will never overlook the opportunity to bad-mouth 'the celebrity,' and I will take every chance to rave about Patricia Fripp."

How do you determine from which sources to accept advice?

Recommendations and their track record.

All of us have failed and learned from it. Do you have a favorite "flop"?

Speaking for gravel quarry workers who were drunk. They would have been better off hiring a stripper.

What did I learn? When an insurance company executive who likes you and your message wants to sponsor you for a safety banquet for blue-collar workers, and there is going to be an open bar, go with your first response, "I do not think I am a fit for the audience." That week I had no other bookings, it was close to home, and the more I protested, the higher the fee went. Overly confident from past successes, I thought, "How bad could it be?" I found out!

You're an excellent speaking coach. What are the traits of an outstanding speaking coach?

Very few great speakers are good coaches. Delivering a good speech does not require the same skills as helping others structure, script, and deliver a speech on a subject that the coach knows nothing about. I have learned from different coaches who specialize in structure and others in performance.

I believe the reason my clients keep coming back is my multifaceted approach. As well as having spoken to audiences of all sizes myself, and being familiar with business and sales, I add best practices from marquee comedians, Las Vegas entertainers, and Hollywood screenwriters to my client's business communications. Over the years, I have developed the ability to ask my clients questions, take their answers, edit and polish them, and put the answers back in their mouths. This way, it is easier for them to remember. We write their speeches conversationally.

What were the biggest obstacles that you faced, and how did you overcome them?

To be honest, I do not perceive that I have experienced any obstacles beyond time management.

However, to generalize:

As a novice, not knowing where to start and getting audiences.

As a beginner, how to adapt a message and make it relevant to multiple audiences.

As a professional, how to manage my time between business and performing.

Suffering from "recency bias." When the phone does not ring, you imagine it never will. When business is superb, you forget the cycles of business. Your demand will go down. We must develop a balanced business model.

As a seasoned veteran, to stay excited and relevant.

What final words and ideas do you want to leave with our readers?

The best part of the professional speaking and training business is the education it provides. We learn a lot about many industries, which makes us more valuable to others. Unlike in Hollywood, a few lines and gray hair add to our credibility.

I'm happy to hear that!

APPENDIX

WE'VE DECIDED on a novel approach to keep this book updated and practical for you on a continuing basis. Please visit my site, http://www.summitconsulting.com, go to the bookstore and click on this book, and you'll find a link to access and download the appendix, which will be updated whenever appropriate with current and new resources.

INDEX

Note: Page numbers followed by *f* indicate figures.

ABOUT THE AUTHOR

ALAN WEISS is one of those rare people who can say that he is a consultant, speaker, and author and mean it. His consulting firm, Summit Consulting Group, Inc., has attracted clients such as Merck, Hewlett-Packard, GE, Mercedes-Benz, State Street Corporation, Times Mirror Group, the Federal Reserve, the New York Times Corporation, and more than 500 other leading organizations. He has served on the boards of directors of the Trinity Repertory Company, a Tony Award–winning New England regional theater, Festival Ballet, and has chaired the Newport International Film Festival.

His speaking typically includes 30 keynotes a year at major conferences, and he has been a visiting faculty member at Case Western Reserve University, Boston College, Tufts, St. John's, the University of Illinois, the Institute of Management Studies, and the University of Georgia Graduate School of Business. He has held an appointment as adjunct professor in the Graduate School of Business at the University of Rhode Island, where he taught courses on advanced management and consulting skills. He holds the record for selling out the highest-priced workshop (on entrepreneurialism) in the 21-year history of New York City's Learning Annex. His Ph.D. is in psychology, and he is a member of the American Psychological Society, the American Counseling Association, Division 13 of the American Psychological Association, and the Society for Personality and Social Psychology. He has served on the board of governors of Harvard University's Center for

Mental Health and the Media. He has keynoted for the American Psychological Association on two occasions.

Alan has been inducted into the Professional Speaking Hall of Fame and concurrently received the National Speakers Association Council of Peers Award of Excellence, representing the top 1 percent of professional speakers in the world. He has been named a Fellow of the Institute of Management Consultants (FCMC), one of only two people in history holding both those designations.

His prolific publishing includes more than 500 articles and 40 books, including his bestseller, *Million Dollar Consulting* (from McGraw-Hill). His books have been on the curricula at Villanova, Temple University, and the Wharton School of Business, and have been translated into German, Italian, Arabic, Spanish, Russian, Korean, and Chinese.

He is interviewed and quoted frequently in the media. His career has taken him to 57 countries and 49 states. (He is afraid to go to North Dakota.) *Success* magazine has cited him in an editorial devoted to his work as "a worldwide expert in executive education." The *New York Post* calls him "one of the most highly regarded independent consultants in America." He is the winner of the prestigious Axiem Award for Excellence in Audio Presentation.

In 2006 he was presented with the Lifetime Achievement Award of the American Press Institute, the first ever for a nonjournalist, and one of only seven awarded in the 60+-year history of the association.

He has coached the Miss Rhode Island/Miss America candidates in interviewing skills. He once appeared on the popular American TV game show *Jeopardy*, where he lost badly in the first round to a dancing waiter from Iowa.